The Archaeology
of
Medieval Ireland

The Archaeology
of
Medieval Ireland

T. B. BARRY

First published in 1987 by
Methuen & Co. Ltd

First published in paperback in 1988 by
Routledge
11 New Fetter Lane, London EC4P 4EE
29 West 35th Street, New York, NY 10001

Reprinted 1994, 1999

Routledge is an imprint of the Taylor & Francis Group

Transferred to Digital Printing 2003

Set by Hope Services, Abingdon

British Library Cataloguing in Publication Data
Barry, T.B. (Terence B.)
The archaeology of medieval Ireland.
1. Ireland. Human settlements, ca 1000–ca 1500.
Archaeological investigation
I. Title
941.5

Library of Congress Cataloging in Publication Data
Barry, Terence B.
The archaeology of medieval Ireland / T.B. Barry.
p. cm.
Bibliography: p.
Includes indexes.
1. Ireland—Antiquities. 2. Ireland—History—1172–1603.
3. Excavations (Archaeology)—Ireland. I. Title.
DA920.B348   1988
936.1—dc19   88–14799
ISBN 0-415-01104-3 (pbk.)

Printed and Bound by Antony Rowe Ltd

This book is dedicated to
Eithne, Stephanie and Maeve,
and to the memory of
Lieutenant Terry Barry (1921–43)

Contents

Figures

Plates

Preface and acknowledgements

I would like to thank my wife, Eithne, who has patiently read through this book and made many helpful suggestions. In this same regard I would like to acknowledge the help and criticism of three of my professional colleagues who have read parts of the typescript and therefore prevented me from making even more mistakes in the interpretation of much archaeological data, Dr Michael Ryan of the National Museum of Ireland, Mr David Sweetman of the Office of Public Works and Mr Roger Stalley of the Department of the History of Art, Trinity College, Dublin.

I also owe a great debt to the typing skills of Mrs Muriel Levingston of the Department of Medieval History and all the typists of the central secretariat of Trinity College, Dublin.

I must acknowledge the stimulus and encouragement given to me by the then head of department, Professor Jim Lydon, all my students who have laboured hard in my special subjects and especially my research students. I am also grateful for the help given by the library staff of the Royal Irish Academy, the Royal Society of Antiquaries of Ireland, and Trinity College, Dublin. Finally I have to thank my editors at Methuen & Co./Routledge for their forbearance and skilful assistance which has allowed this book to see the bright light of day.

Because of the pace of research in medieval archaeology in Ireland some parts of this synthesis are likely to be out-of-date almost as soon as it is published, so the author would welcome additional information which could be included in any future edition. I have tried, to the best of my ability, to cover all aspects of settlement archaeology in medieval Ireland but because most of the available archaeological data relates to the Anglo-Normans the book has tended to concentrate on them, although every effort has been made to investigate the indigenous settlement forms as well. Finally I hope that all my readers and colleagues will forgive any errors of fact, interpretation or emphasis which may have occurred in the text.

The author and publishers would like to thank all the photographers and scholars whose names appear in the lists of figures and plates for permission to reproduce them. In particular we would like to thank the following for their illustrations: Con Brogan (front cover); Brendan Dempsey and Peter Butler of Trinity College, Dublin; Commissioners of Public Works, Dublin; Committee for Aerial Photography, University of Cambridge; Royal Irish Academy; National Museum of Ireland; the Dundalgan Press and the Phaidon Press. Figures 10, 11, 15 and 38 are Crown Copyright and are reproduced by permission of the Controller of Her Majesty's Stationery Office.

The author would also like to thank the following individuals for information and advice which has been invaluable to him in the preparation of this book:

C. Bourke, J. Bradley, M. Cahill, K. Cambell, D. Caulfield, A. Clarke, M. de Buitléir, C. Foley, R. E. Glasscock, B. J. Graham, A. Hamlin, P. Harbison, S. Harbison, V. Jenkins, M. Lawlor, J. F. Lydon, C. J. Lynn, F. McCormick, A. MacDonald, T. E. McNeill, C. Manning, M. Moore, M. Murphy, D. Murtagh, F. Myles, W. O'Brien, R. Ó Floinn, A. B. Ó Ríordáin, E. Plunkett-Dillon, M. Reynolds, M. Ryan, R. A. Stalley, P. D. Sweetman, L. Swan, D. Twohig and P. Wallace.

Thanks are also due to K. M. Davies for the skilful cartographic work in figures 21 and 28. Finally the author would like to acknowledge financial support from the Grace Lawless Lee Fund, Trinity College, Dublin, and from the Archaeological Research Fund of the National Committee for Archaeology, Royal Irish Academy.

Finally, I would like to thank Professor Phillip Rahtz and Dr Robin Glasscock for their advice and encouragement to me as a student to pursue the study of the medieval archaeology of Ireland.

Abbreviations

Acc. Roll Holy Trinity, Dublin	*Account Roll of the Priory of the Holy Trinity, Dublin*
ALC	*Annals of Loch Cé*
Ann. Con.	*Annals of Connacht*
Ann. Inisf.	*Annals of Inisfallen*
Ann. of Ire.	*The Annals of Ireland by Friar John Clyn and Thady Dowling*
Antiq. Jnl	*Antiquaries Journal*
Archaeol. Jnl	*Archaeological Journal*
ASCD	*Archaeological Survey of County Down*
AU	*Annals of Ulster*
BAR	British Archaeological Reports
Bull. GSIHS	*Bulletin of the Group for the Study of Irish Historic Settlement*
Cal. Alen's Reg.	*Calendar of Archbishop Alen's Register*
Cal. Inq. Post Mortem	*Calendar of Inquisitions Post Mortem*
'Cal. Liber Ruber'	'Calendar of the Liber Ruber'
Cal. Pat. Rolls	*Calendar of Patent Rolls*
CBA	Council for British Archaeology
CDI	*Calendar of Documents relating to Ireland 1171–1307*
'Chart. Duiske, Kilkenny'	'Charters of the Cistercian Abbey of Duiske in the County of Kilkenny'
Chartul. St Mary's, Dublin	*Chartularies of St Mary's Abbey, Dublin*
DART	Dublin Archaeological Research Team
Exp. Hib.	*Expugnatio Hibernica*
Extents Ir. mon. possessions	*Extents of Irish monastic possessions*
Frag. Ann.	*Fragmentary Annals of Ireland*
Hist. and Mun. Doc. Ire.	*Historic and Municipal Documents of Ireland*

IHS	Irish Historical Studies
Ir. Arch. Res. Forum	Irish Archaeological Research Forum
Ir. chartul. Llanthony	The Irish chartularies of Llanthony Prima and Secunda
Ir. Geog.	Irish Geography
JCHAS	Journal of the Cork Historical and Archaeological Society
Jnl Kildare Arch. Soc.	Journal of the Kildare Archaeological Society
Jnl Brit. Archaeol. Assoc.	Journal of the British Archaeological Association
Jnl Louth Arch. Soc.	Journal of the County Louth Archaeological Society
Jnl Old Wexford Soc.	Journal of the Old Wexford Society, later Journal of the Wexford Historical Society
Knights' fees	Knights' fees in Counties Wexford, Carlow and Kilkenny (13th–15th century)
Med. Archaeol.	Medieval Archaeology
MSRG Report	Moated Site Research Group Report
NI	Northern Ireland
NLI	National Library of Ireland
NMI	National Museum of Ireland
N. Munster Antiq. Jnl	North Munster Antiquarian Journal
Old Kilkenny Rev.	Old Kilkenny Review
OPW	Office of Public Works
Ormond Deeds	Calendar of Ormond Deeds
PRO	Public Record Office, London
Proc. Camb. Antiq. Soc.	Proceedings of the Cambridgeshire Antiquarian Society
PROI	Public Record Office of Ireland
QUB	The Queen's University of Belfast
Red. Bk. Ormond	The Red Book of Ormond
Reg. St Thomas, Dublin	Register of the abbey of St Thomas the Martyr, Dublin
Reg. Tristernagh	Register of the priory of the Blessed Virgin Mary at Tristernagh
Rep. Dep. Keeper	Reports of the Deputy Keeper of the Public Records of Ireland
RIA Proc.	Proceedings of the Royal Irish Academy
RIA Trans	Transactions of the Royal Irish Academy
Rot. pat. Hib.	Rotulorum patentium et clausorum cancellariae Hiberniae calendarium
RSAI Jnl	Journal of the Royal Society of Antiquaries of Ireland

Song of Dermot	*The Song of Dermot and the Earl*
TCD	Trinity College, Dublin
UCC	University College, Cork
UCD	University College, Dublin
UCG	University College, Galway
UJA	*Ulster Journal of Archaeology*

1 Introduction

This book is broadly aimed at the questioning person in the street as the great Irish archaeologist, Sean P. Ó Ríordáin, intended his now classic *Antiquities of the Irish Countryside*, first published in 1942 and now in its fifth edition revised by the late Ruaidhri de Valera. It is an attempt to synthesize the explosion which has taken place in our knowledge of the medieval period in Ireland, roughly from 1170 until 1531, which has been provided by archaeological excavation and field-work over the last generation or so.

If medieval archaeology is a young discipline in mainland Britain and in continental Europe it is in its infancy in Ireland where the first lecturer in medieval archaeology was appointed at Queen's University, Belfast, only in the early 1970s. That it is such a recent development in Ireland is due in large measure to the history and the politics of the island in the present century and this is probably why the first impetus came from Northern Ireland. The Irish Republic only gained its political freedom from Britain in 1922 and since then Irish archaeologists have naturally tended to concentrate on the prehistoric and the Early Christian periods before the coming of the Scandinavian and later the Anglo-Norman invaders. It was understandable for a new state, finding its way among the community of nations in the troubled early years of this century, to wish to emphasize its own unique cultural identity free from the impact of later invaders and colonizers. But in recent years, with Ireland's increasing involvement with the United Nations and latterly with the EC, a more mature approach has been pursued by her scholars in that there is now a general acceptance of the positive contributions that all newcomers to this island, including incidentally the Celtic influx, have made to its culture and historical development. Thus as a result both of this greater pluralistic approach to the study of Ireland's past and with the growing awareness that historical methods of enquiry were insufficient to ensure answers to all the complex questions about medieval society, lectureships in medieval archaeology were also set up in University College, Cork, University College, Galway, and Trinity College, Dublin.

Perhaps the most symbolic and public example of this change in attitude was the controversy over the future of the Wood Quay site in central Dublin from 1975 into the 1980s. With it came a re-evaluation of the contribution of the Norse settlers to the development of trade in the city of Dublin and indeed of their major contribution to the origins and development of urban life in general on this island. It also inevitably led to an increasing interest in the Anglo-Norman period of urban settlement.

An outline analysis of the settlement and economy of Ireland in the years immediately before 1169 will be the first task to be addressed, because no true appreciation of the impact of the Anglo-Normans can be gained without an examination of the major features of pre-Norman native settlement. A thematic approach to the archaeology of medieval settlement will then be pursued so that the broader issues of continuity, urbanization and the evolution of the economy can be more fully appreciated by an understanding of the material remains of the period. Nevertheless, a chronological framework will be observed as far as possible throughout this thematic approach in order to emphasize medieval archaeology's essential interrelationships with the historical process.

It will soon become apparent that this work concentrates on the *settlements* of the medieval period and only utilizes artefactual evidence in so far as it elucidates the chronology and socio-economic development of the medieval settlement pattern. Thus the very limited archaeological evidence for medieval industry, whether rural or urban, is examined from this perspective. Secondly, the vast majority of medieval excavations have concentrated on Anglo-Norman sites and the documentary sources relating to settlement are almost totally Anglo-Norman so that the bias of this book is towards an examination of Anglo-Norman settlement sites. However, where there is some evidence for indigenous settlement forms in the medieval period I have attempted to weld it into a coherent pattern.

In many respects the medieval archaeologist is in a unique position *vis-à-vis* his colleagues in earlier fields of research as he has to be able to understand the significance and importance of the documentary sources of the medieval period. The documentary assistance given or constraints imposed upon the archaeologist of medieval Ireland are, however, fewer than they might have been because of the destruction wrought upon the Public Record Office in the Four Courts in Dublin in 1922 when it was ignited by artillery shells during the Civil War. This compounded the miscellaneous fires and the general neglect of all types of documents in earlier centuries. Thus for large classes of medieval documents which had no copies in the Public Records Office in London the scholar is dependent upon the published calendared summaries. However, in some cases it is also true that researchers, and especially archaeologists, have often not looked far enough in secondary publications printed prior to 1922 for portions of these now destroyed records. This omission is presently being rectified in the Department of Medieval History in Trinity College, Dublin, where a major research project is being undertaken on the reconstruction of the rolls of the Irish Chancery from both secondary published sources and from material located in other archives.

The following is a very general survey of these medieval documentary sources; those readers who wish to be more adequately informed about the actual records themselves should refer to the works of acknowledged scholars such as MacNiocaill for the Irish annals,[1] Lydon for the Survey of the Memoranda Rolls,[2] Curtis for the Ormond Deeds,[3] as well as the all-embracing compass of such writers as Sweetman,[4] Gilbert,[5] McNeill[6] and Brooks,[7] to name but a few of the most important.

Written sources

It is the records of the central government, especially those of the lordship of Ireland emanating from Dublin, which probably suffered the greatest destruction in 1922. However, these classes of documents are usually of such a general nature that they are of little direct use to the archaeologist digging a particular site unless it had particular royal or important aristocratic connections. These surviving records of the Crown and of the higher nobility have been most usefully employed by those archaeologists who have excavated some of the major medieval castles such as Trim and Limerick and more recently by A. Lynch and C. Manning of the OPW at Dublin Castle. Thus D. Sweetman, also of the OPW, was able to chart the main historical developments of the stone castle at Trim from the mandate of 1224[8] issued by the Justiciar presenting the castle to Walter de Lacy, through the de Geneville ownership and on until the beginning of the fourteenth century when it passed to the powerful Mortimer family. Then, like many other Anglo-Norman settlements, it ceased to be permanently occupied from the middle of the fourteenth century until it was reoccupied in the early seventeenth century by the Confederate forces. It was never again to be used as the residence of a great family as it was throughout most of the middle ages. However, from the surviving records Sweetman was still able to chart the owners of the castle all the way from the Mortimers, who held the liberty until 1425, through the ownership of Richard Plantagenet and then from 1460 when the lands and liberty of Trim passed into the hands of the Crown who held it for the rest of the middle ages.[9] And because it is known from the documentary records that Geoffrey de Geneville made Trim Castle his demesne manor soon after he had been granted the liberty in 1254 Sweetman was able to tie in the first phase of occupation of the castle to Geoffrey de Geneville's ownership from then until his death in 1302. In fact, Sweetman argued, it was during this period that a large plinth was added to the base of the keep to protect it from attack by mining, and either at the same time or slightly earlier the upper portion of the keep was constructed.[10] Sweetman also noted that the only pottery found associated with the temporary structures and post holes for the scaffolding was from Ham Green which indicated that the masons for this major construction job 'may well have come from the Bristol area'.[11]

Sweetman relied for his documentary information upon the great published calendared collection of medieval documents of Ireland by H. S. Sweetman (no relation), the then Deputy Keeper of the Public Records in Ireland, called the *Calendar of Documents relating to Ireland, 1171–1307*, and published in five volumes between 1875 and 1886. The other important published lists and calendars include the *Calendar of the Justiciary Rolls of Ireland, 1295–1314*, published in three volumes between 1904 and 1950, and the *Calendar of Inquisitions Post Mortem*, which include Irish estates of the tenants-in-chief of the Crown, the first volume of which was published in 1904. These major calendars augment an earlier calendar of some of the close and patent rolls of Ireland compiled by Tresham in 1828, which contains various inaccuracies, as well as the *Reports of the Deputy Keeper of the Public Records, Ireland, 1903–21*, which contain extracts from the pipe rolls and other classes of medieval documents under his care. All these published calendars and lists are of inestimable value to the scholar of the medieval past in Ireland as most of the originals on which they were based were totally destroyed in 1922. Also of great use to the medieval settlement archaeologist is the only known surviving Irish pipe roll of 1211–12, translated and edited by Davies and Quinn in 1941, particularly because of the financial information and construction details it gives about major castles and settlements. Apart from some scattered survivals the only other original collections of medieval documents relating to the King's government of his lordship of Ireland to have survived are those which, for a variety of reasons, were kept in London.

There have also been modern collections of different classes of documents such as that of the borough charters of Ireland, with a commentary in Irish, compiled by MacNiocaill in 1964. The two cities of Dublin and Kilkenny have probably the largest number of surviving early urban records that have been edited and published. For Dublin, Gilbert produced the *Calendar of the Ancient Records of Dublin*, covering the period between 1228 and 1841 which was published in nineteen volumes from 1889 to 1944. Records of the medieval city of Dublin also feature prominently in Gilbert's *Historic and Municipal Documents of Ireland, 1172–1300*, which he edited in 1870. One such important document contained in it is the only known early roll of the citizens of Dublin, possibly dating to the end of the twelfth century, which by listing the names of approximately 1,600 citizens has allowed historians to locate their probable origins. Hardly surprisingly, the roll shows that the majority of them came from England, particularly from the south-west. Other citizens came from South Wales and a few from Scottish and French towns.

When the surviving urban records for Kilkenny are examined it immediately becomes apparent that it is the *Liber Primus Kilkenniensis*, a contemporary record of many of the major events affecting the city from 1223 until 1573, that is a source of unparalleled importance. It is a vellum book bound in oak boards which was written in various hands from the middle of the fourteenth century until the 'Liber 2' takes over in 1540. The *Liber Primus* not only reproduces the charters but also records the proceedings of the town courts as well as the elections of the sovereigns and the other officers of the borough, the admission of burgesses, the city's by-laws and the rentals of town property in addition to many other matters that directly affected the ordering of the town in the medieval period. Fortunately for the archaeologist it was edited in 1931 by McNeill for the Irish Manuscripts Commission, and a translation into English and a chronological reordering of it was completed in 1961 by Otway-Ruthven. Unluckily the page references correlating this translation with McNeill's edition were not printed.

Generally the most informative class of documents for the medieval archaeologist are those manorial extents, surveys and accounts produced for the great landowning families of Anglo-Norman Ireland. However, the major problem about the surviving manorial documents is that they are regionally imbalanced. Thus the Ormond estates in Counties Tipperary and Kilkenny are the best documented because of the survival of the family right up to the present day. This has led to the publication by the Irish Manuscripts Commission of such volumes as *The Red Book of Ormond* in 1932. This is a cartulary, probably compiled in the fourteenth century, containing rentals and deeds of the family from about 1192 to 1547. Its publication was regarded as a supplementary volume to the six volumes of the *Calendar of Ormond Deeds*, published between 1932 and 1970, which were designed to cover the medieval portion (1172–1603) of the large number of family documents then in the Muniments Room in Kilkenny Castle.

Other important collections of manorial documents include the *Calendar of the Gormanston Register*, published in 1916, which is basically an entry book of the title deeds of the estates of the Lords of Gormanston in Counties Meath and Dublin, originally compiled at the end of the fourteenth century. Parts of the neighbouring county of Louth, including Dundalk, are also well documented in the *Dowdall Deeds*, which were edited by McNeill and Otway-Ruthven in 1960. There is also a collection of the manorial documents of the Fitzgeralds, dating mainly from the late thirteenth and fourteenth centuries but continuing into the early sixteenth century, collated in *The Red Book of the Earls of Kildare* (recently acquired by Trinity College, Dublin). There is also a modern edition published by the Irish Manuscript Commission in 1965 under the editorship of MacNiocaill. The only other part of the country to have an adequate collection of published manorial documents is again in Leinster and concerns the large estates of the Archbishop of Dublin in Counties Dublin and Wicklow which are contained in the *Calendar of Archbishop Alen's Register* and in the 'Calendar of the Liber Niger'.

The cartularies and registers of several important monastic houses have also survived and these are also important sources for settlement evidence because of the large areas controlled by some of these religious foundations. Significantly, collections of documents have survived for four important houses in the city of Dublin. The *Register of the Hospital of St John the Baptist*, published by the Irish Manuscripts Commission in 1936, contains most of the deeds of the holdings of this Hospital dating from the end of the thirteenth century up until 1486. The original register was almost entirely written in two identifiable hands at the end of the fourteenth century and seems to have been compiled from the original charters of the Hospital. The deeds are grouped together according to their locality, with half of them being from the city of Dublin and its surrounding area and the bulk of the remainder from Co. Tipperary. The other important Dublin religious houses whose medieval documents have survived to a considerable extent were the Cistercian abbey of St Mary's,[12] the Augustinian priory of the Holy Trinity at Christ Church[13] and the house of the Victorine canons at St Thomas's.[14] Other monastic cartularies and registers which contain significant information for the settlement archaeologist include those for the Co. Meath holdings of the Augustinian canons of Llanthony Prima and Secunda,[15] which largely date to the thirteenth century, the register of the priory at Tristernagh, Co. Westmeath,[16] and the charters of the Cistercian abbey of Duiske or Graiguenamanagh in Co. Kilkenny.[17]

The medieval manorial documents of the Augustinian priory of the Holy Trinity at Christ Church, Dublin, are mainly account rolls of the period 1337–46. They are especially important to the medieval archaeologist as they contain some of the most detailed information about the socio-economic workings of several Leinster manors just before the destructive impact of the Black Death. For the archaeologist it is a pity that these manors, and especially their manor houses and associated farm buildings, are now under the modern suburbs of the city of Dublin. For instance, at Grangegorman the accounts describe a hall with rooms off it and a yard with a barn, malthouse, workshop and a cow byre and haggard.[18] At the manor farm of Clonken (Kill of the Grange, Co. Dublin) the buildings were similar and there is also information about their construction, being timber-framed with wattle and daub walls.[19] The accounts related the cost and the time it took to construct these buildings and are therefore of inestimable value to the archaeologist because of the amount of constructional detail that they contain. For instance, the building of the kiln house (probably the potter's house or workshop near the kiln) is recounted in so much detail that it could probably be reconstructed accurately today employing the same materials and to the same dimensions. From the description of the construction work we can tell that it had a thatched roof, similar to all the other identifiable buildings on the manor, supported on four principal rafters. It also had wattle walls probably made weather-tight by mud being thrown against them, as was described in the repair of a cow-house there.[20] The knowledge of the existence of a pottery kiln at this manor is of major importance to medieval archaeologists because only two actual medieval examples, Downpatrick and Carrickfergus, have been found to date in Ireland.[21] The grange itself was a more substantial building as its walls were constructed out of timber weatherboarding 'brought among the Irish', probably from the Dublin mountains.[22]

The other major series of Irish medieval accounts are those preserved among the Minister's Accounts in the PRO in London for some of the greatest English lords who held estates in Ireland.[23] Chief among them are almost a hundred rolls of the accounts of the treasurers and bailiffs of the vast Irish estates of Roger Bigod, Earl of Norfolk and Earl Marshal of England, mostly located in Carlow and Wexford. These accounts have been extensively researched by Mills,[24] Hore[25] and, more recently, by Lyons.[26] In particular the accounts for Bigod's manors in Wexford, and especially the series of them for Old Ross at the end of the thirteenth century, have been extensively studied by both economic historians and archaeologists.[27] They give some considerable detail about the construction of at least one moated site as well as a wealth of information about the socio-economic workings of the various manors controlled by the Bigods in Ireland. However, like all surviving manorial accounts of the medieval period, these documents only inform us about the economic performance of the manor from the viewpoint of the tenant-in-chief. We therefore know next to nothing about all the micro-economies of the tenants of the manors, except where they impinged upon their profitability within the large estates held by the Bigod family. In fact, all the surviving medieval manorial documents really only inform us about the economy and society of those people who actually held land, so for the vast majority of the population of the Anglo-Norman lordship there is no surviving documentary evidence.

The only extant nationwide medieval taxation return is the ecclesiastical taxation of the early fourteenth century.[28] In the six surviving rolls in the PRO in London every Irish diocese is included except for Ossory, Ferns, and part of Leighlin in the Province of Dublin.[29] However, two returns for Ossory are to be found in the fourteenth-century 'Liber Ruber' in Kilkenny.[30] Two taxation returns also survive for Meath, Waterford, Cashel, Emly and Cork, the first from c.1303–6 and the second from c.1319–22. Where this has happened it is very useful for the researcher as it allows him to measure the effects of the Bruce invasion (1315–18) and the contemporary Great European Famine on the lordship of Ireland.[31] There are, of course, many problems in using this source generally to measure the economic performance of Anglo-Norman settlement in the early fourteenth century as it only taxed the temporalities of the Irish clergy. Another major problem relates to the identification of the Irish place-names in the rolls, which were probably written by scribes with very little knowledge of the original name.[32]

However this identification has been made much easier by the transcripts compiled by Reeves in the last century.[33]

There are also several important narrative histories and chronicles which contain much of interest to the medieval archaeologist. Chief among them are the two accounts of the events surrounding the Anglo-Norman invasion of 1169–70. Probably the most important of the two is the _Expugnatio Hibernica_ (Conquest of Ireland) completed by Giraldus Cambrensis in 1189, for which we have a modern translation and edition by Scott and Martin published in 1978. Not surprisingly, as Giraldus was a brother of Robert and Philip de Barry who were involved in the Conquest and were Geraldines through their mother, Angharad, his historical interpretation is very much biased in the family's favour. Nevertheless, especially as he had twice visited Ireland in the 1180s, his observations about the settlement history of the early Anglo-Normans have been found by archaeologists to have been both accurate and informative.[34] His earlier book on Ireland, _Topographia Hibernica_ (Topography of Ireland), translated by O'Meara in 1951, is more descriptive and lacks the precision of his second book but nevertheless still contains much useful contemporary information about Ireland in the late twelfth century.

The second major source is a Norman–French poem, given the title _The Song of Dermot and the Earl_ by Orpen who translated it in 1892. Although its author is unknown the consensus of academic opinion indicates that it was possibly written by a poet in the court of Dermot MacMurrough, maybe even Maurice O'Regan, after 1225. It is valuable, although it is later than Giraldus, because it contains earlier material which was probably transmitted orally to the scribe and also acts as a necessary counterweight to the _Expugnatio_ as it is more complimentary to Strongbow and also contains much information about the MacMurroughs that is absent from the _Expugnatio_. For the archaeologist the detailed account of the subinfeudation of Leinster and Meath has been of great importance in analysing the pattern of early medieval settlement there and in elucidating the main features of early castles such as Trim.[35]

Before briefly examining the Gaelic annals of the period some mention must be made of late medieval Anglo-Irish chroniclers, especially those of Friar John Clyn of Kilkenny and Thady Dowling.[36] The annals of Dowling are of much less importance than Clyn's as they are mainly derived from printed sources with some brief notes on local matters in Co. Carlow. They were not compiled until the early seventeenth century and therefore cannot really be regarded as a primary source for the medieval period. Clyn's annals, on the other hand, were probably written in the early fourteenth century and are important for their eye-witness account of the Black Death in Kilkenny, and in the lordship generally. Indeed it is thought that Clyn himself died of the plague as his chronicle ends in 1349.[37] This chronicle also includes much information about the Gaelic revival in Leinster in the same century, and for all these reasons it is a valuable late medieval source although it has yet to be published in an English translation. The other surviving Anglo-Irish annals are mainly fragmentary without modern editions and are not really so relevant to the archaeologist.[38]

Although some information on settlement and on the socio-economic framework of medieval society is contained in the major Gaelic annals there are many problems associated with their interpretation. The major one is the fact that all these medieval sources were written for a very different purpose to that which the archaeologist is interested in. This is particularly so for these annals, which were often compiled by monks, especially as most entries are brief and often only concerned with a particular region. They are, nevertheless, full of references to both monastic and defensive settlements which often complement the Anglo-Norman sources. They are, as well, our major source of information for that part of the island outside the area of the lordship.

Nevertheless, for the archaeologist a greater use of these annals is often vitiated by the lack of modern editions or translations of many of them. It is a pity that two of the most modern editions, of the *Fragmentary Annals* of Ireland by Radner in 1978 and the *Annals of Ulster* (to AD 1131) by MacNiocaill in 1984, concentrate on the period before the Anglo-Norman invasion. Of the remaining annals the most helpful to the archaeologist are those of Connacht[39] and Innisfallen[40] which have fairly modern translations, while those of Loch Cé[41] and for Ulster after 1131[42] date back to the end of the last century. There is also the largely seventeenth-century summary, the *Annals of the Four Masters*, edited and translated by O'Donovan in 1848–51, which contains much information of value to the settlement archaeologist.

Because of the comparative dearth of surviving medieval documents of a socio-economic nature the archaeologist often has to have recourse to later sources to try to elucidate the probable pattern of medieval settlement in Ireland. Perhaps the most important of these are the seventeenth-century surveys ordered by Cromwell to facilitate the large-scale redistribution of land to his followers. The most important of these is the *Civil Survey* (1654–6), the nearest Irish equivalent to the *Domesday Book*, which can be used in conjunction with the *Stafford Inquisition* of c.1636 for Connacht, and with the maps of the *Down Survey* (1654–6). The major problem for medieval archaeologists in the use of these later sources is the assumption that rural settlement in Ireland was, in effect, largely ossified between the fourteenth and the seventeenth centuries. This assumption is steadily becoming less tenable as research on the later medieval period – notably by K. Nicholls of UCC – gathers pace.[43]

Other socio-economic information and assistance with the evolution of place-names can be gained from a close study of two further seventeenth-century sources. These are the *Books of Survey and Distribution* (1641–1701), which gives some details of the lands forfeited after the 1641 rebellion, and *A Census of Ireland* c.1659, which by extrapolation backwards can give an idea of the probable composition of the medieval population in areas of Ireland unaffected by the later plantations.

Cartographic and later sources

By the first half of the nineteenth century there appeared what is arguably the greatest aid to the field archaeologist in Ireland, the production by the Ordnance Survey of the first edition of a series of maps to the scale of 6 inches to the statute mile for the whole island from 1824 to 1846. These were supplemented by a collection of town plans at an even larger scale. This series, as well as being a work of art in its own right, is of the greatest value to the archaeologist because it depicts the landscape, with its antiquities and field monuments, just before the extensive reorganization of settlements and field boundaries which followed the Great Famine (1845–7). It also captures the Irish landscape before it was dissected by the railways and by the intensification of the road construction network. Perhaps the first edition's most valuable contribution to the field archaeologist is its representation of many earthworks which were especially prone to destruction as a result of processes mentioned above, such as changes in field boundaries. Ironically, this is currently a major problem again in many parts of Ireland as progressive farmers are now securing grants to amalgamate smaller fields into bigger entities and to drain marshy lands. All of these trends threaten the integrity of surviving earthworks in particular as they often border old field boundaries or are situated on less favourable land. However, this problem is being addressed fairly successfully by the OPW which has developed a close liaison between its archaeologists and the Agricultural Advisers of the Department of Agriculture, who make the recommendations on land grants. In 1985 the OPW also produced an informative and excellently designed book, *Irish Field Monuments*, by Manning. This is being circulated to the farming community and to planning authorities in an attempt to inform them about the rich archaeological heritage of Ireland.

The maps in the first edition are also supplemented by the *OS Letters* which were copies of the correspondence between the field-workers, who included the great Gaelic scholars, John O'Donovan and Eugene O'Curry, and the director of the Survey. They are usually in the form of detailed past histories of every parish which often included drawings of many major archaeological and architectural monuments. The succeeding editions and revisions of the 6-inch maps are also valuable in both assessing destruction rates of earthworks in particular and in deciding what is the most accurate representation of a particular monument. In this regard the larger scale 25-inch plans are invaluable.

This nationwide cartographic coverage can be supplemented to a great extent in this century by the growth in aerial photography. Indeed, many of the newest maps are now being made by complex and expensive machines directly from accurate vertical aerial photographs. Some of the first aerial photographs to be used by Irish archaeologists date back to the 1930s.[44] But it is only over the last two decades that they have both become widely available and been extensively used in field archaeology.

Until recently there was no complete photographic cover of the whole of Ireland available to the general researcher. There was a complete vertical cover for Northern Ireland provided by the RAF, but taken at too high an altitude to identify smaller monuments successfully. However, in 1973–7 the National Geographical Institute of France was commissioned to take vertical aerial photographs of the whole of the Republic for the Geological Survey of Ireland. Although they are a little too small in scale for every archaeological purpose (each photograph covers an area of 20 square miles) their definition is of excellent quality. There are also earlier vertical aerial photographs taken by the Army Air Corps, which are also available at the offices of the Geological Survey of Ireland, approximately at the scale of 6 inches to the mile. The major limitation concerns their coverage as it is mostly of the coastline with a few runs inland.

There are also collections of photographs taken specifically for archaeological reasons, the most important being several thousand low-level oblique aerial photographs taken by J. K. St Joseph in the 1960s for the Cambridge Committee for Aerial Photography. Their larger scale and the advantages of the oblique angle in the right kind of lighting conditions mean that they reveal much more of the complexities of earthwork settlements in particular. Their disadvantage is, of course, that as they are usually only of one particular feature they do not provide a comprehensive cover for the country as a whole. Other small archaeological collections are also held by private aerial photographers.[45] Additionally some aerial photography has been undertaken by the OS for archaeologists,[46] and by various commercial companies.[47]

Returning to the last century there is another published source which has become a standard work of reference. This is the *Topographical Dictionary of Ireland* by Lewis, published in two volumes in 1837. Although much of the material about the major towns and villages of the country is derivative there is also systematic information included which is not to be found elsewhere.

There are also local histories of varying degrees of scholarship and accuracy which often include detailed information which is not readily available elsewhere. Perhaps the two most famous are Carrigan's for Ossory, published in four volumes in 1905, and Hore for Wexford, published in six volumes (1900–11). Then there are the important works of modern historical synthesis for the middle ages, notably the magisterial study by Orpen of the Normans in Ireland published in four volumes between 1911 and 1920, still an indispensable tool for any medievalist, Curtis (1938), Otway-Ruthven (1968), Lydon (1972), and Cosgrove (1987). There are also two major paperback series on Irish history whose volumes on the medieval period can usefully be consulted, the Gill History[48] and the Helicon History.[49]

Finally, some short mention must be made of the archives in the major governmental organizations involved in archaeology, although they are not normally available for consultation by the general public. However, arrangements can usually be made for scholars and other serious researchers to consult these archives by special arrangement with the particular institution. In Northern Ireland the accession registers of the Ulster Museum, and the Sites and Monuments Record of the Archaeological Survey of Northern Ireland are perhaps the most accessible archives. In the Republic the National Museum of Ireland has extensive finds registers and a card index, as well as a comprehensive topographical index which contains both published references and unpublished reports on the artefacts and many of the known archaeological monuments in Ireland. A broadly similar National Monument File is also available in the National Monuments Branch of the Office of Public Works, and the Archaeological Survey of Ireland also have important files. There are plans for all these archives to be computerized in the near future which should make data retrieval and the correlation of information very much easier and more comprehensive in nature.

Chronology

One of the main problems facing any archaeologist is the establishment of a secure chronology for both settlement sites and artefacts. For the medieval period there is, of course, a fairly secure general historical chronology based upon the surviving sources. However, this general chronology is not very useful for dating specific sites and so archaeological dating methods are often used, such as the typological dating of artefacts (usually pottery), and especially the use of coin evidence which is often the most precisely dated artefact found on medieval sites. A relative chronology is also usually built up from the broad stratigraphical relationship between layers and structures, although this method only gives a very imprecise relative chronology for site occupation.

More importantly, modern methods of scientific dating have revolutionized archaeological chronology over the last thirty years or so. Initially the radiocarbon method of dating organic matter by measuring the decay rate of the isotope carbon-14 became a common dating technique on many archaeological sites.[50] However its accuracy has been increasingly questioned by the scientific community, especially over the past decade. There have been major disagreements over the exact calculation of the half life of the isotope (the period of time in which the radiocarbon in a particular sample has decayed by one half). There is also the growing realization that the rate at which radiocarbon was produced has not always been uniform. Finally it has been shown that much more radiocarbon occurs naturally, and this has meant that the calendar years computed on the basis of the original radiocarbon dates have been too early. Therefore, in order to compensate for this error all modern radiocarbon dates are calibrated using dendrochronology. Despite these major problems the biggest drawback of this dating method for the medieval archaeologist is that its statistical error can range anywhere from 100 to 400 years.[51] Such imprecision is not acceptable for many medieval sites where the other methods of dating, such as dendrochronology, provide a greater degree of accuracy.

In the light of all this it is hardly surprising that the scientific analysis of tree-ring growth, or dendrochronology, has assumed paramount importance on the many medieval sites which have timber remains upon them. The accuracy of this method is such that M. Baillie of QUB has been able to date many samples of oak timbers in the Dublin excavations to an accuracy of ± 9 years, as long as the sapwood was present in the sample.[52] He has also been able to construct for Ireland the world's second longest tree-ring chronology from 5289 BC until the present day, and also to relate it to neighbouring tree-ring chronologies.[53] Currently only oak samples can be dendrochronologically dated. This is a minor disadvantage when compared with the problems related to accurate radiocarbon dating, especially as oak was commonly used for many medieval wooden structures.

Therefore, by a combination of traditional methods of dating such as typology and stratigraphy with those of dendrochronology and radiocarbon dating the chronological basis for our understanding of the broad development in material culture in medieval Ireland is becoming much more secure. There are other scientific methods of dating which are not so relevant to the medieval period although archaeomagnetic techniques might usefully be employed to date kiln sites in Ireland.[54]

Other scientific techniques are also proving valuable to the medieval archaeologist such as the use of low-level oblique and vertical aerial photography to elucidate the complexities of the often tenuous medieval settlement earthworks on the Irish landscape. The increasing use of infra-red film and infra-red linescanning is also likely to bring much more information about these sites to the attention of the archaeologist.[55] Other remote sensing devices such as ground soil radar, proton-magnetometers, and resistivity surveys are also of critical importance to the archaeologist to give him some idea of the lay-out of a buried settlement before he, in effect, destroys it by excavation.[56] In this connection, the development of sampling techniques is also of great importance to the archaeologist of the future both in preserving some part of every excavated site for future generations, and also in the random or systematic sampling of many sites rather than a concentration on one large site to the exclusion of several more typical examples.[57]

Thus there is a considerable range of sources from which it is possible to piece together the economy and social structure of Ireland between AD 1000 and the later middle ages; and although much of the evidence is inevitably patchy, as has been shown, and in some areas has been barely analysed, the foundations have been laid for a fuller understanding of the material culture of the country during the medieval period.

2 Pre-Norman settlement c.1000–1169

Introduction

Although this book is mainly concerned with the archaeology of the period after the Anglo-Norman invasion of 1169 it is very important that some account be taken of indigenous settlement forms before their arrival. All too often in the not too distant past Anglo-Norman settlement was treated as though it existed in a spatial vacuum whereas it is becoming increasingly apparent that the Anglo-Normans often built their settlements on or beside existing Irish structures. There were, of course, many entirely new settlements because it is probable that there was also an influx of settlers who had to be housed somewhere, although the full extent and density of this still has to be fully examined. In the following chapters it will be seen that the Anglo-Normans reused ringforts for their own mottes or ringwork castles, and that many of their towns or villages were located close to Early Christian monastic sites. Thus it is important to study, if only in a general fashion, the broad pattern of this pre-existing settlement. This in turn means that the rich artefacts of the Early Christian period, especially in metalwork and stone sculpture, for which Ireland is internationally famous are only mentioned if they have a direct bearing on the socio-economic or chronological development of the settlement sites under discussion. Any reader who wishes to pursue this aspect of Early Christian archaeology further should consult the text and bibliography in M. F. Ryan (ed.), *Treasures of Ireland* (1983).

Rural settlement

The present consensus of academic opinion is still that Ireland was predominantly a rural society in pre-Norman times and that the patterns of settlement were dispersed, i.e. settlements were located out of earshot of each other. The commonest settlement type was the ringfort, which is also generally known by two Irish terms, *rath* (earthen fort) and *cashel* (stone fort or enclosure), which is most commonly found in the west where stone is more easily available as a building material. At its simplest it has been defined by Ó Ríordáin as 'a space most frequently circular surrounded by a bank and fosse'.[1] However, this simple definition does not encompass the large diversity of such sites, ranging from the largest tri-vallate examples with strong banks and fosses to small simple features with insignificant banks and ditches. Their ground plans also vary, sometimes quite markedly, from the ubiquitous circle and occasionally two or more examples are to be found located close to each other. They make up the most widespread type of relict earthwork to be found on the Irish landscape, with estimates of between 30,000 and 50,000 surviving in the first edition of the Ordnance Survey 6-inch maps of the 1840s.[2] Thus it is interesting to speculate as to how many were still surviving in the landscape when the Anglo-Normans landed in Ireland at the end of the twelfth century.

Despite recent researches on this important settlement type by historical geographers such as G. F. Barrett, and by medieval archaeologists such as M. J. O'Kelly and C. J. Lynn there still remains much to be elicited about its chronology and function. With the general lack of information about ringforts in the surviving written sources of the period, which are mainly literary, or law tracts or annalistic writings, archaeological investigation assumes a primary importance. Although the totality of excavations number fewer than 120 sites, a small statistical sample, their random distribution would indicate that we do now possess a typical picture of their chronology and function. However, the archaeological evidence produced by many of these sites has often been either non-existent or undateable. Nevertheless, of the sites which have produced useful data, it would appear that ringforts can be broadly dated to the first millennium AD, and often functioned as defended farmsteads of one family grouping. Some others, such as Garryduff in Co. Cork (fig. 1), functioned as metalworking centres[3] whilst other smaller examples served as pens to protect cattle, valuable assets in pre-Norman Irish society.

It is also difficult to know, given the small sample of excavated sites, how many ringforts of the national total were occupied simultaneously. This together with our lack of knowledge of the size of the population at the time means that it is only possible to guess whether or not the entire population was living in these defended farmsteads or whether there was another complementary nucleated settlement form, the existence of which is hinted at in the surviving law tracts. But before the problem of undefended settlements in pre-Norman Ireland is examined it is necessary to review some of the major conclusions on the nature and chronology of the ringfort produced by archaeological methods of enquiry.

The areal size of ringforts has been measured in some parts of the country as a result of various surveys, such as those for Counties Donegal, Down, Louth, Meath and Monaghan, the barony survey of Ikerrin in Co. Tipperary and *Corca Duibhne* (Dingle peninsula) in Co. Kerry,[4] and Barrett's

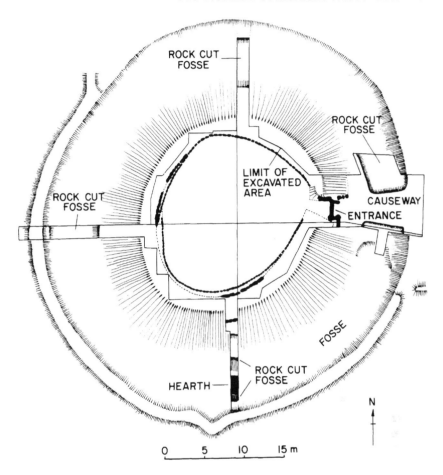

Figure 1 Plan of ringfort at Garryduff I, Co. Cork

specialized surveys of ringforts in the Dingle peninsula of Co. Kerry and part of south Co. Donegal.[5] They have all shown that ringforts broadly vary in size from around 15 m in diameter to a few which are as large as 80 m. However, the median diameter would be somewhere around 30 m. Inside these fosses and banks archaeologists have found evidence for mixed farming but often with the emphasis on cattle rearing. At other sites there has been evidence of industrial activity, especially ironworking, as well as spinning and weaving. And at some of the larger ringforts there has been evidence of specialization in metalworking as well as glass production.

A more detailed analysis of their chronology reveals that the majority of excavated sites were occupied in the last half of this first millennium AD, i.e. from around AD 500 to 1000. However, both the origins and the final phase of ringfort construction have been the subjects of much academic debate which is still not resolved satisfactorily. It has been put forward by O'Kelly that their origins can be found in the Bronze Age and that they were an important feature of the Early Iron Age.[6] But, more importantly for the subject of this book, there is evidence of occupation and, less certainly, the logical possibility that some were constructed *after* 1169. Barrett and Graham first put forward the above hypothesis based mainly upon their study of the 1840s distribution of this settlement type, especially in the Pale areas of Counties Louth and Meath.[7] They found that the known distribution of ringforts was much denser in those regions which were west and north of the probable line of the Pale boundary, and they sought to try and explain this either by the removal of ringforts as a concomitant to the more intensive agriculture introduced by the Anglo-Normans in the areas under their control or, more controversially, through the continued construction of such settlement forms in medieval times in areas on the periphery of dense Anglo-Norman settlement. Incidentally, the areas of lower densities of ringforts also correspond fairly closely with concentrations of the place-name element 'town' which, according to T. Jones-Hughes, indicates regions which experienced 'the most durable impact of Anglo-Norman colonisation and settlement'.[8]

There is no doubt that on the eve of the Anglo-Norman invasion there were numerous examples of ringforts surviving in the Irish landscape. What effects the Anglo-Norman invaders had on them, and also the problem of their chronology, will be examined later on. However, at this stage, the difficult question must be posed as to whether these ringforts were the only permanently occupied settlement forms in pre-Norman society or whether any other types of identifiable permanent settlements existed along with them. Because of the general lack of both archaeological and written evidence it soon becomes apparent that there is no definitive answer to the complexity and totality of the pre-Norman rural settlement pattern.

One of the major 'rogue' factors is the extent to which Irish society at this time dwelt in transitory settlements, migrating from place to place as the seasons changed. K. W. Nicholls has investigated this phenomenon, especially in the later middle ages,[9] and D. O'Corráin has done the same for the pre-Norman period.[10] It is, at this stage, impossible to calculate the full extent of these types of settlement because, by their very nature, they do not leave much of a trace on the landscape which could be identified archaeologically.

Thus we are left with a consideration of a variant of the ringfort form, the *crannóg*, and also with the possibility of the existence of two types of nucleated settlement in a rural environment, the so-called 'proto-clachan' and the major Early Christian monasteries. The crannóg is essentially a habitation site on an island in a lake, and in many cases the island itself was artificially created by accretions of soil, timber, stones and even occupation debris. It was often delineated either by wooden palisades or by stone walls and its origins are to be found in the Neolithic period.[11] Some of the most important excavated examples originated in the later Bronze Age and occupation of this type of settlement continued at least until the seventeenth century where they seem to have been used as defended strongholds in the wars of that period. However, the burden of archaeological evidence would tend to indicate that relatively few crannógs were occupied in the Anglo-Norman period. Whether this conclusion would help those researchers who maintain that ringforts also went out of fashion after the late twelfth century is difficult to say because of the much smaller total number of known crannógs (around 1,000)[12] and also the very small percentage that have been archaeologically examined. The evidence could also be stood on its head in order to bolster the argument that the Anglo-Normans were so successful in stabilizing the eastern half of the island that the necessity for living in these damp and often very inaccessible protected sites was largely obviated.

There have been some sites with medieval occupation strata, such as the crannóg at Island MacHugh, Co. Tyrone, where there seems to have been a considerable habitation in the thirteenth and fourteenth centuries.[13] But there were severe problems in interpreting the evidence for the dating of the earlier period of occupation, and the exact stratigraphical relationship between the early medieval occupation strata was difficult to establish. Some valuable research has been completed by Baillie in dating the probable age of some crannógs in Ulster by dendrochronological analysis of their oak timbers. He concludes that in the very near future absolute dating will be available for these sites of the first millennium AD.[14]

The economy of crannógs was very similar to that found in ringfort excavations. It was essentially mixed farming on the lands surrounding the lake and it is surprising that crannóg dwellers did not seem to have taken advantage of the fish and other food resources of the lake itself or the marshland around its edges. It has been suggested by excavators such as C. Bourke that the inhabitants of crannógs probably existed on a diet of meat and dairy products which was varied by recourse to wild fruit and vegetables.

Some of the smaller crannógs such as the one at Lough Faughan, Co. Down, have produced evidence for an agricultural economy dominated by livestock from their earliest levels right up to the medieval period. Despite the difficulties posed to the archaeologist by their location it is obviously important for more of them to be investigated archaeologically, as is currently happening at Moynagh Lough, Co. Meath, to balance our present archaeological evidence for the pre-Norman rural settlement pattern which is almost wholly based on findings from the excavation of ringforts.

Another major class of dispersed enclosed settlement inhabited in the pre-Norman period was the hillfort which has a broadly prehistoric origin but which obviously acted as a focus for settlement in some cases right up until the modern period. In contrast to the smaller ringforts, hillforts were principally defensive sites, with some of them possessing religious or ceremonial significance, and generally functioned as tribal rather than family centres. As there are only about sixty probable hillforts in Ireland it cannot really be argued that they made up an important class of settlements in the immediately pre-Norman period, except for examples such as those at Armagh and Downpatrick which must have acted as foci for later urban settlements. Of the other excavated hillforts it would seem that most of them were long abandoned before the start of the eleventh century although there would appear to have been some examples of very tenuous reoccupation in the medieval period.

Another major class of enclosed settlement forms surviving into the immediately pre-Norman period consists of the promontory forts which are to be found in such profusion especially on the western coastline. They are usually easily recognizable by their earthen or stone banks and their fosses which cut off access both to coastal or inland promontories. Yet again the problem with any interpretation of their probable function and chronology is the insufficiency of the archaeological data base. In all only six promontory forts have been excavated in recent years and it is unlikely that any of these were occupied in the century before the coming of the Anglo-Normans. At Dunbeg in Co. Kerry, the most recently excavated example, a ruined *clochaun* or beehive hut, with two occupation layers, yielded radiocarbon dates suggesting that it was probably occupied some time in the tenth or eleventh centuries;[15] but as at the other excavated sites there was generally extremely limited evidence for any sustained occupation of the fort (fig. 2). Thus it is still uncertain what particular role these settlements fulfilled in pre-Norman society.

Finally there is also a large number of unclassified enclosures, rectangular, sub-rectangular and trapezoidal, which have been examined by various archaeological surveys. Some of them may date to the immediately pre-Norman period such as those which are clearly visible on the ground in Counties Louth, Meath, Monaghan, Kildare and Westmeath.[16] Thus the possibility exists that after further surveys have been published and when some of these enigmatic enclosures have been excavated new classes of pre-Norman settlement forms will become apparent.

As Proudfoot has correctly pointed out there were probably other non-enclosed dispersed settlements in rural Ireland before 1169. But it is precisely sites lacking either an enclosing bank or fosse that are the most difficult to trace in the field. Probably the most important of this type of settlement are undefended, nucleated settlements of farm houses and out-buildings which, in a later period, were given the name 'clachan' by that most distinguished geographer of Ireland, E. Estyn Evans. In theory, according to the contemporary law tracts, pre-Norman Irish society comprised two major classes of people: the free farmers who probably lived in the ringforts and farmed lands of around 30 ha, and the lower orders who lived in separate settlements. It is in examining these latter settlements that we leave the sphere of archaeological evidence and venture into the much more uncertain world of place-name analysis because there is as yet no secure evidence that clachans existed in Ireland before the seventeenth century, when the earliest estate maps were drawn. Only one clachan has been partially excavated, that at Murphystown in Lecale, Co. Down, and the results for the dating of its origins were inconclusive. However, there was some limited evidence of occupation on the site from 'Early Christian or medieval times' but not in a form that could be identified as any form of proto-clachan, to use V. B. Proudfoot's designation.[17]

The use of place-name evidence, therefore, to try to resolve this problem was developed by Proudfoot, one of Evans's research students, who developed an earlier suggestion by MacAirt that the place-name element *baile*, which has been anglicized to 'bally', of which many examples survive as townland names in Ireland, could be equated with these early nucleated settlements. Proudfoot had noticed during his research on the settlement history of Co. Down that the distribution of *baile* townlands was complementary to those areas with high densities of ringforts. Thus he concluded that these two densities could be combined to give a truer picture of the total population density of pre-Norman Ireland.

But statistical tests on this hypothesis applied by G. F. Barrett to three

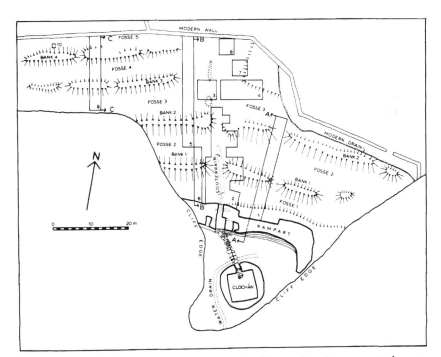

Figure 2 Plan of Dunbeg promontory fort, Co. Kerry, showing excavated areas

other regions – southern Co. Donegal, the Dingle peninsula of Co. Kerry, and Co. Louth – have produced conflicting evidence which would tend to suggest that the original Co. Down evidence is not necessarily applicable elsewhere in the country. From her research it would appear that only in the Dingle peninsula are ringforts and *baile* townlands complementary.[18] Of course, it must also be remembered that one of the main problems about establishing this complementary relationship over the whole island is the very late date of our major source of information about the actual areas of these townlands – the first edition of the OS 6-inch maps of the early 1840s.

Townlands themselves probably date back to the twelfth century at least, as is revealed by two surviving land grants from Co. Down. That townlands were being formed even earlier than this is suggested by several pre-twelfth-century charters such as the ones incorporated into the Books of Kells and Armagh.[19] The problem therefore which bedevils any modern researcher is the extent to which these townlands have changed in areal size from their inception until they were first mapped in the early years of the nineteenth century.

In the two twelfth-century land grants surviving for Co. Down about half of the listed denominations of land can be identified with modern townlands.[20] However it does not appear that the scholars have fully established whether the townland names in question refer to the same extent of land in the twelfth century as their present areal extent. It would seem from Barrett's researches into the development of the townland network of southern Donegal and in the Dingle area, using documentary evidence from the middle of the seventeenth century onwards, that there was considerable variation in this. She found that in some areas the townlands remained fairly unchanged but that in other locations there was significant sub-division. She concluded that 'considerable linguistic changes and fluctuations in townland boundaries are evident, whilst subdivision and the creation of new townlands from marginal areas and common lands also led to the introduction of new place-names'.[21] If this conclusion were extrapolated for the country as a whole, and there is no reason to doubt its nationwide validity, it would strongly suggest that the existence or otherwise of a *baile* townland name does not indicate the presence of a nucleated settlement of the clachan type.

Even were present-day townlands the same area as their pre-Norman predecessors there would still be a major problem in attempting to explain the precise meaning of the word *baile*, as it could mean either a piece of land, a homestead or a cluster of houses.[22] Also, in some cases, although the name is most frequently found in areas of intensive Anglo-Norman settlement, it is also located in areas reoccupied by the Irish in the later middle ages. In a valuable article utilizing a geographical approach to Irish place-names study T. Jones-Hughes has also concluded that *baile* townlands fall into his 'hybrid zones' where both Anglo-Norman and Irish cultures 'met, intermingled and struggled for supremacy'.[23] Thus, as the late

D. Flanagan noted, the existence of a *baile* townland name does not always suggest a settlement unit but can also simply mean a small portion of land.[24] In the finality, perhaps there is only a survival in the continuity of the tradition of such unenclosed nucleated settlements rather than any survival of settlements *in situ*, given the probable flexibility of this particular settlement form.[25]

Clachans, whatever their antiquity, have survived in parts of Ireland as diverse as Donegal in the remote north-western corner of the country and in the south-east, such as at Kilkenny and Wexford. Proudfoot defined them as 'a cluster of farm houses and associated outbuildings usually grouped without any formal plan'.[26] The agricultural system associated with these settlements is usually known as 'rundale' whereby the better lowland soils were cultivated in an openfield system in which each farmer held his land in scattered strips and which was continuously cultivated, while the 'outfield' was often cultivated every two to four years. In many cases the inhabitants of these clachans were related to each other and they all enjoyed grazing and peat-cutting rights in common on the unenclosed uplands nearby. The optimum size of these settlements has never been fully established but, according to Proudfoot, clusters of between thirty and forty houses were common in Donegal in the nineteenth century and in a few cases up to a dozen houses still survive (pl. 1).

Plate 1 Modern clachan at Lenankeel, Co. Donegal

Another important component of these pre-Norman settlements, both dispersed and nucleated, are the fields which must have been associated with them. There are, of course, many problems in first of all identifying these features and then in dating them. Obviously the field systems associated with the clachans cannot be dated before the seventeenth century because of the lack of a secure chronological framework for the clachans themselves. In the 1960s, however, a sustained programme of low-level oblique aerial photographs which were taken by J. K. St Joseph produced numerous examples of apparently early field patterns, especially in the east and west of the country.[27] More recently in the west of Ireland the Archaeological Survey in Co. Galway has discovered numerous early field systems, some of which seem to be associated with surviving cashels.[28]

In her intensive study of the ringforts of Co. Louth, Barrett has also found several definite examples of field systems related to ringforts as a result of studying St Joseph's collection of aerial photographs. At Whitecross she identified a large bi-vallate ringfort crop-mark 'set within and adjoined to the eastern edge of a large elliptical enclosure, approximately 120 m . . . in length and 90 m . . . in breadth at its widest point'.[29] Further, according to Barrett, there were signs of this enclosure having been realigned and slightly enlarged, and along its southern edge there was evidence of a circular building. At another site at Ballynahattin a possible ringfort crop-mark is adjoined on its eastern side by a crescent-shaped annexe with two entrances. As similar enclosures have been found elsewhere in Ireland Barrett suggested that they were either an extension of the original domestic quarters of the ringforts or an associated cattle enclosure. She also found three more examples of ringforts set either within or in close proximity to comparable enclosures in her study of Co. Louth. As she remarked, all these enclosures suggested 'a predominantly pastoral economy'.[30]

Barrett also located several ringforts which appeared to be surrounded by 'small irregular cellular field boundaries'.[31] She also located some examples of ringforts where fragments of field boundaries remain close by but which cannot be definitely linked chronologically with them. Of course a major problem in the identification of this aerial evidence is whether a particular feature is a subsiding enclosure to the ringfort or whether it is actually a field. There have, however, been a few excavations which have attempted to resolve this problem, such as at Cush in Co. Limerick where Ó Ríordáin found that associated with a cluster of six small conjoined ringforts, and a rectangular enclosure which contained five house sites, there were fields which were almost certainly contemporary with the ringforts as their stone boundaries were actually attached to them in some cases. However, there is some dispute as to the date of these features, ranging from the Early Iron Age to the Early Christian period.[32]

There is, as yet, no archaeological evidence to support this theory that both enclosed and open fields coexisted in the pre-Norman period. The written sources are not particularly helpful in this instance because all they do is to confirm the presence of both cereal and cattle production in the pre-Norman period. They do not give any real evidence of the comparable importance of the one compared to the other or of how these two types of agriculture were practised and organized in any detail.[33]

There are two other features usually associated with the pre-Norman Irish rural landscape: the souterrain and the horizontal mill. The souterrain or 'artificially built cave'[34] is often found in association with ringforts and other enclosed settlements of the pre-Norman period such as promontory forts (fig. 3). They are found throughout the country but have only recently been studied in any detail by P. Gosling for Co. Louth. He found that of the 250 examples known in Co. Louth there were high concentrations in the area to the west and north of the town of Dundalk.[35] He attempted to establish a chronology for these problematic structures as well as to identify their main functions. Although they are not confined to Ireland, being found also in western Cornwall, Scotland and Brittany, very few datable finds have been located in association with them. The second major problem is that they also vary greatly in both size and plan, so much so that it has been difficult to isolate their major functions. In Cornwall the *fogous* (souterrains) are nearly always found in association with surface features, including 'rounds' which are broadly similar in function to the ringforts. Thus it has been asserted that they were probably used for storage rather than for any defensive reason. Undoubtedly, some souterrains were used as safe hideaways for the inhabitants of nearby surface settlements because they contain either traps or some form of obstruction to confuse any intruder, such as the fine example at Donaghmore, Co. Louth. We are also

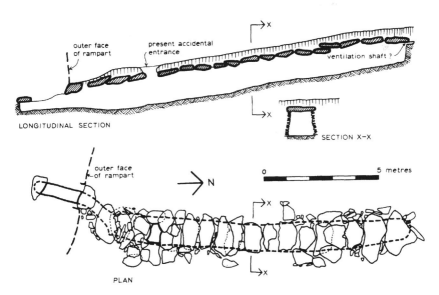

Figure 3 Souterrain at Dunbeg, Co. Kerry

lucky to have a dendrochronological date of AD 822 ± 9 for the oak posts which originally supported a roof of oak planks in the chambers of a souterrain at Coolcran, Co. Fermanagh.[36]

Horizontal mills are also an important feature of the pre-Norman landscape for which there is some archaeological evidence, mainly in the form of surviving timbers in waterlogged deposits. As Baillie has stated, 'The simplicity of construction and the freedom from gearing made the horizontal mill ideal for use in peasant communities.'[37] He also observed that although there are recorded instances of their use in the nineteenth and even in the twentieth centuries there is, as yet, no evidence for their being constructed in the medieval period.[38] Altogether he was able to date eleven examples using dendrochronology, and all of them fell within a 300-year period, from AD 630 to AD 926 ± 9.[39] Interestingly, these dates fitted in broadly with the earlier radiocarbon dates obtained by the late A. T. Lucas for similar structures in the 1970s.

If we now leave these secular rural settlement forms and examine the ecclesiastical settlements it soon becomes apparent that here too there is a wide variety of both morphology and function. It is only in the recent past that scholars have produced evidence to change our older notions about the place of the Early Christian monastery in contemporary Irish life. More and more it is becoming apparent that not all of the monasteries were of the Skellig Michael-type, comprising small communities eking out an existence in isolated locations where they could commune more easily with God. In fact, it has been argued that the most successful of them, such as Glendalough, Co. Wicklow, and at Kildare to name only two, took on true urban functions as the centuries progressed and large numbers of people, both lay and ordained, were attracted both to their thriving religious centres and to the increasing economic activities surrounding them. They developed to such an extent that urban geographers, such as R. A. Butlin, began to call the largest 'proto-towns'. In the context of this book, then, I will be examining them purely as settlement types and will not be concentrating on their important contribution to the development of religious life in Ireland.

Most scholars of the Early Christian Church in Ireland would now probably agree that by the eleventh century the most successful monasteries had outgrown their original purely religious functions, and this was possibly also an accidental result of the eighth-century Céle Dé movement which sought to separate the religious core of the monastery from the lay accretions that grew up around it. The only problem from the archaeologist's point of view is that most of the evidence currently available is based on literary sources as no large eastern monastery has yet been excavated, probably because most of them are still used as Christian burial places. There have recently been some small-scale excavations around Glendalough in preparation for the erection of various amenities by the Office of Public Works for visitors. However, none of these excavations produced horizons or artefacts which were of use in interpreting the historical development of the monastery itself.[40]

If we deal with the isolated monasteries which have been excavated, first of all, it immediately becomes apparent that they were often small in area such as the complex and important site at Reask on the Dingle peninsula of Co. Kerry, which was excavated by T. Fanning from 1972 to 1975 for the Office of Public Works. Within an irregular oval-shaped dry-stone enclosure wall, with dimensions of 45 by 40 m, there were revealed paths, drains, subdivisions, a small stone oratory, the foundations of several *clochauns* (circular stone beehive huts) and a cemetery of lintel graves. The initial settlement here enclosed within the cashel-type wall was identified by Fanning as probably that of a 'Christian community of, say, the fifth to seventh century AD'.[41]

The second main phase of occupation which could not be accurately dated seems to have extended from the seventh/eighth century to the twelfth century AD and could possibly have been a mainland version of the other famous monastic enclosures on the islands of Skellig Michael or Church Island in the same county (on which there was a limited excavation by A. Lynch of the OPW in 1986). The conjectural reconstruction by K. O'Brien (pl. 2) graphically illustrates how the settlement probably appeared during this second phase of occupation. The sanctuary area to the right of the low wall which sub-divided the settlement probably included a structure that could be interpreted as the abbot's dwellings. The large conjoined beehive huts in the foreground were the last *clochauns* to be built on the site and it was suggested by Fanning that the reuse for ironworking of the other buildings in this outer area could have been undertaken by the occupants of this structure.[42] Interestingly enough, after the *clochauns* and oratory were abandoned a portion of the site was used as a *ceallunach*, or burial place for unbaptised infants.

Plate 2 A conjectural reconstruction of the Early Christian enclosure at Reask, Co. Kerry

One major interpretative problem which exercised the mind of Fanning at Reask, as well as other scholars of the Early Christian period in Ireland, was whether such a site was monastic in character. Although the cross-slabs, burials, slab shrine and oratory were definitely ecclesiastical features, none of the small finds, with the possible exception of the sherds of amphorae found during the excavation, could be regarded as being ecclesiastical. He draws a parallel with the excavation by O'Kelly at Church Island,[43] and thus suggests that these sites were secular Christian settlements rather than monastic communities. That there were eremitical monastic communities in isolated locations, especially in the west of the island, cannot, however, be doubted. And Fanning, along with other scholars of this period, maintains that it was the Anglo-Normans rather than the Vikings who disrupted this type of settlement.[44]

Finally there are over 600 ecclesiastical enclosures, not necessarily of monastic origin, which have been located by researchers such as D. L. Swan. By using aerial photographs, cartographic evidence and place-name study he has found that their densest distribution is in the central part of the country, with the counties of Roscommon, Galway and Clare having the highest densities of such sites (fig. 4). Morphologically they are usually circular or oval enclosures of earth and stone, averaging from 90 to 120 m in diameter, which makes them much larger than even the largest ringfort. Excavations at sites such as Kilpatrick, Co. Westmeath, indicate that they were mainly habitation sites with burials only occupying a small area within the enclosure.[45] The weight of place-name evidence, especially in the south-west of Ireland which has been extensively studied by V. Hurley, supports a pre-twelfth-century date for most of these sites.[46] Undoubtedly, however, some of these enclosures would still have been occupied at the time of the Anglo-Norman invasion of Ireland.

Urban settlement

We must now move on to a brief discussion of the two types of urban settlement in pre-Norman Ireland. There has always been little doubt about the importance of the Vikings who set up most of the major ports of the eastern seaboard to act as market centres for their large northern European trading empire from the tenth century onwards. However, only the series of excavations in Dublin have produced a sizeable quantity of both structures and artefacts of the Viking period, with some limited evidence being found on the Lady Lane site at Waterford of occupation in the Scandinavian period. Other excavations in ports such as Cork and Wexford, which are known to have had Hiberno-Norse occupation, did not produce any archaeological traces of this period of their history. But the question of a second major component of urban settlement in pre-Norman Ireland, some of the larger monastic centres, has only recently been examined by scholars and the archaeological evidence for this is almost non-existent.

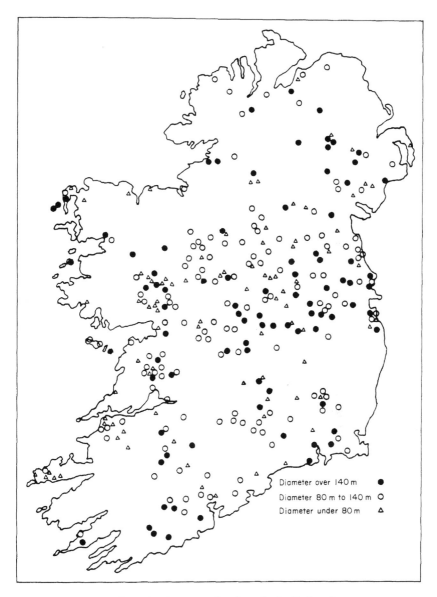

Diameter over 140 m   ●
Diameter 80 m to 140 m   ○
Diameter under 80 m   △

Figure 4 Distribution map of early ecclesiastical enclosures

There is, nevertheless, limited evidence for some kind of urban character
in the larger monasteries from the written sources of the period. But the
nature of these sources, mainly annals and law tracts, makes their
interpretation extremely difficult, especially for something as tangential to

urban + religious (???)

their original purpose as evidence of urbanization. For instance, the annals relate the destruction of many houses in Armagh in AD 912, three streets in 1112, and twenty houses and four streets in 1166,[47] and other sources make it clear that at about the same period the settlement was divided up into 'thirds' or suburbs where merchants, students and craftsmen were to be found. But despite several excavations in Armagh[48] there is still no definite archaeological evidence for its urban character in the pre-Norman period. Other annals refer to the workshops of comb-makers in Kildare which were probably similar to those found in the Dublin excavations.[49] Also, the mid-seventh-century description of Kildare by Cogitosus is of a *civitas* or town without walls but with *suburbana* (suburbs) and also with boundaries. Thus, in the words of the most recent work of synthesis on urbanism in this period in the non-Roman world: 'From the tenth century onwards places such as Armagh, Clonard, Clonmacnoise, Derry, Downpatrick, Kells and Kildare had urban attributes, though their main function was still religious.'[50]

As has been stated above the vast increase in our present understanding of the material culture of Scandinavian urban settlements in Ireland has come as a result of the excavations in Dublin over the last quarter of a century or so. It is a pity that there has yet to be a comparable number of excavations of another Scandinavian urban settlement in Ireland with which the finds and structures discovered in Dublin can be compared. Thus it is not possible at present to be sure whether they are typical or atypical for areas under Scandinavian influence in Ireland generally. The Dublin excavations have all taken place in the immediate vicinity of Christ Church Cathedral and the Castle in the city centre. The first historical evidence for Scandinavian settlement in the vicinity of Dublin was the annalistic reference to the establishment of a Viking *longphort* in AD 841, although the original source was a late one and not that reliable.[51] It was originally thought that one of the two timber-revetted curving earthen banks found in the Fishamble Street area of the large Wood Quay site could have been part of this *longphort* but the excavator, P. Wallace of the National Museum of Ireland, dated its construction to the middle of the tenth century.[52] Indeed none of the modern excavations have produced any evidence for ninth-century Scandinavian activity within the city centre. Thus Wallace has argued that the early medieval city of Dublin was probably founded in the first quarter of the tenth century by a new generation of Scandinavians from Britain whose numbers included both Anglo-Saxon and indigenous Irish.[53]

The only finds from an earlier period were located as a result of railway construction work in the western suburb of the city at Islandbridge, Kilmainham in the nineteenth century when a group of Viking burials were discovered. The major problem with any interpretation of this possible cemetery site is that it was not excavated utilizing modern archaeological methods and thus there is no known plan of the burials or, indeed, of where the site was exactly located. The finds associated with both male and female skeletons include weapons, shears, tongs and a sickle along with other iron household objects. These finds were broadly dated to the ninth century mainly by typological analysis of the brooches. This has led scholars such as J. Graham-Campbell to suggest that the original Scandinavian *longphort* was located close to this cemetery in Islandbridge, further upstream of the river from the present centre of the city.[54]

The first modern excavation of pre-Norman artefacts and horizons was directed by M. Ó hEochaidh of the OPW in a small area within the ward of Dublin Castle in 1961–2. Although this excavation has yet to be published it is known that deeply stratified deposits were found underneath the medieval castle horizon going back to the tenth century. The waterlogged remains of planked pavements and wicker screens were uncovered as well as pre-Norman barlip pottery and a tenth-century strap tag.

Since then all the later major excavations in the city outside Dublin Castle have been carried out by the National Museum of Ireland (fig. 5), and have produced numerous artefacts and structures of the Hiberno-Norse period in the city. This means that any attempt to summarize the main findings of this series of complex excavations is an almost impossible task to accomplish adequately in the space available, especially with regard to the many thousands of artefacts recovered. All that I can advise is that the reader reads the published papers of two of the excavators, B. Ó Ríordáin

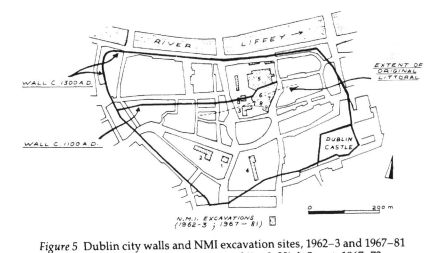

Figure 5 Dublin city walls and NMI excavation sites, 1962–3 and 1967–81
1. High Street, 1962–3, A. B. O'Ríordáin; 2. High Street, 1967–72,
A. B. O'Ríordáin; 3. Winetavern Street, 1969–71, A. B. O'Ríordáin;
4. Christchurch Place, 1972–5, A. B. O'Ríordáin; 5. Wood Quay, 1974–6,
P. F. Wallace; 6. Fishamble Street, 1975–6, A. B. O'Ríordáin, and 1977–8.,
P. F. Wallace; 7. Fishamble Street, 1975–6, 1978–80, P. F. Wallace; 8. John's Lane,
1978–9, P. F. Wallace; 9. Fishamble Street, 1980–1, P. F. Wallace

and P. F. Wallace, as well as of other writers such as H. B. Clarke and A. Simms which are included in the bibliography. However, it must be stressed that despite the activity in Dublin since the early 1960s only an area of approximately 10 per cent of the walled city has been scientifically excavated.

What the excavations have done, along with the researches of A. T. Lucas and K. Hughes, is to allow a dramatic reassessment of the Scandinavians in the history of early medieval Ireland. No longer are the Scandinavians thought of solely as plunderers of monasteries and notorious agents of destruction of the culture of Early Christian Ireland. From the artefacts and the structures recovered from the Dublin excavations we can now see the inter-mixture of Irish and Scandinavian cultures which made up the Hiberno-Norse city. Although some of the closest parallels with Dublin are to be found in the Scandinavian city of York, which is also currently undergoing large-scale excavation,[55] the city was also strongly influenced by Anglo-Saxon culture and society.

Due to the waterlogged nature of the sites there has been excellent preservation of both the foundations of post-and-wattle houses and workshops of the period, along with property boundaries and wooden and stone pathways and streets. The houses were often sub-rectangular in plan and ranged in size from around 3.80 by 3.20 m, up to 8 by 6 m. Some of them had benches surrounding a central hearth and in their associated levels a wide range of everyday domestic articles and ornaments of the tenth and eleventh centuries were located. Anglo-Saxon coins, stamped, glazed and cooking wares of pottery were found along with hundreds of bone combs, Irish souterrain ware, gaming pieces of carved walrus ivory, dyed woollen garments, shoe leather, and carved bone trial-pieces in Ringerike, Geometric and other designs, as well as brooches, rings, bracelets and pins. The baked clay crucible fragments, slag and vitreous matter as well as the trial or motif-pieces of bone, all indicate the importance of metalworking in the city, along with the making of bone combs, weaving and leatherworking. These are, however, only from the industries that have left some archaeological trace in the city and so it still gives us only an incomplete picture of the society and economy of the Hiberno-Norse city.

In the Fishamble Street area next to the Wood Quay site proper (fig. 6) Wallace has been able to chart the development of around fourteen house plots from c.AD 900 until 1100.[56] He has been able to show the continuity of these plots of land around the houses that probably bordered onto a street from Hiberno-Norse into Anglo-Norman times. This excavation also produced many artefacts such as Saxo-Norman pottery which showed the close connection that already existed between Dublin and England, especially with the western areas of that country, in the two centuries before the coming of the Anglo-Normans. Glazed Andennes ware and the red painted wares of Normandy were located in the organic refuse dumped behind the city wall built across the Wood Quay site to stabilize it from the pressure of

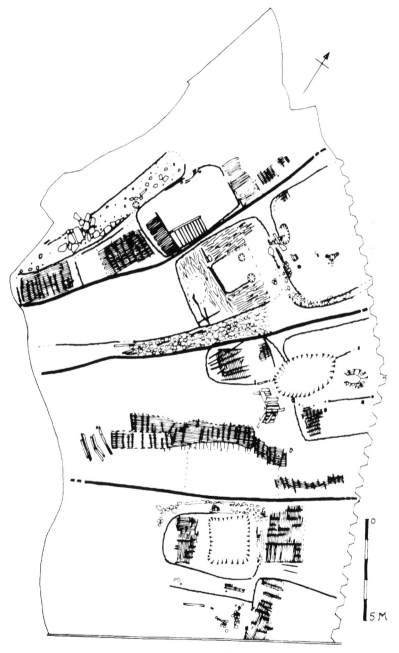

Figure 6 Simplified plan of four house plots of the eleventh century at Fishamble Street, Dublin

the tides. These revealed that 'Dublin was part of an active Franco-Norman trading network long before the Norman invasion of 1169'.[57] It is also interesting to note that Wallace decided to date the first stone wall here to around 1100.

The only other urban excavation to produce possible evidence of Scandinavian occupation was the site at Lady Lane in Waterford excavated by M. Moore of the OPW in 1982–3. Historically it is thought that the Norse King Sitric founded a settlement at Waterford, although the actual origins of the city can probably not be dated until the arrival of a Viking fleet in AD 914. The site was located at the sharp point of the triangular area that was thought to encompass the Scandinavian area, at the junction with the walls of the thirteenth-century extension to the city (fig. 7). The earliest features exposed were a number of post-holes dug into the natural clays

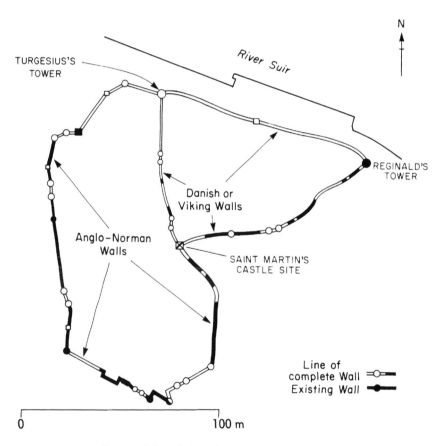

Figure 7 Map of Waterford city walls and towers

which were congregated into two clusters and which Moore interpreted as houses similar in plan to the three-aisled or four-post type which predominated in Dublin. Unluckily no artefacts were located which could help date these two structures although he was able to say that they probably pre-dated the twelfth century as one of them was partially destroyed by a defensive ditch which was definitely in use by then. Using an analogy with Dublin, Moore was able to suggest that another property existed between the two houses, which as it was built further west was destroyed by later developments.[58] The defensive ditch which ran north to south across the site was over 7 m wide at its north end and appeared to become narrower as it progressed southwards. Moore found no traces of an internal bank as it was destroyed when the city wall was erected some time at the end of the twelfth or the beginning of the thirteenth century. A small post-and-wattle hut, probably used to house an animal,[59] was erected upon the deposits in the ditch which were produced by natural silting and also the result of the inhabitants throwing their rubbish into it.

Very little in the way of archaeological evidence was found at this site to illustrate the socio-economic activities of the city in the Hiberno-Norse period. However a quantity of metalworking slag was found in the vicinity of the ditch but no hearths or furnaces were located, so Moore has suggested that the slag was probably being dumped into the ditch from metalworking inside the city itself.[60] Other finds from the ditch were animal and fish bones as well as some eleventh- and twelfth-century pottery sherds. Unlike Dublin, however, the building of the city wall here and the erection of another post-and-wattle house with a rudimentary hearth are more likely to have taken place *after* the Anglo-Norman invasion.[61] However, this later date is dependent upon our present understanding of the chronology of English and French green-glazed wares of pottery which may well be altered in the light of future research.

There have been further small-scale excavations in Waterford in 1985 but they have, as yet, produced no additional evidence for Scandinavian activity in the city. What is obviously needed is a programme of excavation in the historic core areas of other Viking ports such as Arklow, Wexford, Limerick and Cork to provide comparative material with which the Dublin and Waterford finds can be seen in context. Also some attempt should be made to locate inland Viking settlements to see how far the Scandinavians penetrated into the countryside outside the major coastal ports. Most of our evidence to date on Scandinavian penetration is based on coin or silver hoards and the occasional Viking burial.

The picture of indigenous settlement in Ireland on the eve of the Anglo-Norman invasion is both complex and confusing, both because of the lack of archaeological excavations and because of the scarcity of documentary sources before the twelfth century. Nevertheless, Ireland's landscape seems to have been dominated by the dispersed defended farmstead, the ringfort, with the possibility of the existence of some type of undefended nucleated settlements. Recent research has also indicated that some of the larger monasteries were functioning as urban areas from the tenth century onwards although the documentary evidence has yet to be confirmed by archaeology. And the long series of excavations in Dublin have also revealed the variety and richness of Scandinavian culture in Ireland as well as stressing the importance of the Vikings' establishment of these urban nuclei which traded with most of northern Europe from the tenth century onwards, and which became some of the major ports of the country in the centuries that followed.

3 Anglo-Norman military fortifications

Until fairly recently it was thought that the initial phase of the Anglo-Norman invasion of Ireland was marked by the construction of mottes or motte-and-bailey earthen castles at strategic locations throughout the country to consolidate the position of the invader. A motte can best be described as a mound of earth, usually artificially raised, with a fosse around its base. Contiguous to it there was often a bailey, commonly a sub-rectangular or crescent-shaped earthwork delineated by a bank and a fosse, as can be seen at Granard, Co. Longford (pl. 3). However, recent research by archaeologists has revealed that this pattern of military earthworks constructed by the Anglo-Normans is much more complex than would appear at first sight. As well as the suggestion by T. E. McNeill that mottes were probably built in areas which were always under the control of the indigenous population in Ulster,[1] there is some evidence to show the colonizers were not averse to constructing their mottes on top of the defended farmsteads of the 1st millennium AD, the ringforts,[2] or indeed to refashioning these ringforts into military ringworks.[3] As can be appreciated by any field-worker, there are immense problems in trying to identify an Irish ringfort from an Anglo-Norman ringwork from surface morphology alone.[4] Even excavation cannot always answer this question because of the frequent lack of occupation levels and artefacts in these classes of earthworks.

If first we examine the available archaeological evidence for motte construction in Ireland it immediately becomes apparent that the number of such castles which have actually been excavated is very small, with much of the work having been carried out in Ulster. The first published distribution map of mottes in Ireland was completed by Orpen in 1911 and shows all the mottes that were known to him, whether surviving or destroyed, in relation to the topography of the island.[5] Then in 1973 R. E. Glasscock mapped 340 mottes extant in Ireland which had no stone buildings on them, 184 in the Province of Leinster, 128 in Ulster, 24 in

Plate 3 The motte and bailey at Granard, Co. Longford, from the air

Munster and only 4 in Connacht.[6] These figures must be regarded as being minimum totals as they were arrived at mainly from cartographic research, except for Ulster where McNeill visited the sites on the ground, and further research (by Graham in Counties Meath and Westmeath,[7] the Archaeological Survey of Ireland in Counties Louth and Meath,[8] and D. A. Caulfield in Co. Kilkenny[9]) has revealed higher numbers of mottes than Glasscock's original county totals. Nevertheless, the greatest density of mottes are still to be found in the eastern half of the island as shown on Glasscock's map (fig. 8). Of the mottes that have been excavated most of the evidence would date their construction to some time in the period 1170 to 1230. In Co. Down, where the great majority of excavation has taken place, the occupation dates that have been produced all fall into the twelfth or early thirteenth centuries. But these excavations have usually been concentrated on the summits of the mottes so that the current state of our knowledge as regards

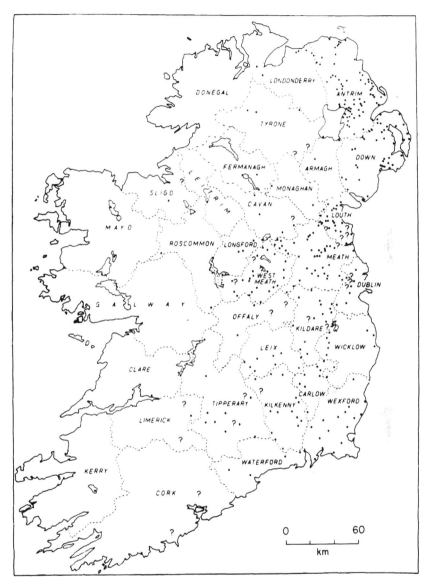

Figure 8 Distribution map of surviving mottes in 1973

the chronology and structures of the baileys and other subsidiary features is very rudimentary.

In the larger towns most of the mottes were superseded by stone castles, as happened at Athlone, Co. Westmeath, where a substantial castle built by de Grey in c.1210 replaced a motte probably built before 1199.[10] That this was not always the case can be seen in Drogheda where the Anglo-Norman motte, called 'Millmount', still dominates one section of the town.

From an archaeological point of view, because of the concentration by excavators on the summits of these mottes very little is known about their actual construction. If we go back to the Bayeux Tapestry, woven some ten years after the Norman victory at Battle in 1066, we can see the well-known representation of the motte that William caused to have built at Hastings soon after his arrival on the coast of England (pl. 4). It shows a perfect reversed stratigraphy with clear-cut horizons of earth one above the other, but when P. A. Barker came to excavate the motte that still survives there he found that it was composed almost entirely of sand which would have been a very unsuitable structure.[11] This led historians and archaeologists to wonder whether the Hasting's motte representation on the tapestry was purely stylistic or whether there were originally two mottes there. The first interpretation has been given added weight for Ireland as a result of the researches and excavations on several sites where it would seem that mottes were often constructed by a ring-bank being built first and then filled in until the appropriate height was reached. At Lorrha motte in Co. Tipperary E. Talbot investigated a very rough and ready section through the mound and found that the soil horizons dipped towards its centre suggesting that it had been built in this way.[12]

At another site, that of Dunsilly in Co. Antrim, McNeill excavated a motte, 4 m high and 8 m in diameter at its top, which was built on an earlier ringfort (or rath) which had three major phases.[13] Here a house of the third and final phase of rath construction was covered by the motte which was also constructed in three stages. The site was first levelled by the laying down of a thick layer of clay and boulders and then a surrounding ditch was dug and its spoil piled along its edge to produce a small ringwork which included a section of the rath bank. The final stage was the tipping of the earth derived from scarping the bluff on which the rath was originally built against the stable rath bank until the desired height of the motte was reached. (Interestingly, the archaeological evidence, or lack of it, further revealed that this motte was never used.) Again, this is an example of the Anglo-Normans utilizing indigenous earthworks to facilitate the construction of their mottes. At Rathmullan in Co. Down, C. J. Lynn discovered that the motte constructed on top of an earlier ringfort had also been erected by gradually heightening a bank around the perimeter of the site until the hollow centre could be safely filled in (fig. 9).[14] But at two roughly exposed motte sections in the south of the country, Old Ross, Co. Wexford,[15] and Kells, Co. Kilkenny,[16] there was no apparent evidence of the construction of any type of ring-bank.

The evidence for structures on top of the mottes is also very slim despite the programme of excavation by D. Waterman in Co. Down. At Lismahon, where a platform rath was converted into a motte in c.AD 1200, the remains of a house, approximately square in plan with rounded corners, was located

Plate 4 The motte at Hastings in the Bayeux Tapestry

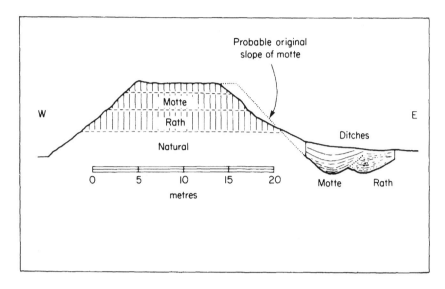

Figure 9 Simplified section of Rathmullan raised rath and motte, Co. Down
(after Lynn 1981–2)

on top of the mound.[17] Waterman paralleled it with other houses dating to the first millennium AD, probably because of the lack of comparable medieval structures found in an Irish context. Along with this house and attached to it he found evidence of a wooden tower (fig. 10), presumably erected for defensive purposes, which he likened to the much more substantial tower found by Hope-Taylor on top of the motte at Abinger, Surrey, in England.[18] The remains of another wooden tower surrounded by a palisade and a timber and earthen breastwork were found by Ó hEochaidh of the OPW in 1964 during the excavation of a motte at Lurgankeel in Co. Louth.[19] But the most common features identified on the summits of mottes in Ireland have been weapon pits, such as those found at Clough Castle and Lismahon in Co. Down,[20] and traces of wooden palisades around the peripheries of the mottes such as were located at Dromore and Clough Castle, again in Co. Down (fig. 11).[21] But on many other mottes no structural features have been identified, although coins, iron objects and pottery of the twelfth and thirteenth centuries have been found at, for example, Ballyroney and Castleskreen, both in Co. Down.[22]

In recent years there has also been a rekindling of the arguments over the origins of mottes which so exercised the minds of Orpen and Armitage at the start of the century. Waterman suggested from the finds of native pottery that Lismahon was always in Irish hands and that they could have built the motte on top of their earlier platform rath.[23] The possibility that the indigenous population could have constructed mottes in imitation of

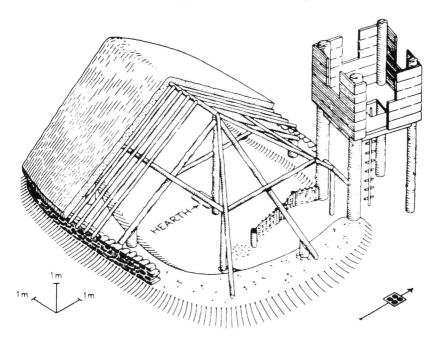

Figure 10 Conjectural restoration of the house and tower at Lismahon,
Co. Down

nearby Anglo-Norman examples was also put forward by McNeill in his
study of the Anglo-Norman settlement of Ulster when he found that 17 out
of a total of 128 mottes were to be found west of the River Bann.[24] McNeill
also remarked that few of the Ulster mottes possessed baileys and, where
they did, the feature was a fortification for a military garrison rather than
functioning as a residential or manorial centre. He further maintained that,
in comparison with England, motte ownership in Ulster extended relatively
far down the social hierarchy and suggested that the form might represent
an appropriate adaptation of the hall and manor to the dispersed Irish land-
holding system.[25]

At Big Glebe in Co. Derry a recent excavation has uncovered evidence
that mounds very similar to the later mottes were being built in the Early
Christian period in Ireland.[26] The mound there was oval with a flat summit
20 m in diameter and over 7 m in height above the surrounding land. The
perimeter of the mound was delimited by a roughly circular wall of
unmortared loose stones. At the highest point of the mound and away from
the perimeter wall the burnt outlines of a circular house, 8.50 m in diameter,
was revealed. There was also a paved entrance to the house on the eastern
side and numerous internal stakeholes and pits. When the mound itself

was fully excavated a sloping ramp and a dry-stone retaining wall were exposed. The mound had been erected in one continuous sequence, probably with the use of the ramp and the short length of wall which enabled a larger volume of soil to be carted up to the summit than would have been possible by hand.

There is also the problem of the 'raised' and 'platform' raths mainly located in Ulster, and especially in Co. Down, where several have been excavated. This immediately raises the question as to whether these were mainly a northern feature or whether more detailed fieldwork will reveal more of them elsewhere in Ireland. Some examples have been tentatively identified outside Ulster by the Archaeological Survey of Ireland, such as the half destroyed example at Castletown Kilberry, Co. Meath.[27] Nevertheless, the majority of 'raised' raths excavated in Co. Down provide evidence of

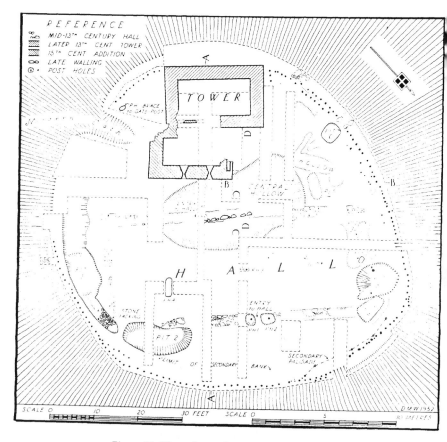

Figure 11 Plan of top of motte at Clough Castle

some use in the medieval period. These earthworks can be identified in the field as they are usually more than 3 m in height above the surrounding ground level and they lack the fosse and internal bank of the typical ringfort. There seem to be two major factors behind their raised profiles, the first illustrated by the example at Dromore, Co. Antrim, where the excavation revealed that the site was located on the top of a glacial *kame* (small gravel mound),[28] while at Ballynarry in the same county the mound was raised by continuous occupation over a long period of time, in this case up until the thirteenth century.[29] On the other hand, a 'platform' rath is an earthwork which has been deliberately heightened by human labour. Many of these sites, such as Lismahon in Co. Down, and Ballingarry, Co. Limerick, were heightened in the thirteenth or fourteenth centuries and were located in areas either controlled by the Anglo-Normans or within their sphere of influence. Thus it has been suggested that these fortifications possibly represent the transformation of an indigenous settlement form into an imitation of the imported Anglo-Norman mottes and it is therefore often difficult to distinguish between them in the field.[30] Several examples of impressively sited ringforts, usually on the crests of drumlins and a possible variant of these 'raised' or 'platform' raths,[31] have also recently been identified by the Archaeological Survey of Ireland in Co. Monaghan.

Despite such sites as Big Glebe and the existence of 'raised' and 'platform' raths the broad chronology for the construction of mottes in Ireland is still thought to range from the end of the twelfth century to the first quarter of the following century, and there is documentary evidence for the erection of the motte and wooden tower at Roscrea, Co. Tipperary between 1213 and 1215.[32] Occupation on top of some of these mottes went on in some fashion right through the medieval period. At Lismahon there was evidence of occupation in the fourteenth century, while at Clough Castle a later tower house was sited on top of the motte.[33]

The types of military earthwork introduced by the Anglo-Normans into Ireland are, however, much more complex than their erecting mottes on existing ringforts or at strategic natural locations. There is now mounting evidence that they built their own military ringworks where the main defensive element was not the height of the mound but was the peripheral palisade bank and ditch, as well as the fortified gate tower. It is hardly surprising that these ringworks have not been noticed, since their surface morphology would have been virtually indistinguishable from the indigenous ringforts. If the motte distribution map (fig. 8) is re-examined it soon becomes clear that there are several surprising gaps in their distribution in areas that were known to have been extensively settled by the Anglo-Normans. The major lacunae are the counties of Waterford, Limerick, east Kerry and southern and eastern Co. Cork. The lack of mottes in these regions cannot be explained away either by agricultural destruction, because there are other eastern counties with intensive agricultural activity that do have high motte densities, or by the lack of field-work, as only the province of Ulster has been satisfactorily covered. It is in these areas that archaeologists like D. C. Twohig[34] have suggested that we look for Anglo-Norman military ringworks.

Ringworks were a fairly common earthwork of the early medieval period in both Normandy and Britain. It had been calculated that in England for every one ringwork there were, on average, 3.7 mottes.[35] But ringworks were more densely distributed in parts of England and Wales, such as parts of South Wales, and it is significant to note that many of the Anglo-Normans who conquered Ireland came from this part of Wales. Often it would seem to have been just the result of personal preference as to whether a motte or a ringwork was erected at a particular location in their homeland and this was probably the case in Anglo-Norman Ireland as well.

Before we examine the archaeological evidence for the presence of such ringworks in Ireland it is instructive to look at the contemporary literature of the Anglo-Norman invasion. In his two works on Ireland, *The Topography of Ireland* and *The Conquest of Ireland*, Giraldus Cambrensis includes much valuable information on the fortifications that were constructed in the first phase of the settlement. According to Giraldus one of the first castles built in Ireland was erected by Fitzstephen at Ferrycarrig in Co. Wexford. It has often been assumed that this castle was of the motte-and-bailey type,[36] but Giraldus used the word 'municipium' in his description which is translated as 'fortress' rather than castle.[37] The only element in the defences of the fortress that Giraldus mentions is the *fossata* or fosse.[38] The site characteristics as described by Giraldus are also closer to those of a ringwork on the Penmaen model in Wales[39] rather than those of a motte. He described it as being 'built . . . on a steep crag . . . and improved by artificial means a place naturally protected'.[40] Writing in the early twentieth century Orpen also concluded that it was likely that no motte was erected at Ferrycarrig but that a 'promontory castle', comprising an earthen rampart, wooden palisade and fosse, was built around a level space on top of a rock outcrop, now marked by a Crimean War monument.[41] In 1984 I. Bennett excavated a section across the fosse which revealed the base of a possible dry stone rampart on the fosse's interior edge. It also showed that the fosse itself was rock-cut as the topsoil cover was very thin. There was some charcoal staining located at the base of the fosse, along with one sherd of imported thirteenth- or fourteenth-century pottery.[42]

At Trim Castle in Co. Meath until the excavations by P. D. Sweetman in 1971–4[43] it was generally thought that the mound on which the later stone keep was standing was an original motte (fig. 12). But Sweetman found that this mound was caused by the presence of a stone plinth which was a later addition to the keep. In the south-west section of the castle ward Sweetman found the two terminals of a fosse which probably ran right around the keep with a free-standing stone structure situated in the gap between these two fosse ends. Although much more excavation would be necessary to confirm it, the remains that have been uncovered so far point to a military

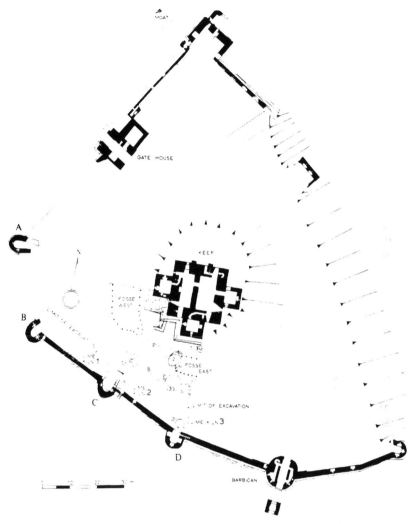

Figure 12 Plan of Trim Castle, Co. Meath, showing excavated area

ringwork being constructed here rather than a motte prior to the construction of the stone castle. The account of the building of the castle by Hugh de Lacy is also recorded in the near contemporary Norman–French poem, *The Song of Dermot and the Earl*, in the following lines:

> Then Hugh de Lacy
> Fortified a house [*meisun*] at Trim
> and threw a trench [*fosse*] around it,
> and then enclosed it with a stockade [*hireson*][44]

Interestingly enough this is a clearer description of the major element of a ringwork castle rather than that of a motte.

There are also five archaeological sites where the earthworks uncovered by excavation are likely to have been ringworks. At Pollardstown, some 1.25 km west of Newbridge in Co. Kildare, Fanning excavated the remains of what looked like a typical ringfort with a fosse and double bank.[45] Because of gravel workings only the western third of the fort survived so that the excavation was only of a very small portion of the defences and part of the interior. No structures were located and the stratigraphical evidence indicated that the construction of the fort and the habitation deposits were broadly contemporary. But what surprised the excavator was the range of finds, none of which were what would be normally expected from a ringfort, as all of them were of Anglo-Norman date. Most of them also had a military connection, being twelfth- or thirteenth-century iron arrowheads similar to ones found in Clough Castle and Seafin Castle, both in Co. Down. Fanning also found two medieval stirrups, nails of 'fiddle-key' form for horseshoe usage, and a medieval buckle. The range of these artefacts would point to a twelfth- to fourteenth-century occupation date for this site and led Fanning to wonder whether the earthwork was a military ringwork located close to the motte-and-bailey castles of Oldconnell and Morristown-biller.

Another supposed ringfort at Castletobin in Co. Kilkenny was excavated in advance of a road-widening scheme to the immediate north of the town of Callan. The earthwork had an internal diameter of 52 m and was delineated by a ditch some 8 m in width. Only small squares and trenches were opened during the excavation so the only features found were late field drains and cobbled flooring in the south-west quadrant, and a hearth and well to the south-east. But most important of all, the foundations of a strong stone and mortar gate tower were uncovered in the western ditch of the site, broadly similar to the gate tower located by Alcock at Penmaen in South Wales.[46] Because of the complete absence of finds of an Early Christian date the excavator tried to maintain that the medieval finds were from a secondary occupation layer. It is much more likely, however, that this site is another Anglo-Norman ringwork and so the medieval finds are probably from the primary occupation.[47]

One of the most intriguing sites is that of Beal Boru in Co. Clare, situated on the River Shannon above Killaloe, which O'Kelly dug in the 1960s and which he interpreted as being an unfinished motte built on top of an earlier ringfort.[48] He was able to demonstrate, mainly from coin evidence and despite the interference of a grove of trees which had to be left in place, that the occupation of the primary ringfort continued until the later part of the eleventh century. Then early in the thirteenth century the ringfort was reused by the Anglo-Normans when they heightened the ring banks. O'Kelly, using evidence from the *Annals of Clonmacnoise*, concluded that this secondary construction was, in fact, an unfinished motte. But other writers, notably Talbot[49] and Twohig,[50] have suggested that the Anglo-Normans were not trying to construct a motte here on the Dunsilly or Lorrha model but rather that they were building another ringwork.

Sweetman has also identified a 'large ringwork', trapezoidal in shape, as part of a complex of medieval earthworks excavated by him beside the Clonard river in Co. Meath.[51] In one of the three small cuttings opened by him on the eastern edge of this possible ringwork he found part of its wooden palisade and a few sherds of thirteenth/fourteenth-century pottery. Then at Ferns Castle, Co. Wexford, he located a small portion of a rock-cut fosse to the east of the castle's fosse, 1.2 m deep and 2.5 m wide. He found some late thirteenth- to early fourteenth-century pottery sherds over the fill of the fosse.[52] Thus he interpreted the fosse as probably being part of the fort recorded in the *Annals of the Four Masters*: *sub anno* AD 1160 which was constructed by Dermot MacMurrough, High King of Leinster. However, it is also possible that this may have been part of an Anglo-Norman ringwork castle erected on the site before the construction of the stone castle in the early thirteenth century.

Apart from these five excavated sites there is other archaeological evidence to suggest that the later stone castle and keep at Adare, Co. Limerick (fig. 13), are not located upon a ringfort but rather upon a ringwork.[53] Both the siting of an earthwork on low-lying ground so close to the River Maigue and the finding of artefacts from the early medieval period in the moat in the nineteenth century would point to this latter interpretation. Again if it were an earlier ringfort it is surprising that none of the finds from the moat proved to be of Early Christian date. If the enclosure over which the later Desmond keep and inner ward were constructed is a ringwork then it follows that there are probably other sites where the same sequence was followed. Such sites could include Raheen Castle, Co. Limerick, where there are the remains of a castle inside a roughly circular contemporary earthwork which had a maximum diameter of 35 m,[54] and Rahinanne Castle, near Ventry on the Dingle peninsula of Co. Kerry, where a late medieval tower is located at one side of a large circular enclosure which has a fosse over 6 m in depth.

It has even been suggested recently that such sites as Piper's Fort, Farranfad, Co. Down,[55] could have been a ringwork rather than an unfinished motte-like structure in an area which was always under Irish control. Here a trial excavation revealed that the 'unfinished mound' had been piled over a pre-Norman occupation layer which had produced souterrain-ware-type pottery. The facts that the floor of the hollow in the middle of the mound was cobbled and that there was some evidence for a light timber palisade around the periphery of the mound indicate the possible existence of a ringwork rather than an unfinished motte.[56]

Twohig has examined many of the early Norman castles in Co. Cork in an attempt to locate some ringworks which would help to explain the gaps in the distribution of mottes in this area. He has, up to now, managed to locate

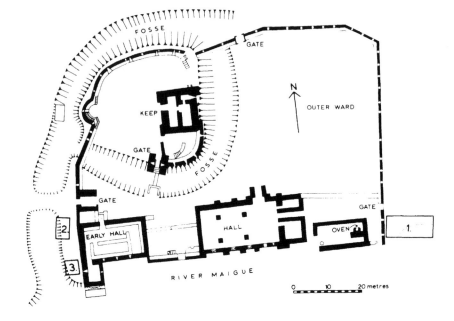

Figure 13 Plan of Adare Castle, Co. Limerick, showing areas excavated by
Sweetman in 1975

three such ringwork castles – 'Dunamark one of the best examples of a
ringwork I have seen in either Britain or Ireland',[57] Castleventry where he
saw evidence of a stone built gate-tower similar to the one at Castletobin in
Co. Kilkenny, and Castlemore Barrett which had a hall keep built within
the ringwork in *c.*1250, and to which a tower-house was added in the
fifteenth century.

Altogether forty-five possible ringwork castles have been identified to
date in Ireland (fig. 14). However, if the broadly comparable proportion of
3.7 mottes to one ringwork in England and Wales, as estimated by King and
Alcock,[58] is used as a guide for an Irish total the figure should be well over
100. The final total will probably be higher as the 1:3.7 proportion of
ringwork castles to mottes is based on only those mottes in Ireland that
have survived up to 1973 and do not have later stone buildings on them, as
compiled by Glasscock largely from cartographic sources.[59] Perhaps the
proportion might be as high as 1:1 in some parts of the country, as many of
the Anglo-Norman invaders were from Welsh counties, such as Glamorgan-
shire and Pembrokeshire, which had these proportions.

As can be appreciated the picture that we now have of the initial pattern
of Anglo-Norman earthworks in Ireland is a much more complex one than

hitherto realized. Giraldus Cambrensis himself must take some of the blame for over-simplification as he intimated that the Anglo-Normans avoided the dwelling places and fortifications of the Irish and built anew. In fact, as has been shown, not only did the Anglo-Normans construct motte-and-bailey castles at strategic locations to dominate the surrounding countryside but they also appear to have reused indigenous ringforts, as well as constructing their own ringworks. That the picture is not clearer is due in large measure to the lack of comprehensive excavations of any but a very small number of Anglo-Norman military earthworks. There is also the problem of the existence of a significant number of earthworks which cannot be easily classified, such as the thirteen rectangular and sub-rectangular enclosures as well as medieval field systems which were located by the Archaeological Survey of Ireland in Co. Louth.[60]

If the pattern of military settlement in the Anglo-Norman-held areas is complex, the situation in the regions which were always under Irish control is very uncertain, again mainly due to the lack of historical and archaeological evidence. There is increasing evidence that the indigenous ringforts were occupied throughout the middle ages and on into the post-medieval period as shown, for example, by the excavation of Thady's Fort and Garrynamona at Shannon Airport, Co. Clare.[61] There has been a great deal of debate on the question of whether these ringforts continued to be constructed after the coming of the Anglo-Normans. In their study of the distribution of known ringforts in Co. Meath, Barrett and Graham found that the areas of greatest concentration were in the western fringes of the country which were always under Irish control throughout the medieval period.[62] The Archaeological Survey of Ireland has also found that in Counties Louth, Meath and Monaghan the densities of ringforts and mottes are largely complementary.[63]

However, several archaeologists would maintain that the evidence from the small number of excavated examples just does not bear out these conclusions.[64] Lynn maintains that of the eighty published excavations of ringforts which had appeared by 1975, sixty produced finds of Early Christian date and only three produced actual medieval occupation layers.[65] He further concluded that it was the dislocation of settlement by the Vikings that caused the abandonment of the construction of ringforts on any large scale, rather than the influence of the Anglo-Normans.[66] It would seem that this theory is probably less tenable than that of the medieval dating of some ringforts both because of the lack of direct evidence and because of more recent research on the impact of the Vikings on Ireland and the rest of Europe. This indicates a reduced scale of destructive Viking activities and emphasizes instead the industry and trade patterns that they developed in Ireland.[67] Perhaps an improved classification, based on more extensive field-work and further excavations, might help to provide some more information on the chronology and function of the

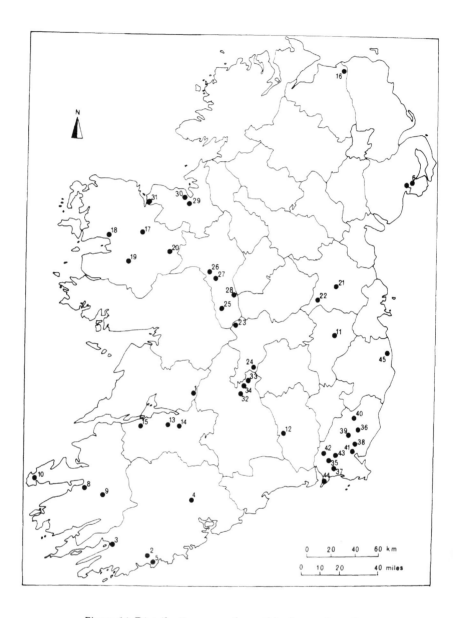

Figure 14 Distribution map of possible ringwork castles

References Site 1: O'Kelly 1962a; Twohig 1978. Sites 2, 3, 4, 23: Twohig 1978. Sites 5, 8, 9, 17, 18, 19, 20, 25, 26, 27, 29, 30, 31: B. J. Graham, personal communication, 1986. Sites 6, 41: *Exp. Hib.* Site 7: Waterman 1959b; *ASCD*; Twohig 1978. Sites 10, 14: Fanning and O'Brien 1973–4. Site 11: Fanning 1973–4; Twohig 1978. Site 12: *Excavations 1974*; Twohig 1975. Site 13: Rynne 1961; Twohig 1978. Sites 15, 28: T. Fanning, personal communication, 1980. Site 16: McNeill 1980. Site 21: Sweetman 1978a. Site 22: Sweetman 1978b. Site 24: G. Cunningham, personal communication, 1982. Sites 32, 33, 34: Stout 1984. Sites 35, 36, 39: I. Bennett, personal communication, 1984. Sites 37, 38, 42, 43, 44: Colfer 1986. Site 40: Sweetman 1979. Site 45: L. Simpson, personal communication, 1985.

Key to figure 14

Figure 14 reference	Site name	Townland	OS maps 6"	OS maps ½"	National Grid
1	Beal Boru	Ballyvally	45	18	R 665741
2	Castleventry	Castleventry	134	24	W 296425
3	Dunnamark	Dunnamark	118	24	V 998502(?)
4	Castlemore Barrett	Mourneabby	42	21	W 573924
5	Rathbarry Castle	Castlefreke	143	24	W 323354
6	Downpatrick	Downpatrick	37	9	unknown
7	Piper's Fort	Farranfad	37	9	J 434434
8	Killorglin	Killorglin	56	21	V 781965
9	Parkavonear	Parkavonear	66	21	V 934927
10	Rahinanne Castle	Rahinanne	42	20	Q 369015
11	Pollardstown	Pollardstown	23	16	N 775151
12	Castletobin	Castletobin	26	18	S 423452
13	Adare Castle	Adare	21	17	R 471468
14	Raheen Castle	Raheen	13	17	R 596493
15	Shanid Castle	Shanid Upper	19	17	R 243453
16	Mount Sandel	Mount Sandel	7	2	C 859319
17	Ballylahan Castle	Ballylahan	61	11	M 274980
18	Burrishoole	Carrowkeel	67	11	L 970956
19	Castlecarra	Castlecarra	100	11	M 172756
20	Lough Mannin	Mannin	92	11	M 460847
21	Trim Castle	Manorland	36	13	N 802567
22	Clonard	Mulphedder	47	13	N 656449
23	Clonmacnoise Castle	Clonmacnoise	5	15	N 007304
24	Dungar	Dungar	43	15	S 151919
25	Dundonnell Castle	Dundonnell	51	15	M 895381
26	Oran	Carroweighter	34	12	M 778693
27	Rathbrennan	Rathbrennan	39	12	M 839658
28	Rinndown Castle	Warren	46	12	N 009541
29	Ardcree	Ardcree	26	7	G 645230
30	Buninna	Buninna	13	7	G 597312
31	Castleconor	Castleconor	22	6	G 260241
32	Battery	Borrisnafarney	22	18	S 048756
33	Oldcastle	Oldcastle	17	18	S 100832
34	Summerhill	Summerhill	23	18	S 076815
35	Ballygarvan	Ballygarvan	40	23	S 782194
36	Ballyorley Upper	Ballyorley Upper	21	19	T 070452
37	Boley Castle	Boley	40	23	S 798167
38	Castlesow	Castlesow	32	23	T 028288
39	Dunanore	Dunanore	26	23	S c.966364
40	Ferns Castle	Castleland	15	19	T 023499
41	Ferrycarrig	Newtown	37	19	S 979278
42	Finshoge	Finshoge	34	23	S 746250
43	Rathnageeragh	Rathnageeragh	35	23	S 799213
44	Templetown	Templetown	49	23	S 756035
45	Kilmartin Castle	Ballyvolan Lower	19	16	O 287018

ringfort as it is such a vital component in the pattern of rural settlement in Ireland.

Obviously, there must have been some displacement of population, with the great Anglo-Norman lords carving out estates and manors for themselves and their followers in the agriculturally richer eastern half of the island. But surviving fourteenth-century manorial extents, such as that for Cloncurry in Co. Kildare, reveal that the unfree elements of medieval society, the *betaghs*, most of whom were probably Irish, lived in their own settlements within the bounds of the Anglo-Norman manors. Perhaps some of these settlements were the medieval precursors of the clachan, a type of nucleated settlement present in Ireland from the post-medieval period which may have had its origins in the pre-Norman period (see chapter 2). But it is unlikely that the Anglo-Normans would have allowed them to inhabit or refortify any of the large multi-vallate ringforts which still existed because of the military threat that these might have posed to Norman rule. Indeed, as has been shown above, the Anglo-Normans refortified some of these ringforts themselves both for their own strategic reasons and also, possibly, to deny them to the Irish. It has also been suggested by Barrett and Graham that one of the contributory factors for the apparently lower density of surviving ringforts in eastern Ireland is that many of them were levelled, either deliberately or as a result of the intensive agricultural activity of the Anglo-Normans.[68]

Finally, in any examination of the pattern of military-type earthworks in Irish areas the whole question of the nature of the *caistel* or *caislen* sites recorded in the annalistic sources for the early twelfth century at places such as Ballinasloe, Co. Galway; Collooney, Co. Sligo; Athlone, Co. Westmeath; Tuam, Co. Galway, and Ferns, Co. Wexford must be examined.[69] It is of great interest to the historians and philologists of this period that the descriptive noun for military strongholds in the annals undergoes a significant change from *dún* or *ráith* to *caislen* in the twelfth century. This has led some scholars to suggest tentatively that this development could be linked to the existence of some of the elements of incipient feudalism in Ireland broadly parallel with the rest of Europe at that time, as Ireland was in close contact with England and the rest of western Europe in the twelfth century.[70] This suggestion can only be tentative because, as far as the present author can ascertain, no trace of these fortresses survived above ground level to be recorded at a later date and there is also no archaeological evidence for their construction and occupation.

Nevertheless, earlier researchers such as Leask have suggested that *caislens* were probably built of wood as the annals recorded that the Ballinasloe example was burnt by a 'casual' fire in 1131,[71] while the Athlone *caislen*, probably built by Turlough O'Connor in 1129 on the eastern side of the River Shannon to protect his bridge, was burnt by thunderbolts in 1131.[72] In this second case the fortress must have been rebuilt as it was again destroyed in 1133 or 1135 before its final destruction in 1155 during further dynastic struggles.[73] Thus it is conceivable that although the buildings inside the fortification were wooden the actual defensive perimeter could have been of earth or stone. But whether they would fit into the Royal Archaeological Institute's definition of a feudal castle as 'a fortified residence which might combine administrative and judicial functions but in which military considerations were paramount'[74] will have to await the testimony of the spade. However, it is significant that the term *caistel (caislen)* is also used to refer to early Norman castles in Ireland, such as Richard Le Fleming's motte at Slane, Co. Meath.[75]

Anglo-Norman stone castles

Soon after the Anglo-Normans consolidated their military position along the eastern seaboard of Ireland at the end of the twelfth century they began to erect permanent stone edifices at important settlement centres. Arguably the earliest castle erected by them was at Carrickfergus in Co. Antrim, which is still the best preserved early medieval castle in Ireland (pl. 5). However, the evidence for the first phase of construction of the castle in about 1178 relies heavily upon an *interpretation* of the historical rather than archaeological evidence. McNeill has interpreted a reference in Giraldus for 1178, where he describes the retreat of John de Courcy from a defeat in 'Fir Li' to a castle, as referring to Carrickfergus rather than Downpatrick.[76] This first castle would probably have consisted of a polygonal stone enclosure which now makes up the present inner curtain wall cutting off the landward approach to the platform of dolerite rock on which it is located in

Plate 5 Carrickfergus Castle, Co. Antrim

Belfast Lough. Then in about 1182 the construction of the impressive rectangular stone keep was begun but, again, it is not possible to be sure how long it took to be completed. However, from a study of the surviving fabric and the documentary sources it would appear that it was probably completed by 1210 at the latest.[77] The importance of this castle to the Anglo-Normans in Ulster can be seen by the entry in the pipe roll of 1211–12 showing its garrison to be forty men, twice the size of any other castle in Ulster.[78] This document is also very informative about the functions of the three floors of the keep: the first or entry floor was probably a guard-chamber giving access to the all important well, the second probably housed the retinue of John de Courcy, and the top floor functioned as the lord's principal chamber.[79] There have been some limited excavations at Carrickfergus but they were limited in area and only addressed themselves to trying to answer specific problems such as to expose a blocked postern gate.[80]

The other major early Norman castle at Trim in Co. Meath is, in fact, the largest in the country (pl. 6). Building in stone probably began here some time at the beginning of the thirteenth century. Again, like Carrickfergus, the dating depends on architectural features and on limited documentary sources. Sweetman's excavation of a substantial part of the *bawn* to the south-west of the keep while providing much valuable information about the twelfth-century earthwork castle did not assist with the dating of the keep.[81] Sweetman has suggested that the reason that the keep is historically outmoded can be found in the dispute between Walter de Lacy, Earl of Meath and King John in about 1210 which may have caused a delay in the

Plate 6 Trim Castle, Co. Meath, from across the River Boyne

completion of the top part of the keep until *c.*1220.[82] The curtain wall to the north with its square towers was completed before the dispute, and the southern line of wall with the round tower was added in the 1220s. The two stages of keep construction can be seen clearly from inside the main hall as the springers for the original lower roof are clearly visible. The surviving windows in the keep are also different, with the ones in the upper part of the building having square heads while those at the bottom are of rounded sandstone moulds.

The great bulk of finds from the excavation came from the late thirteenth to the early fourteenth century and have been linked by Sweetman with the occupation of the castle by Geoffrey de Geneville from 1254.[83] He also investigated several of the towers of the curtain wall which were also filled with late thirteenth- to early fourteenth-century pottery, including some sherds of polychrome ware.[84] These finds reveal a considerable amount about the general standard of living in the upper strata of Anglo-Norman society at the time. Sweetman calculated that the large number of pottery sherds represented up to 800 jugs and 100 cooking vessels, the bulk of them of Irish origin. He also maintained that the majority were probably manufactured in Trim itself. The imported pottery sherds all revealed the major trading areas of Europe that did business with Anglo-Norman Ireland – Ham Green pottery from near the port of Bristol, as well as Saintonge and polychrome wares and green-glazed and north-west French wares, all from the western seaboard of France.[85] Although metal objects were scarce in relation to the amount of pottery, probably partly due to the chemical composition of the soil, some very fine pieces were located whose best parallels were objects found on an English royal site, King John's Hunting Lodge at Writtle in Essex.[86] Among the more 'exotic' samples were a decorated knuckle guard from a knight's leather glove, a decorated mount probably from the cover of a valuable book, and a small bronze bell. Leisure activities were also represented by small gaming pieces of antler and by rough-outs for bone dice. These types of find are not so common on village and other rural medieval sites of lower social status, and therefore reflect the importance and the wealth of the de Genevilles and their successors.

Archaeologically, it would seem that Trim Castle fell into disuse in the second half of the fourteenth century as was evidenced by the filling in or the partial infilling of the towers, the gatehouse and the fosse.[87] Its ceasing to be a residence coincided with a general period of decline in the fortunes of the Anglo-Norman colony occasioned by the Great European Famine (1315–17), the Bruce Invasion (1315–18) and the Black Death (1348–50). Trim Castle again came into the historical limelight in the seventeenth century when it was reoccupied by Confederate forces in the Cromwellian wars.

Of the other early Norman castles with a rectangular keep isolated within a ward – such as Greencastle, Co. Down, Adare, Co. Limerick, Maynooth, Co. Kildare, and Athenry, Co. Galway – only Greencastle has had any large-scale excavation. At Adare parts of the fosse and the area to the immediate south of the early-thirteenth-century hall were excavated by the owner in c.1860, and the artefacts located were dated mainly to the fourteenth century. Then in the late 1970s Sweetman located a small mooring area to the east of the curtain wall, which was dated to the late thirteenth to early fourteenth century by the finding of Saintonge pottery.[88]

C. Foley of the OPW excavated just outside the southern wall of Athenry Castle in 1972 to try and locate a moat there. No evidence of such a feature was found, probably because this side of the castle was already well protected by the town wall, which projected southwards, and by the river.[89] The excavations at Greencastle started in 1951 when Waterman and Collins elucidated the outer defences, then in 1968–9 Warhurst excavated in the east and north sides of the ward, and finally in 1970–1 Lynn investigated the east fosse.[90] It was probably built by Hugh de Lacy by the middle of the thirteenth century to provide accommodation for him and his successors *en route* for Dublin and also to protect the northern terminal of the ferry across Carlingford Lough to another impressive castle at Carlingford itself (pl. 7). According to McNeill its defensive layout closely resembles Skenfrith Castle in Gwent, close to de Lacy territory in Wales, which was largely rebuilt in the 1220s.[91] Like Skenfrith it lacks a fortified gatehouse, the circuit of its curtain wall is trapezoidal, and its three-quarter round towers are similar to those of the Welsh castle although only three have been traced. Inside the ward is a solid rectangular keep, some 21 m long by 12 m wide, which was extensively rebuilt in post-medieval times.

At the southern end of the eastern fosse a wall straddling it was uncovered in 1970–1 and has been interpreted as being a dam to build up

Plate 7 King John's Castle, Carlingford, Co. Louth

the water level within it. However, the builders of this feature must have forgotten about the extremely porous nature of the bedrock on the site.[92] In this fosse green-glazed English-style pottery was located beneath a layer of masonry rubble thought to be the result of the sacking of the castle in the 1260s, while above it only native cooking-pot sherds were recovered. Many iron objects, including nails, knives and a short sword blade, were also found above this masonry layer and have been tentatively dated to the period between the end of the thirteenth and middle of the sixteenth century.[93]

Whereas all the early-thirteenth-century castles discussed above had rectangular keeps the castle at Dundrum in Co. Down has a massive round keep, which was probably in existence in 1211 if we are to believe the Irish pipe roll for that date which mentions a 'magne turris' (large tower) there.[94] Excavations in 1950 revealed that the original phase of the castle, built around the 1180s, comprised a multi-angular curtain wall on the hill top, with probably a timber building in the interior.[95] The next period of work at Dundrum after the construction of the keep is represented by the building of an impressive gatehouse on its south-western side in about 1260, the design of which has been compared with the one at Pembroke Castle.[96] Probably in the fifteenth century another circuit of curtain wall was added to the south-west (fig. 15).

The circular keep at Dundrum is only one of a whole series which became popular in Europe at the start of the thirteenth century probably as they were more defensible in that they lacked any awkward angles which could be reduced by an enemy's siege weapon. Indeed, in 1215 Rochester Castle in Kent fell to King John after one of the four square towers at the angles of the keep was demolished by siege weapons attacking its exterior angle.[97] It is more likely that the fashion spread from Welsh castles such as Longtown in Monmouthshire whose keep was built by the de Lacy family possibly as early as 1187–8, and Pembroke which was erected by William Marshal, lord of Leinster, in about 1200. Perhaps the finest circular keep in Ireland of the few that remain is the one at Nenagh in Co. Tipperary which rises to almost 30 m, although the top quarter was added in the nineteenth century. It has been dated to around 1200 and attributed to Theobald Walter, the first Earl of Ormond, and formed an integral part of a pentagonal curtain wall which has still to be revealed by excavation.

There are also several possible examples of polygonal keeps in Ireland but none of them remain as intact as the cylindrical examples discussed above. For instance, the strategically placed castle at Athlone guarding access to the bridge across the River Shannon on its Connacht bank originally possessed such a keep, probably built in the early thirteenth century. It is, however, difficult to see this now because of all the rebuilding that has gone on in the castle since the middle ages.[98] At Shanid in Co. Limerick there are also the remains of another polygonal keep within surrounding curtain walls. Half of the keep is still at its full height of 11 m,

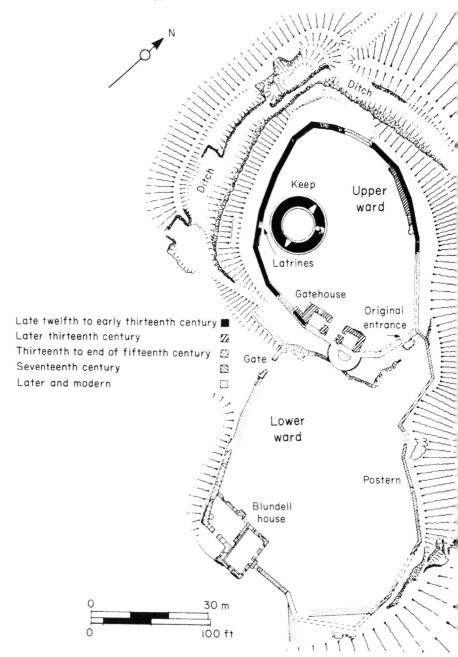

N

Keep

Upper
ward

Ditch

Ditch

Ditch

Latrines

Gatehouse

Original
entrance

Late twelfth to early thirteenth century ■
Later thirteenth century ▨
Thirteenth to end of fifteenth century ▨
Seventeenth century ▨
Later and modern ▢

Gate

Lower
ward

Postern

Blundell
house

0   30 m

0   100 ft

Figure 15 Plan of Dundrum Castle, Co. Down

and its internal diameter is some 7 m with walls 4 m thick. Although the castle is not mentioned before 1230 in the sources its design is earlier in date, and this is yet another site where an excavation might give us a more precise date for its construction.[99] In Castleknock in Co. Dublin there are the fragmentary remains of Tyrell's castle which is shown as having a polygonal keep in 1698 in a drawing by Francis Place.[100]

One of the major functional problems of the cylindrical or polygonal keeps was the difficulty of inserting into them a residential hall of an adequate size and proportion. There were two answers to this problem. The first was the continued use of rectangular keeps such as at Athenry, Co. Galway, and Maynooth, Co. Kildare; two examples of this anachronistic usage of a rectangular keep in the thirteenth century have been excavated. The castle at Seafin in Co. Down was excavated in the 1950s by Waterman and consists of a polygonal stone ward, about 30 m across, which reutilized the banks of an earlier hilltop rath, with a rectangular keep attached which was dated to the second half of the thirteenth century by pottery found in a layer contemporary with the occupation of the keep.[101] It has been identified as being probably the castle of 'Magh Cobha' which was known to have been built by the Justiciar in 1252, destroyed by Brian O'Neill in the following year, and refortified in 1254.[102] The other excavation was directed by Manning of the OPW at Glanworth in Co. Cork. This mid- to late-thirteenth-century castle of the Roche family was badly destroyed by General Ireton's artillery in the 1649 campaign. It comprises a rectangular keep within a trapezoidal curtain wall and the excavation concentrated on the keep and the western half of the curtain. Although Manning was unable to date the keep closely he located the remains of the original gatehouse near the centre of the western curtain wall which was later blocked and eventually, probably in the late fifteenth century, converted into a large tower-house.[103] The other solution was to construct a separate hall within the outer curtain wall, such as the one, probably made of timber, at the north-east side of the ward of Dundrum Castle.[104]

The conflict between the two major functions of a castle, its military and residential needs, was resolved in the thirteenth century by abandoning the idea of separate keeps and concentrating instead on increasingly strong outer walls. Thus the domestic buildings were contained within the protective perimeter wall. This new development was not to be found all over the country because there existed a small group of castles – mainly in Leinster – whose main features were a square keep with round towers at each angle and probably a rock-cut fosse. There are a few English parallels such as the castle at Nunney in Somerset but these all date to the later fourteenth century and it is also difficult to date the surviving Irish examples very closely. However, it is possible that either a castle which is now destroyed or one of the surviving examples acted as an exemplar for the others. Perhaps the best preserved example is Ferns in Co. Wexford which was excavated by Sweetman for the OPW from 1972 to 1975 prior to conservation work.[105] It was disappointing that no medieval occupation evidence was located in the keep's interior although it was revealed that whereas the northern side of the keep was founded on bedrock the southern half was on boulder clay. Sweetman's explanation for this was that the southern portion could have incorporated the original defences of MacMurrough's fort erected in the area in the 1160s.[106] The excavation of the two remaining towers, the southern fosse and part of the eastern fosses produced mainly medieval pottery and some other small finds but no precise dating for the construction of the castle. Typologically the window loops on the towers of Chepstow Castle are the same as those at Ferns which would indicate that it was completed by the first quarter of the thirteenth century by one of the Marshals. Sweetman also found the remains of a drawbridge in the south fosse and speculated that there must have been another on the east side because of the evidence of another entrance there. He also interpreted the existence of a projecting wall at the east side on the rock causeway as being part of an outer ring of defences to defend the two gateways, such as exists at Lea Castle in Co. Laois.[107] Like Trim and other castles in Ireland it would seem that the fosses were silted up and the castle itself was in a state of disrepair by the beginning of the fourteenth century. Later occupation, probably by the Kavanaghs who held it from 1360 to 1539, was indicated by fifteenth-century pottery and pieces of cut stone (probably the result of repairs done to the fabric).[108]

The earliest pottery found was local crude ware, which still had a good glaze on it. Sweetman postulated that it was probably of early-thirteenth-century date as it was stratigraphically lower than the sherds of Saintonge polychrome which, he argued, can roughly be dated in Ireland to the years 1280–1310. Because this local ware was probably made on a slow potter's wheel (unlike the local Trim pottery which was presumably influenced by France) and because there were also very few English imports it looked to Sweetman as though there were no appreciable external influences on it.[109] What was even more surprising was the low percentage of imports – around 3 per cent – among the pottery sherds at Ferns, of which the largest amount was from southern France with only a tiny number of Ham Green ware sherds.[110] This could be interpreted as showing how insular Ferns and its region was in the high middle ages in comparison with Trim, and how its pattern of external trade was with the south of France, probably through the declining port of Wexford.

The bulk of the other small finds reflected the military nature of the site – four arrowheads, of which two were armour-piercing types, one horseshoe, and part of a dagger. Surviving iron objects were scarce and poorly preserved partly, perhaps, because of the high acidity of the fosse's fill. Other medieval finds included a plain leather scabbard and two pieces of silk, obviously imported from either France or England. Some idea of the inhabitants' diet was also obtained by a study of the animal bones – mainly cattle, pig and sheep, with some deer and horse – and from three samples of the black organic fill of the fosse. They also seem to have enjoyed blackberries or raspberries and strawberries as well as wild vegetables such as chickweed and nettles.[111] Increasingly this environmental evidence, where it survives, is being analysed to give the archaeologist a broader spectrum of life in the medieval period.

Plate 8 The remaining western side of Carlow Castle

Another castle of this type at Carlow (pl. 8) was probably built either by William Marshal the elder, or by his son who succeeded him in 1219. It has been suggested by Stalley that Carlow might be the earliest one of this group although only the western wall and towers survive, the rest having been blown up in 1814 in order to make way for a lunatic asylum.[112] There is a Beranger drawing from the late eighteenth century which shows the keep virtually intact, with small round-headed windows, which would fit with a date early in the thirteenth century. Perhaps an excavation here might provide some kind of answer. Other examples, all as yet unexcavated, of this type of keep are Terryglass, Co. Tipperary, possibly built by the Butlers of Ormond, and Lea near Portarlington, Co. Laois, which can be roughly dated to the middle of the thirteenth century when it was occupied by the Fitzgeralds; and it is possible that two other castles, in Wexford and in Enniscorthy, Co. Wexford, were also originally of this type.

If we accept that the development of the keepless castle was mainly a phenomenon of the later thirteenth century in Ireland it is interesting to note that the castles of the three major cities of Dublin, Limerick and Kilkenny, all royal castles, probably conformed to this type early in the century. Not surprisingly Dublin castle has been the most altered over the centuries as it has been the centre of government administration. Thus the only surviving parts of the original castle are the base of the Bermingham Tower, the Wardrobe or Record Tower, some of the southern curtain wall and a fragment of the bridge found during the recent excavation there. Leask described the layout of the castle from a late-seventeenth-century plan as being five-sided, with massive towers at each corner and a small central tower or towers at an obtuse angle on the south curtain. All major authorities agree that it was probably substantially completed by the first half of the thirteenth century. It is especially frustrating that there exist early-thirteenth-century descriptions of some of the buildings in the castle but it is as yet not possible to work out where they would have been. In the winter of 1961–2 there was a limited excavation by Ó hEochaidh of the OPW in conjunction with building work which followed the demolition of the Cross Block, and parts of the eastern and northern curtain walls and the north-eastern corner tower were uncovered and recorded. Many thirteenth-century pottery sherds were found in association with these features as well as animal bones, oyster shells, and other refuse of the medieval period. At a lower level buildings and artefacts of the pre-Norman period of the city's occupation were also uncovered.[113] Major excavations by the OPW also took place in the castle from 1985–7 in advance of the construction of an EEC Conference Centre there. During these excavations A. Lynch revealed the base of the rebuilt Corke Tower and also excavated the 22m-wide castle moat from which she located a wide range of artefacts from the thirteenth to the eighteenth centuries. Traces of pre-Norman structures were found on the outside edge of the moat. She also exposed the moat area at the Bermingham Tower where the curtain wall meets the city wall. C. Manning also excavated the site of the La Touche Bank in front of the Genealogical Office and located the original medieval causeway into the castle.[114]

There has also been a limited excavation of 'King John's Castle' in Limerick built on the eastern bank of the River Shannon, probably to protect the city's bridge which gave access to it from Thomond (pl. 9). Like the other castles of this type it is almost square in plan, with towers at all four angles, the south-eastern one being replaced by a large bastion in 1611. The entrance is guarded by two smaller gate towers on the north side and the 1976 excavation directed by Sweetman for the OPW took place in a small area on its north-west angle.[115] As well as finding the foundations of eighteenth-century barrack blocks Sweetman located at least two walls of a rectangular building, possibly a hall, close to the curtain wall. He dated it to at least as early as the end of the thirteenth century because sherds of Gloucestershire, Ham Green and Saintonge green-glazed pottery were found in association with it.[116] Again, we can only hope that a much larger excavation will be undertaken on Limerick Castle in the near future to try

Plate 9 King John's Castle, Limerick

and recover more evidence of the medieval structures within its walls.

The castle itself has been dated to the beginning of the thirteenth century largely because of an entry in the Irish pipe roll of John in 1212 which stated that £733 16s. 11d. was required to repair it, a very substantial sum indeed. It is probable, along with most other Irish castles, that it went into decline in the fifteenth and sixteenth centuries until it was reoccupied in the seventeenth century. We must be careful, however, not to over-stress its early decline until we have positive archaeological evidence for a much larger area within its curtain walls.

There have also been minor excavations at two more examples of this type of castle, Roscrea in Co. Tipperary and at Kilkenny. Roscrea Castle was probably built near the motte which was erected around 1214–16, a very late example.[117] Its plan is that of an irregular polygon with a rectangular gate tower and two other D-shaped towers. According to Leask, the gate tower can be dated architecturally to around 1280 and the rest of the castle can hardly date to before the middle of the thirteenth century.[118] The excavation concentrated on the south-west tower, which was found to have been gutted in the nineteenth century, and on a contiguous portion of the fosse which was dated to the thirteenth century by pottery evidence.[119]

Kilkenny Castle has been much changed over the centuries and the two small excavations within it have not elucidated its original medieval form. Like Roscrea it was probably sited near a motte castle erected by Strongbow in 1172 to control the crossing of the River Nore. The trapezoidal castle of stone with massive drum towers was probably built soon after 1204 when William Marshal the elder succeeded to Leinster.

When we move on to examine the archaeological evidence for the important group of castles built in the later thirteenth century, it is salutary to record that only one, Ballymote in Co. Sligo, has been excavated in recent times. Like Roscommon and other major castles of this group its main surviving feature is the remains of a powerful gatehouse with projecting half-round towers on each side of the entrance. The castle is almost square in plan with a three-quarters round tower at each angle and a D-shaped tower in the middle of the east and west curtain walls. Sweetman's excavation concentrated upon these corner towers, the gatehouse and on the site of a possible postern to the south. The castle is generally dated to c.AD 1300 because of a reference in the Annals of the Four Masters to it being built by Richard de Burgo, but in 1317 it fell to the Irish and remained in their hands until 1584.[120] The excavation revealed that although a postern gate was planned on the south side, and tie stones can be seen in place for one along the curtain wall, it was probably never built because of the events of 1317. Sweetman also found that there was no proper moat on the south side although there was a very shallow depression in the bedrock which was 9 m wide and which could appear to the uninitiated to be a strong deep moat as it was always full of water which seeped upwards through the bedrock. He uncovered the foundations of the eastern tower of the gatehouse which had been slighted in the seventeenth century, and he also noticed that both towers had a double 'skin' of exterior walling to make it more difficult for them to be breached.[121]

The paucity of artefacts and occupation levels reflects the history of this castle in that it appeared never to have been occupied for any appreciable length of time after its capture in 1317, although seventeenth- and eighteenth-century pottery has been recovered there. The gap in occupation evidence for the fifteenth and sixteenth centuries here is similar to the pattern to be found at other major Norman castles, such as Ferns, Co. Wexford and at Limerick. We obviously need to look elsewhere for another type of fortification that was being occupied in these two turbulent centuries.

It would be valuable to investigate this pattern of occupation further by an archaeological excavation of arguably the most impressive and probably strategically the most important of these castles (fig. 16). Like so many other castles built in Ireland at this period, Roscommon Castle was built on church land, in this case land belonging to the priory of St Coman at Roscommon. It was begun in 1269 by Robert de Ufford the Justiciar who was looking for a strong defensive site to build a castle which would overawe Connacht, and the presence of a lake there (called 'Lochanen') was ideal as a defensive barrier to the west. However, it was recorded that this earliest structure was virtually demolished by Aedh O'Connor and his forces in the 1270s. Thus the impressive remains are those of the castle

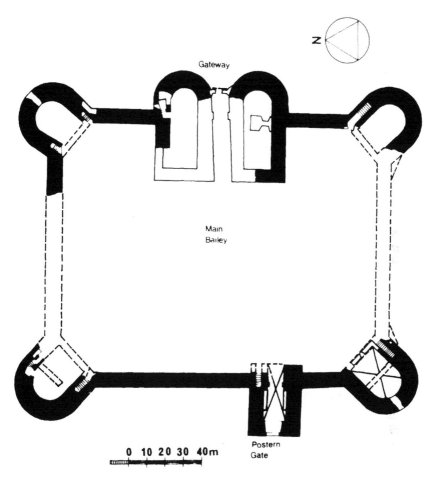

Figure 16 Plan of Roscommon Castle, Co. Roscommon

which was rebuilt in the 1280s to the latest military specifications as they predate the construction of Harlech Castle in Wales by around three years.[122] This was a costly enterprise as can be seen from the records for 1280 when de Ufford accounted for £3,000 2s. 5d. spent on his three Connacht castles, that is the refurbishment of Athlone and Rinndown, Co. Roscommon, and, more significantly, the building of Roscommon itself.[123] The layout of Roscommon is that of an almost rectangular court, 50 by 41 m, with strong D-shaped towers at each angle, an impressive gatehouse in the centre of the eastern curtain and a smaller postern on the western wall. Like Ballymote it was used both by the Anglo-Normans and by the Gaelic O'Connors during the middle ages as a stronghold until windows and other residential features were incorporated into it in the 1580s.

About 16 km north-west of Roscommon lies an even larger castle at Ballintober, Co. Roscommon, which Leask concluded was probably built by Richard de Burgo at the beginning of the fourteenth century, using Roscommon as a model. It is nearly square in plan, 76 by 84 m, with polygonal corner towers and an external fosse. The gateway is also similar to Roscommon being in the eastern curtain but is of a smaller scale.[124]

One other castle of this type has been excavated, Ballyloughan in Co. Carlow, by L. de Paor in 1955 for the OPW. This castle is not as impressive as the other described above, possibly because very little remains of it above ground level apart from its gate-tower which has two nearly circular external towers and which stands in the centre of the south wall, as well as the remains of rectangular towers at the south-west and north-east angles. The ward itself is square in plan, 46 by 46 m, but the lines of the curtain wall can only be identified by low grass-covered mounds. Before the excavation it had been broadly dated by Leask to the thirteenth century by reference to the squared irregularly coursed granite block masonry of the surviving buildings.[125] The limited excavation carried out during the course of conservation did not provide much evidence for the chronology of the castle as a whole.[126] But the finds, mainly pottery, were dated to the fourteenth century and included a silver finger-ring which had good fourteenth-century English parallels. The pottery included both imported and locally made wares, but with the absence of any known local kiln in Leinster, de Paor was unable to identify the provenance of the latter. More positively the excavation indicated that there was a fosse around the castle which was filled in during the fourteenth century and was linked by him to the capture of the castle by the MacMurrough Kavanaghs. Because of the lack of documentary evidence for the origins of the castle and because a large part of Co. Carlow was under the control of the MacMurrough Kavanaghs in the fourteenth century de Paor further suggested that it might have, in fact, been built by them much in the way that Ballintober was probably erected by the O'Connors.[127] The north-east tower was also found to have been a later addition to the curtain wall which was abandoned at the end of the medieval period when, as we know from documentary evidence, the castle itself was still in use. This tower was then reused as an out-house of the seventeenth-century house which was built on the side of the hill overlooking the castle.[128]

All the evidence presently available would indicate that there was a hiatus in the building of major stone castles from about the end of the first quarter of the fourteenth century to the following century. Although there were probably repairs and alterations to pre-existing structures it is not altogether surprising that no new ones were begun. In Ireland, as in much of the rest of Europe, the years 1315–17 were marked by the Great European Famine, with massive crop failures and animal murrains, but in Ireland this coincided with the warfare and devastation of the Bruce Invasion which affected much of the island. The dislocation of society and of the economy of the Anglo-Norman colony was further exacerbated by the coming of the bubonic plague, the Black Death, from 1348 until 1350 which killed from a quarter to a third of the population, especially in the more densely populated Anglo-Norman urban areas. These events were, not surprisingly, taken advantage of by the indigenous Irish who all through these later centuries were steadily pushing back the frontiers of the colony to the area around Dublin and eastern Leinster.

The English Crown, usually a major instigator of castle building, was also having to deal with problems of plague and crop failures in England along with the prosecution of wars against Scotland, Wales and, more importantly, the Hundred Years' War against France. Thus the King was only interested in Ireland for the supplies of men, victuals and finance for the successful prosecution of these entanglements. It was probably due to a combination of all these factors that the major era of castle building in Ireland was over, although there are a few examples of large castles still being built in the fifteenth and sixteenth centuries, such as the impressive Cahir Castle, Co. Tipperary, constructed by the powerful Ormond family on a rock island in the River Suir. What replaced them were smaller stone structures known as tower-houses which were a cross between a fortified building and a residential house for one family unit. With the increasing breakdown of centralized authority in the later middle ages and the growth in power of the greater Anglo-Irish families such as the Ormonds and the Fitzgeralds such large castles which had been so much a feature of the landscape in earlier centuries were no longer necessary. Despite the success of these tower-houses – it has been estimated that there are at least 3,000 in the country which are mostly concentrated in the west – we have until recently known very little about the date of their inception or even their origin.[129] But research has now thrown some light on these very important components of the post-Black Death settlement pattern and this will be dealt with in chapter 7.

This chapter has included a very wide sweep of all the major known types of medieval fortifications in Ireland, starting with the earthwork castles, the mottes and ringworks of the initial military invasion of the late twelfth and early thirteenth centuries and concluding with a review of our present knowledge of the development of the impressive feudal fortresses of stone that succeeded them. As a result of the lack of contemporary documentation of most of the earthwork castles it is the archaeologist alone who can elucidate their origins, the periods of occupation and the socio-economic status of their inhabitants, although their destruction by agricultural development in the present century has increased. Our knowledge is still very limited by the small number of mottes to have been scientifically excavated. Many of these excavations were only small-scale investigations while others were on mottes that had already been largely destroyed, such as Lurgankeel in Co. Louth, and none have attempted to examine the areas immediately outside the castle ditches in order to see whether a particular settlement grew too big for its perimeter defences or whether other buildings developed around the protection afforded by its defences. In only a few cases have there been detailed excavations of the motte itself to observe the method of its construction. On the question of the existence of military ringworks and other possible Anglo-Norman military earthworks, only recently have published studies even admitted the possibility of their existence in Ireland. Much remains to be accomplished in both identifying them morphologically in the field, especially given their similarity with pre-Norman ringforts in the contemporary landscape, and in instituting a programme of research excavations to elucidate their occupational evidence.

When archaeological methods of enquiry into stone castles are analysed it soon becomes apparent that the majority of excavations have been carried out in order to facilitate conservation works on these monuments rather than on research excavations aimed at trying to answer particular academic questions. Thus these often limited excavations have not usually been able to challenge or add very much to our knowledge of them acquired by a study of the surviving records or from architectural studies of their remaining fabric. Perhaps the most valuable contribution made so far by the modern excavator is in the analysis of the provenance and the dating of the finds discovered in the medieval occupation layers of these castles. The vast majority of such finds has been of pottery which has revealed both the surprisingly large-scale local manufacture of cooking pottery – although only two medieval pottery kilns have so far been actually located in Ireland – and the range and quality of the imported glazed wares. Their distribution and quantity show that the Anglo-Norman colony was part of a much larger trading area, with Bristol as the major English port trading with Ireland closely followed by Chester, with strong connections with the whole of the eastern seaboard of France, especially the southern ports involved in the wine trade. Excavation evidence has also shown that, not surprisingly, there were regional differences within Ireland, not only between Leinster and Ulster but even between the counties of Wexford and Meath. The de Genevilles, an important and influential Anglo-Norman family, obtained their fine table ware and wine jugs for their castle at Trim from eastern France and from the productive Ham Green potters who exported their wares to Ireland via Bristol, the second port of the kingdom. On the other hand, at Ferns the Marshal family seemed to rely almost exclusively on locally made pottery.

Several of the excavations, such as at Ferns, have also provided valuable evidence of the diet of their inhabitants from animal bones and also from seeds and other environmental evidence surviving in occupation layers. At Ferns Castle in the thirteenth century cattle bones were predominant with pig and sheep also being important components in the diet of the inhabitants. Further north, on the motte of Rathmullan in Co. Down in the same century, almost a quarter of all the bones were of rabbit but as there were no signs of chewing, burning or the breaking of these bones it was suggested that the animals were brought whole to the site where they were possibly skinned for their pelts.[130] Rathmullan is a very important site for any assessment of the dietary regime of pre-modern times because of the large amount of faunal remains surviving there from the Early Christian period to the later middle ages. It was also found that, unlike at Ferns, cattle declined in importance, with pigs becoming more important and sheep bones also increasing in frequency in the medieval occupation layers.[131]

The almost universal picture provided by the excavation of these military sites has revealed that there is usually evidence of occupation in the late twelfth and into the thirteenth century, followed by a general lack of such evidence throughout most of the fourteenth, with some sites being reoccupied in the following centuries. Indeed some of the mottes, such as Clough Castle in Co. Down, had a tower-house erected on their summits. This problem over the evidence of settlement in the 'troubled' fourteenth century will be examined in more detail in chapter 7 because it is inconceivable that the population was so decimated that it left hardly any trace. It is unlikely that there was a complete discontinuity in settlement at every location, although in a time of mounting disorder and economic recession large areas of these castles would obviously have been uninhabited. What is needed is larger-scale excavation if we are to hope to answer these puzzling questions allied with a re-evaluation of our typological dating of medieval artefacts, especially the pottery, to see whether the period in which they were in use could be slightly extended to help fill in part of this medieval 'Dark Age'.

4 Anglo-Norman rural settlement

It is with 1169 and the consequent Norman settlement that we find the establishment of a network of nucleated settlements throughout most of Ireland. However, along with the introduction of the typical medieval village with the homes of the peasants grouped around the church and the manor house, so typical of settlements in lowland England at that time, we also have the setting up of what Glasscock called 'rural boroughs'.[1] Although this term is not wholly satisfactory[2] it is a convenient one to describe settlements no larger than a contemporary English village but which possessed a charter of rights confirmed on the burgesses either by the Crown or, more commonly in Ireland, by great lords. These rights or 'liberties' were usually modelled on the charter given to the small town of Breteuil in Normandy in which the inhabitants were given their own court and the right to tax themselves outside the feudal jurisdictions that covered the rest of Anglo-Norman Ireland. As Otway-Ruthven has remarked, the proliferation of these charters was obviously intended to entice intending settlers away from over-populated England into the 'new frontier' of Ireland.[3] This was nothing new in medieval Europe as exactly the same process was being encouraged in the newly conquered Slavic territories of the East.

How successful this campaign was we shall probably never know because of the dearth of any kind of medieval population statistics for Ireland. Even the total number of such foundations is not yet known, despite the fieldwork of Glasscock,[4] Graham[5] and Bradley.[6] Thus our archaeological knowledge for all but the largest medieval Irish towns is minimal, and only portions of four possible medieval rural nucleated settlements have been excavated in Ireland up to the present. The earliest was Caherguillamore, Co. Limerick, where Ó Ríordáin and Hunt, while investigating earlier settlements in the area in the late 1930s, excavated two late-medieval house sites out of a complex of around twelve in 1940 (fig. 17).[7] They were identified by aerial photography, an early use for such a useful

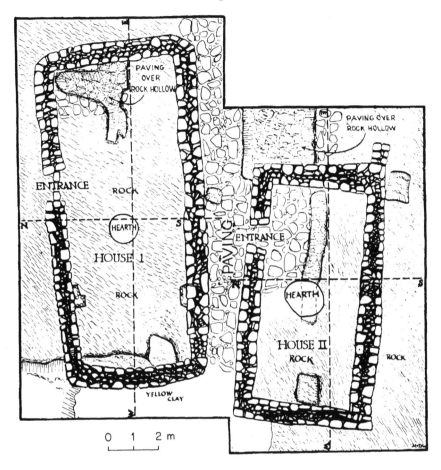

Figure 17 Plan of two medieval houses at Caherguillamore,
Co. Limerick

archaeological tool, as these particular earthworks did not appear on the OS maps. Amid a landscape rich in archaeological features such as old roads, forts and associated field boundaries there were two groups of houses although the two archaeologists suspected the presence of some others in the four townlands under study west of Lough Gur, the famous complex of prehistoric sites in Co. Limerick. On the ground these houses showed up as rectangular structures with grass-covered banks marking their walls.

This excavation has revealed important information on everyday life in rural Ireland in the later middle ages. Both the structure and finds are similar to those found on the excavations at English deserted medieval villages (DMVs). Both houses, which were side by side, were traditional peasant long houses with an entrance to the west, probably single-storied and with a central hearth. The walls were stone faced with a filling of rubble and earth, and the floor was the natural limestone bedrock. As on so many other sites there was no trace of the materials used to roof these houses, although it is probable that it was of thatch. The larger of the two houses (House 1) was built before the second one because this later one is built on its habitation refuse.

The finds date the occupation of these houses from the late thirteenth to the sixteenth century, although it is probable that a re-examination of the pottery fragments in the light of later research might date them back a century earlier. All the finds would suggest a thriving agricultural community with a large number of iron objects predominating, such as keys, knives, shears and buckles as well as bronze strap-ends and horse ornaments. Bone awls and needles as well as stone spindle whorls, whetstones and querns were also found in great numbers. The best dating evidence for the occupation of the site was provided by a late issue silver penny of Edward I (1272–1307) found on the rock floor of one of the houses. This fits in well with the earliest surviving reference for a castle and 'vill' and half a carucate (60 acres) of land at a place called 'Cahir a Gillimo' in an inquisition post mortem for the year 1287.[8]

The remarkable conclusion that we can draw from Caherguillamore is that its form and layout with a sunken way and long rectangular houses is exactly what you would expect from a manorial village in the eastern half of the country that was firmly within the Anglo-Norman manorial economy. It is difficult without the advantage of contemporary analyses of bones, seeds and other environmental factors to be sure of precisely the type of agriculture practised here. However, several informed guesses can be made both from the surviving finds and the present topography of the area. We know from the excavation report that the soil cover at Caherguillamore was very thin so that it is most unlikely that arable farming predominated. It is much more probable that stock-rearing, especially of sheep, would have been the mainstay of this village's economy. Ireland was a noted exporter of wool to England in the thirteenth century and the presence of shears among the finds would tend to reinforce this conclusion. The finding of the remains of a rowel spur and parts of horse trappings would also suggest that horses were used by the community either to pull the plough or as beasts of burden, or perhaps as transport for the lord.[9]

In fact, according to the one paragraph in the report dealing with animal bones the authors remark that there were more bones of horses than is usual among comparable collections. But the most plentiful bones were those of oxen (perhaps used to pull the plough) and pig, with sheep or goat bones in lesser numbers.[10] This does not necessarily mean that sheep were not important in the economy of the village as it could indicate that they were exported live and were not important in the everyday diet of the inhabitants.

At Leighmore, Co. Tipperary, some 9.6 km east of Thurles, where there was an early monastic site with two churches surrounded by a complex of earthworks, Glasscock completed two seasons of excavation in 1968–9. He was guided by earlier excavation by Leask and Macalister in which they uncovered the remains of two seventeenth-century cottages to the north of the larger church, and by several low-level oblique aerial photographs taken by St Joseph. Unluckily the results were inconclusive as to the extent of medieval occupation at the site but revealed the base of a round tower and more evidence of seventeenth-century settlement. What Glasscock found puzzling was the total lack of occupation material from either the Early Christian period or from 1200 to 1500.[11] This should serve as a warning to any archaeologists that extensive rectilineal earthwork patterns do not always indicate the presence of medieval houses and their associated field systems. Nevertheless, the extensive earthworks at Kiltinan, Co. Tipperary (pl. 10), with its hollow ways and rectangular house platforms would be an ideal candidate for an excavation to see whether it was a medieval nucleated settlement, especially as the site has recently been disturbed by ploughing.

Plate 10 Aerial photograph of a possible deserted medieval village or borough at Kiltinan, Co. Tipperary, showing hollow way and possible house platforms

A possible medieval grange or manor house was excavated in 1973 for the OPW by C. Foley in Jerpoint Church, Co. Kilkenny, close to the site of Newtown Jerpoint, a deserted medieval town. Two substantial rectangular buildings with stone footings were found superimposed on one another on an artificial alluvial platform probably constructed to keep them above the flood-plain of the nearby Arrigle river. The second building contained the remains of a collapsed staircase and arch which indicated that it had more than one floor. The range and sophistication of the small finds such as a bronze finger-ring, two bone gaming pieces, Saintonge pottery and some sherds of Ham Green ware would all indicate a fairly high standard of living.[12]

If this grange or manor house is related to the nearby deserted settlement of Newtown Jerpoint it would make this one of the largest medieval earthwork complexes in Ireland. It is located about 3.2 km south-west of Thomastown on the opposite bank of the Little Arrigle river from the still imposing remains of Jerpoint, one of the most influential Cistercian abbeys in Ireland. The town was probably founded in c.1200 and called 'Nova Villa Jeriponte', which immediately begs the question as to the probable location of an earlier settlement. Unhappily, no trace of the Old Town seems to survive except for a townland name. But for the Newtown the first edition of the OS 6-inch map, surveyed in the early 1840s, reveals the outlines of probable peasant houses and their associated garden plots with their long sides parallel to at least two streets, as well as a ruined church, the base of a tower, and a later tomb (fig. 18). Modern aerial photographs now reveal much more degraded earthworks because of the destruction caused early in the last century by the collecting together in large heaps of most of the stone foundations of the houses (pl. 11). The fact that the layout of the town was so clearly visible to the Ordnance surveyors in the early nineteenth century, if English experience is anything to go by, would indicate that it was probably a post-medieval desertion. This would fit in almost exactly with the historical evidence which indicates that it was probably deserted between 1608, the last mention of the Provost of Jerpoint,[13] and c.1656 when Petty's Map was made, showing no trace of either a town or the bridge across the River Nore, the maintenance for which the burgesses of the town received a grant of pontage in 1375. According to local tradition, this desertion in the first half of the seventeenth century was caused by a severe plague.

Because of the extensive remains, Glasscock rightly commented that 'Newtown Jerpoint is an extremely important site for future large scale excavation'.[14] But even without an excavation we can learn a tremendous amount about the settlement from one or two early-fourteenth-century inquisitions, as well as a manorial extent for 1289, which have survived.[15] Armed with all this information and with the results of a research excavation the archaeologist should be able to produce almost a complete picture of life in this town at the start of the fourteenth century. Most scholars think that it was probably founded around 1200 either by Earl William Marshal the elder, or more likely by Griffin Fitzwilliam, brother of Raymond le Gros. It is not difficult to suggest several reasons why the

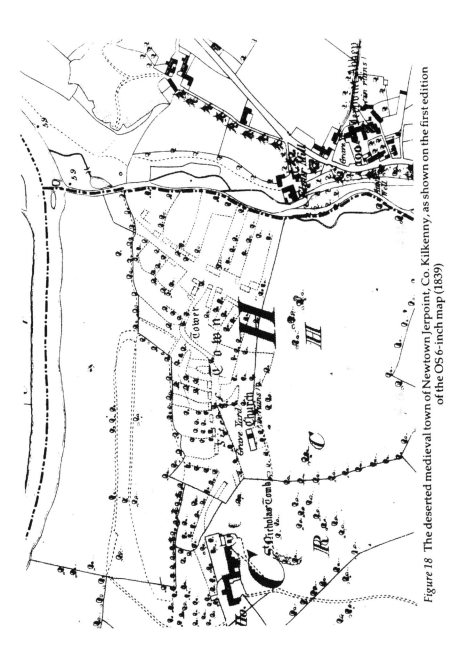

Figure 18 The deserted medieval town of Newtown Jerpoint, Co. Kilkenny, as shown on the first edition of the OS 6-inch map (1839)

Plate 11 Aerial photograph of Newtown Jerpoint, Co. Kilkenny, showing the
ruined church (right foreground), the sunken way, house sites and plots.
Jerpoint Cistercian Abbey can be seen to the top right of the settlement

'Newtown' was sited where it was (fig. 18), the most obvious being its
location close to the prosperous Cistercian abbey of Jerpoint on the other
bank of the River Nore, founded in the previous century. There was
probably a bridge at Newtown long before the grant of 1375[16] so that with
its control over this important crossing, plus its trading relationship with
the abbey, the town could not but prosper. However, with the suppression
of the abbey in the early fifteenth century the fortunes of the town probably
started on the long road to decline, unless the citizens were able to adapt to
their new circumstances and find other trading outlets.

It is more than a coincidence that the known burgage rent for Newtown
was 22s. 6d., which works out at 22.5 burgage plots, as the 1289 extent
actually stated that the rent for each plot amounted to 1s. a year, and the
number of house sites recorded on the OS map is 23, an incredibly close
correlation with the medieval figure (fig. 18). Thus it would seem, without
being able to test its validity by archaeology, that each burgage holding had
a house upon it. Furthermore, in the 1289 manorial extent the principal
landowners number 22, although they probably cannot all have had

burgess status because a few of them owned only one acre or the third part of a *messuage* (dwelling house and plot). It is a frustration of medieval social history that these burgesses would probably not have kept records, so that it is virtually impossible to correlate their names with the plots that we can see in the map. But by an examination of the surviving fabric of the more substantial buildings and by a study of the documents we can produce a fairly full account of the economic and social development of Newtown throughout the middle ages.

From the map it would seem that the surviving house foundations are all of the typical longhouse plan so common in deserted medieval village excavations in England. The majority of them have their long side parallel to the sunken ways that mark the two principal streets through the town. These sunken ways were probably caused by wheeled vehicles compressing the unmetalled roadway during the medieval period, and these are also found in other parts of medieval Europe in similar locations. We actually know a little about the internal arrangement of one of these houses because the owner of the land in the 1860s, a Mr Edward Hunt, had one of them cleared out in the presence of the Rev. James Graves, a local antiquarian, who gave a report of their findings to the Royal Society of Antiquaries of Ireland. From this report it can be seen that the house was made up of a large kitchen with a red tiled floor and a fireplace, separated by an internal partition of mud plastered with mortar from two smaller clay-floored rooms. A fragment of a bottle as well as some window glass were found in association with this house, as well as a key which had been found nearby two years previously.[17] Without illustrations or detailed descriptions of these finds it is impossible to date them, although the presence of fragments of window glass could indicate that these artefacts came from the last phases of site occupation, probably in the seventeenth century. From earlier in this account where it details the removal of the foundations of many of these houses in order to clear the fields for potato planting in the 1840s it is made clear that the walls were of stone.[18]

The only structure of the town to remain above ground, apart from the foundations of a later tower, was the parish church dedicated to St Nicholas which is a late-twelfth- to early-thirteenth-century nave-and-chancel church. Although it is now in ruins it still retains its unusual groin-vaulted rood gallery as well as a residential tower, both probably of fifteenth-century date. In the overgrown graveyard there is a much eroded thirteenth-century tomb with the effigy of an ecclesiastic, as well as a large circular stone block with a square socket on its top. This has been interpreted, probably correctly, as the base of the market cross which would have originally been located at the junction of the two main thoroughfares of the town. The ruined piers of the bridge over the Nore are still supposed to be visible at low water, but there are now no visible traces of the tower and gate at the southern end of this bridge which were mentioned in 1375, and for the repairs of which, along with the bridge itself, the Provost and

Commons of Newtown Jerpoint were given the right of levying certain tolls and customs for ten years on all saleable commodities.[19]

Finally, we can infer the existence of a mill, where the inhabitants of the town and the manor had to get their corn ground, from the 1289 extent as 'Wyn the miller' is the first owner of land to be named in it.[20] Perhaps the medieval mill was sited on the eastern side of the Nore where the flour mill is now shown in the OS first edition map, although it would have been more secure on the town side of the river. From this same source we know that they brewed at least twelve gallons of beer which was worth 4s. so it is possible that there was also a small brew-house in the town. But the one building that is nearly always found in deserted medieval villages in the rest of Europe, the manor house, neither appears in the documents nor can be identified cartographically at Newtown. Perhaps it is one of the larger house plots but only excavation will answer this question. Alternatively, it could either be the buildings excavated by Foley at Jerpoint Church,[21] or it could possibly be located underneath the later Jerpoint House to the west of the town.

From the manorial extent of 1289 it can also be seen that along with the 22 burgesses there were at least 30 free tenants holding land in Newtown. If we use the accepted household population multiplier of 5[22] it can be estimated that the population of the town must have been at least 250, but it is not clear how many other people who did not own land were also living in the town. Some of the free tenants were also listed as 'the son of' or 'the daughter of' so we do not know whether they were, in fact, part of the family of another landowner on the list or of someone who had died before the extent was completed. For reasons such as these a total population figure can only be, at best, an estimate of the true figure. It highlights one of the major problems of the use of medieval documents by historians, namely that the reasons that the documents were originally drawn up were very different from the questions which the modern researcher wants them to answer. In this case, a manorial extent merely lists the principal landowners, their holdings and their rentals; it does not set out to list the total population.

The later history of the town can also be charted from documents such as the extents taken at the time of the dissolution of the abbey of Jerpoint in 1541 where it is stated that one burgage with five gardens and another burgage called 'Marschalls corte', which were in the hands of the abbey, were not to be granted to the Earl of Ormond.[23] This reveals a continuity of over 200 years as one of the burgesses in 1289 was one 'Ricardus Marscall' whose burgage plot still retained the name of his family over two centuries later.[24] But by 1595–6 we find that the names of the inhabitants of the 'Long Street' of the town were probably all Irish, as distinct from the predominantly English names of the early fourteenth century. There seems to be no continuity in the actual names of the tenants for none of the seven listed in 1596 are to be found in the medieval extents.[25] The last known historical reference for the settlement dates to 1614 when at least six 'cottiers of the Longe Street in Jerpoint' are listed in the Ormond Deeds.[26] Unlike the situation in the thirteenth century all the names are now firmly Irish, and it must have been shortly after this that the town was finally deserted. The reasons behind this desertion are still not known except that there is a popular tradition that a severe plague decimated the inhabitants. Historically it is known that bubonic plague visited Kilkenny city in 1650, the same year that two large Cromwellian armies joined up in Gowran.[27] Any one of these events or, indeed, a combination of both of them could well have meant the end of the small borough of Newtown Jerpoint located close by. Alternatively the town could have been in slow decline ever since the suppression of the abbey in 1541, and eventually just faded away in the middle of the seventeenth century when its last remaining inhabitants moved elsewhere, perhaps to the walled and towered town of Thomastown nearby. Thus Newtown Jerpoint's arch rival for the control of trade across the river Nore throughout the middle ages had at last triumphed.

Another of the very few rural medieval settlement sites to have been excavated which produced evidence for medieval house types was the investigation by R. M. Cleary of an area due east of Bourchier's Castle on Lough Gur, Co. Limerick, in advance of the construction of a car park there.[28] She located the foundations of four hut sites of unknown date but which were probably earlier than the thirteenth century, and ditches which might have been part of a medieval field enclosure system. The foundations of two medieval houses were also located. The slightly earlier sub-rectangular one (14.5 m long by 7.6 m wide externally) probably dated to the first half of the thirteenth century, had no traceable internal partitions and possessed a hearth and ash-pit along its south-west wall (fig. 19). The second house was roughly rectangular in plan, 12 m wide and 22 m long, and had a door in its western side. It was divided into two rooms with the smaller room projecting some 2.4 m beyond the wall of the larger room on the north side. As the foundation trench of the large enclosure on the south-east side of the rectangular house had cut through the north-west wall of the first house Cleary suggested that the second house was later in date, possibly being occupied during the latter half of the thirteenth and the beginning of the fourteenth century.[29] She found them difficult to date from the artefacts alone as the two collections were so similar, although the pottery sherds provided a rough chronological framework. A stone-built hearth site and a corn-drying kiln were also associated with the yard enclosure.

The nearest equivalent to these houses were those at Caherguillamore, mentioned above, although the lack of excavation of this type of site in Ireland makes the finding of a closer parallel an impossible job at the present state of our knowledge. It is possible that these two houses were part of a village clustered around the thirteenth-century Fitzgerald Castle which is thought to lie underneath the later Bourchier's Castle. These

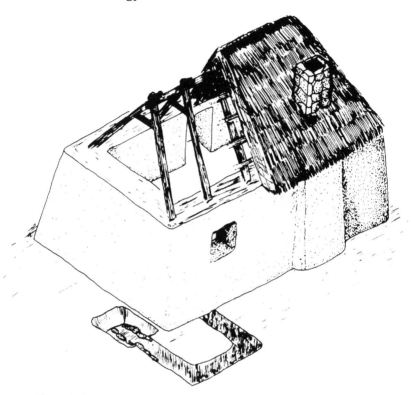

Figure 19 Tentative reconstruction of the earliest medieval house near
Bourchier's Castle, Lough Gur, Co. Limerick

Anglo-Norman tenants may well have been the predecessors of the
sixteenth-century settlement which was described in 1583 as 'divers other
edifices, or cottages with adjoining gardens where dwell divers tenants'.[30]

The excavation in 1982 of a small part of a rectangular earthwork at
Tildarg, Co. Antrim, located on a south-eastern slope of Big Collin
mountain also produced a rectangular house platform of medieval date.
Slight traces of three smaller possible house sites were also located in the
earthwork's interior, and other ones were located to the east of the site by
aerial photography. The excavated platform was rectangular in plan,
approximately 16 by 6 m, with rounded corners and abutted straight into
the northern bank of the earthwork. According to N. F. Brannon, the
excavator, the house platform was only slightly larger than the first house at
Caherguillamore and was 'one of the Irish medieval house forms as
illustrated in late 16th and 17th century pictorial maps'.[31] However, the
house was probably in use in the thirteenth century as a single radiocarbon
sample was calibrated to *c*.AD 1265, and the finding of everted-rim cooking
pottery clearly indicated that the house was medieval in date.[32] Brannon

also suggested that there was field evidence of a possible deserted medieval village about 0.8 km away from this earthwork.[33] If this were proven it would turn out to be the first example so far located in Ulster.

Surviving documentary sources, field-work and cartographic analysis have also been employed, in the absence of excavation, by A. Simms to elucidate the settlement pattern of Duleek in Co. Meath. She was able to show that, unlike Newtown Jerpoint, Duleek was sited on a pre-Norman ecclesiastical settlement probably dating back to the fifth century. Simms chose it as a case study 'Because of the exceptional quality of the documentary evidence in the "Irish Cartularies of Llanthony Prima and Secunda"'.[34] These were drawn up because a grange was founded from the monastery of Llanthony Secunda in Gloucestershire at Duleek in the twelfth century, and an extent of 1381 also survives for this manor. From these documents Simms was able to illustrate, using the OS 6-inch sheet as a base, that the early ecclesiastical site was enclosed by a circular enclosure, which formed the core of the later Anglo-Norman expansion, in rectangular tofts (house plots) arranged along the axes of Main Street and Lahrix Street. She also concluded that because the names of several townlands, as well as the majority of field names, are of Irish origin, the Anglo-Normans reused pre-Norman territorial subdivisions.[35] Since this study she has also investigated the medieval origins of the village of Newcastle–Lyons, some 17 km south-west of Dublin, where not only is there a church of medieval origin but also an adjoining motte as well as relict features which could be interpreted as long-strip field patterns so common in the open-field system of lowland medieval villages in England. There are also at least two tower houses of late medieval date surviving within the village.[36]

That there is much more scope for this approach to medieval nucleated settlement studies in Ireland is shown by the earlier translations and commentaries upon other surviving manorial documents, such as the fourteenth-century extents for Lisronagh, Co. Tipperary, and Cloncurry, Co. Kildare.[37] Both manors also included burgesses holding plots as well as other land, in both cases 240 acres in area. Nothing is now known of the location of these plots, although at Cloncurry the motte still survives in the landscape. There is also a reconstruction of the buildings around the motte at Cloncurry included in the article by O'Loan because of the detailed information on them included in the original extent.

Documentary, cartographic and fieldwork evidence has also been successfully combined by R. Meenan in a postgraduate study of the medieval village settlement-pattern of Co. Westmeath.[38] Of the 150 possible deserted medieval villages in the county, house remains were only found at thirteen locations. Unlike the situation in more easterly counties such as Kilkenny and Tipperary the layout of these settlements was generally irregular. Meenan also suggested that the lack of identifiable village sites might have been caused by the major Anglo-Norman landholders locating their manorial centres at pre-existing population centres, and that in some cases the Anglo-Norman manorial settlement pattern was dispersed, especially in areas that were on the borders of the lordship.

However, archaeological research has taken place over recent years on the manor houses which had moats around them, as the moats have often survived to the present century. But our knowledge of the other main features of the medieval village is still largely based upon documentary evidence and by looking at parallel village excavations in Britain and on the Continent. The same problem of survival also applies to manor houses that lacked moats around them as they cannot be identified in the present-day landscape with any degree of certainty, probably because many of them have been obliterated by farming developments since the middle ages or lie underneath modern farmyards. So we only possess a one-sided knowledge of these manor houses from the beginning, added to which up to 50 per cent of all moated sites have been destroyed since the first edition of the OS 6-inch maps was produced in the 1840s. Thus it is impossible to assess how many manor houses, whether moated or not, were in existence in the first two centuries of the Anglo-Norman colony.

It has generally been accepted that the best term to use for this type of site is 'medieval moated site' as it encompasses all rectangular earthworks bounded by banks and moats of medieval date, whether they enclosed a major house or simply a garden or cattle pen. Limited archaeological excavations of some of these sites as well as detailed cartographic research in nine counties has confirmed that Irish examples are broadly similar in date to English sites, mainly of the thirteenth and fourteenth centuries. The major difference, however, lies in their distribution pattern and thus in their primary functions. The sites are often concentrated along the probable border areas of the Anglo-Norman colony where the settlers were often under pressure from the indigenous population who, not surprisingly, were very keen to reoccupy the best agricultural land which had been appropriated in many instances by the Anglo-Norman invaders in the twelfth and early thirteenth centuries. This was especially so in the later middle ages when economic and political decline in the colony gave impetus to the so called 'Gaelic resurgence'.

Thus, unlike the situation in lowland England where moated sites are almost invariably to be found in villages of medieval origin, whether deserted or still surviving, moated sites in Ireland are found in isolated areas, usually over 3.4–8 km away from the nearest known medieval nucleated centre.[39] Of course, their isolated location may be more apparent than real in many cases as research upon deserted medieval villages in Ireland is also in its infancy. Nevertheless, it is obvious that in the conditions of lawlessness which pervaded the border areas of the colony, isolated Anglo-Norman farmers needed the water-filled moats and earthen banks topped by a palisade to protect themselves and their cattle and goods both from Irish cattle raiders as well as from their lawless Anglo-Norman neighbours. The relative poverty of the colony as well as the often limited occupation on some sites may also explain why there are so few examples of double or even more complex enclosures in Ireland in comparison with the situation in England.[40]

These 'square raths' were recognized and illustrated by such scholars as the Rev. D. Moore, one of the principal members of the Kilkenny Archaeological Society and Mr George Du Noyer of the Geological Survey, in the first half of the nineteenth century. But it was not until Westropp published his comprehensive survey of the forts of Ireland in 1897 that it was realized that these 'rectilinear forts' were to be found over most of the country, and especially in Leinster. However, like other scholars of his day, Westropp thought that these earthworks were merely a variation of the circular ringfort, and thus probably dated from the Bronze to the Iron Age.[41] It was Orpen who first suggested that these 'rectangular platforms' were probably medieval in date and belonged to the period immediately after the mottes were constructed, a remarkable conclusion which has since been borne out by later archaeological and historical research.

On the other hand his assertion that they were concentrated in counties Mayo, Galway and Roscommon was disproved when Glasscock had all 'rectangular earthworks' which appeared in the first edition of the OS 6-inch maps (1832–40) mapped in 1970 (fig. 20). He found that the majority of the 750 mapped examples were to be found in southern and eastern counties, not surprisingly as they are supposed to be Anglo-Norman settlement forms. But whereas the counties with some of the most dense distributions, such as Tipperary (139) and Wexford (118), were on the periphery of the colony, the counties in the heart of the later Pale, such as Dublin, Meath and Louth, also had very small numbers of such earthworks. This has led later researchers such as Barry to conclude that moated sites in Ireland were concentrated in the areas of 'interface' between the colonists and the indigenous Irish.[42] On the other hand, there are also puzzling concentrations in regions like the Ballyvaughan valley in Co. Clare and in north Co. Mayo where there was little or no known Anglo-Norman settlement. In Co. Clare it has been convincingly argued by E. Plunkett-Dillon that what the Ordnance surveyors were mapping there were small rectangular fields.[43] These examples reveal the drawback of cartographic sources and emphasize that all mapped features need to be checked in the field before any definitive statements can be made about them.

The virtual absence of moated sites in Ulster is not surprising if McNeill's contention is accepted that the tenuous military hold the Anglo-Normans exercised there required them to utilize mottes as protected settlement centres rather than the more lightly defended moated site. A good modern parallel would be to compare the fortress-like perimeters of RUC police stations in Northern Ireland with their counterparts in the Republic. Despite there only being fourteen examples of moated sites in the seven most northerly counties, there has been one recent excavation of a rectangular earthwork at Carnaghliss, Co. Antrim, which could be medieval

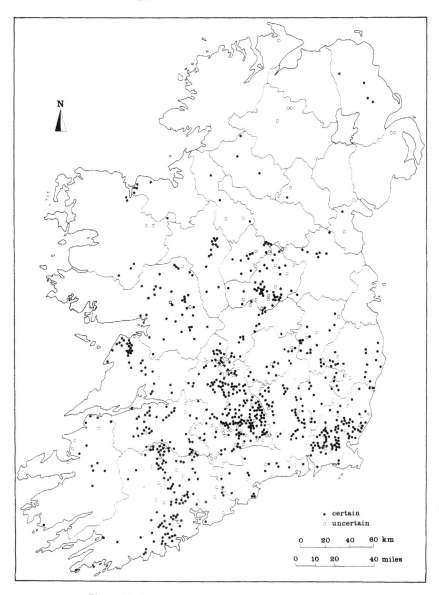

Figure 20 Distribution map of rectangular earthworks

in origin.[44] Apart from the sites surveyed by the Archaeological Surveys of Ireland and of Northern Ireland and by the University Colleges of Cork and Galway there have been complete field surveys by Barry for Counties Wexford, Carlow, Kilkenny and Tipperary in the early 1970s; for Co. Wicklow in 1979, and preliminary surveys by him for Co. Waterford in

1978, and for Counties Cork and Limerick, published in 1981, but based upon field-work carried out some ten years earlier.[45] For the four south-eastern counties surveyed in the early 1970s Barry found that the resulting distribution pattern largely coincided with that shown by Glasscock, but for Co. Cork he found that around 30 per cent of the rectangular earthworks marked on the OS maps were probably not moated sites.[46] Their distribution in Co. Cork is particularly important in that it illustrates the concentration of sites along the borders of the Anglo-Norman colony with a definite linear distribution separating west and east Cork, from Bandon in the east through Kanturk and on into Co. Limerick to the west (fig. 21).

There is only one known medieval documentary reference to a moated site in Ireland but luckily it is a very detailed one which shows how such a site was built. In the accounts of various provosts for the manor of Old Ross, Co. Wexford, for the two account years 1282–3 and 1283–4 all the costs and wages for the construction of the wooden palisade and the digging of the moat around the haggard (farmyard) of 'Ballyconnor', which was probably an out-farm of the manor, are detailed. Apart from the detailed figures which allow a fair assessment of its size, 7,056 sq m which makes it a large example of its type, the account rolls list that as two oxen were stolen by robbers in 1283–4 eight out of the total stock of thirty-six in the manor were thenceforth to be kept within the safety of its moat.[47] This is again a good illustration of one of the main functions of the moat and palisades to be found around Anglo-Norman farms in isolated locations.

The excavation evidence, although limited to six sites, has been remarkably consistent with regard to their chronology and function. The earliest recorded excavation of a possible moated site in Ireland was carried out by Ó Ríordáin in the late 1930s when he put trial sections across one of two conjoined rectangular platform forts at Ballynamona, Co. Limerick and located one sherd of green-glazed pottery of fourteenth-century date along with other glazed pottery sherds and animal bones of pig, young calf and ox. Because of the small-scale nature of the dig the only published reference to it takes the form of a short note.[48] Thus it was not until 1967 that the first certain medieval moated site was excavated by Glasscock at Kilmagoura in Co. Cork prior to its removal by an agricultural improvement scheme. The impressive site (pl. 12) which had an interior area of some 2,640 sq m, as well as a 3.7 m-wide water-filled moat fed by a leet from a nearby stream, was originally part of a much larger earthwork enclosure which had been levelled in recent times. From the excavation it appeared that the moated site had been erected on virgin territory, as the first phase of site occupation was only marked by the remains of the fires of the men who constructed the moat. The second phase was represented by a spread of soil, some 30 cm thick, over the interior of the site and by a trodden stone pathway, but no discernible remains of any structures. The traces of habitation were most apparent in the third phase when the centre of the platform was raised again, possibly to provide a foundation-raft for a stone building, but no

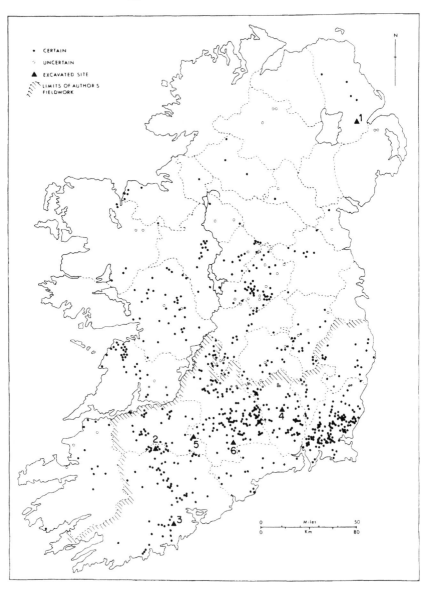

Figure 21 Distribution map of moated sites. 1. Carnaghliss, Co. Antrim;
2. Kilmagoura, Co. Cork; 3. Rigsdale, Co. Cork; 4. Kilferagh, Co. Kilkenny;
5. Ballynamona, Co. Limerick; 6. Ballyveelish North, Co. Tipperary

wall foundations or floor levels were located. However, a flagged pathway,
sited on top of the phase-2 path, led towards this area which was
surrounded by stone lined drains and cobbled surfaces. Perhaps one

Plate 12 The moated site at Kilmagoura, Co. Cork, under excavation

explanation for the absence of any structure here could lie in the technique used in its construction, as a timber-framed building resting on large wooden sill plates may have left little trace on the original ground surface. Glasscock did find fragmentary stone foundations, probably of outbuildings, which included a small rectangular building in the north-east corner of the platform.[49]

The major problem that Glasscock faced in trying to interpret this site, apart from the lack of structures, was the lack of dating evidence for any of the major phases of site occupation. The small finds which were located were either undatable, such as the wooden dish fragment found in the moat or the base of a rotary quern, or were surface finds like the late-sixteenth-century rowel spur and four sherds of post-medieval pottery. He did, however, find the foundation-timbers of the original entrance causeway in the western moat beneath the modern cattle track. This revealed a continuity of use for this portion of the site which probably spans some five centuries. Before he had the results of a radiocarbon date from a sample from these timbers Glasscock had already suggested that the site might be dated to the late thirteenth or fourteenth centuries. An uncalibrated radiocarbon date of AD 1225 ± 70 indicated that the causeway was probably in use some time from the late twelfth to the thirteenth centuries, soon after the Anglo-Normans conquered this region. The small number of small finds was interpreted as showing that the site was not intensively occupied for very long.

The other Co. Cork moated site at Rigsdale was excavated in 1977 by Sweetman of the OPW prior to the proposed erection of a new Garda station.[50] As can be seen from the plan of the excavation (fig. 22) the northern and southern sides of this small single platform site were already badly damaged by a road and laneway. Indeed, from its surface features

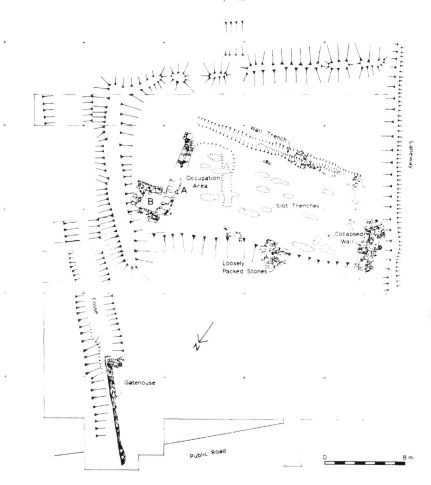

Figure 22   Plan of Rigsdale moated site, Co. Cork

alone it could not be identified as a moated site because the fosses on the remaining two sides were silted up, and so it was only as the direct result of the archaeological excavation that it could be positively identified as such. What was remarkable was that this site, in the same frontier zone as Kilmagoura, produced broadly the same chronology and the lack of occupation evidence in the medieval period. But Sweetman was far luckier than Glasscock with his finds because he was able to date the occupation of Rigsdale with much more precision. The most important finds in this respect were two Edward I pennies which could be dated to around 1300, one slightly worn example found under the eastern bank while the second more worn one was found in association with Saintonge polychrome pottery sherds.[51] This type of pottery has been dated in Ireland to between 1280 and 1310.[52] Thus there is a secure date for this site between the end of the thirteenth and the start of the fourteenth century.

The remains of three structures were also found at Rigsdale: part of the plinth of a probable gatehouse in the eastern fosse; an unfinished large rectangular stone structure (20 by 8 m internally) which was probably a hall; and to its immediate east a probable stone garderobe structure, again never completed. All the indications are, therefore, that this site was probably only occupied by the men who were building it. Thus, as I have argued elsewhere, both Rigsdale and Kilmagoura could have been abandoned in the 1320s as a result of the co-ordinated attacks on the colonists in Cork by the first Earl of Desmond in alliance with Dermot MacCarthy.[53]

The most recently excavated sites in the southern half of the country were revealed only as a result of archaeological investigations by the Department of Archaeology of UCC along the route of the proposed gas pipeline from Cork to Dublin in 1982. No surface traces remained of the site at Ballyveelish North near Ballyclerahan in Co. Tipperary, which was only identified by aerial photography. The excavation by M. G. Doody of UCC revealed a single rectangular site, 1,000 sq m in area, with a 3 m-wide moat and two partially stone-built houses as well as two other wooden structures. The small finds, although again few in number, are classic for medieval rural settlement sites in Ireland. They include two green-glazed sherds of pottery of thirteenth- to fourteenth-century date, several sherds of thirteenth-century cooking ware, pieces of iron nails, some quern stones and a variety of animal bones.[54]

At Kilferagh, Co. Kilkenny, part of another probable moated site was excavated in advance of the gas pipeline. Here a stone-built grain drying kiln was located in association with a house and yard within a double moated enclosure. Unlike all the other moated sites so far excavated in Ireland this one produced great quantities of both indigenous cooking potsherds and imported pottery as well as iron objects, animal bones and much charcoal and carbonized seed. Not surprisingly the date given by the excavator for this site's occupation was from the thirteenth to the early fourteenth century.[55] All the indications are that the Anglo-Norman occupation on this site in a securely controlled part of the colony was intensive although, as at the other sites, there is no sign of habitation after the middle of the fourteenth century. This again underlines the settlement discontinuity probably caused by the economic and social problems of the age, such as the Black Death and the Bruce Invasion.

All six excavations on probable moated sites have, therefore, produced broadly similar chronological data. Their principal functions have also been broadly similar, even if the finds have been very limited in numbers on the majority of sites. They probably all functioned as centres of manors from where the particular Anglo-Norman landowner of the region controlled the feudal system of agriculture. Even chance finds retrieved after ploughing can be useful in dating a site such as 'Killeeshal Fort' in Co. Carlow, a typical single-enclosure rectangular moated site of 1,558 sq m in area, which overlies part of an earlier oval earthwork. If this earlier earthwork is a large ringfort it is significant that one of the objects recovered was a bronze armlet terminal of Early Christian date, while the other finds were of medieval date, such as sherds of native cooking pottery and some green-glazed jugs, all of which can be dated to the thirteenth and fourteenth centuries. Two of the iron objects can be paralleled with examples from Clough Castle in Co. Down, namely a small iron hoe and an iron buckle. Bronze strap-tag protectors, an iron key and some animal bones and teeth were the other objects recovered.[56] This assemblage of finds recovered at random after ploughing makes one wonder what could be located there by a research excavation. It would also be extremely valuable if the stratigraphical relationship between the possible large ringfort and its moated site successor could be worked out and perhaps dated chronologically by the associated finds or by scientific dating methods.

At Galbally in Co. Wexford the ploughing up of the interior of a perfectly square single enclosure of 2,500 sq m in area produced a small polished stone with one rounded and one flat end. Close examination of this stone in the NMI did not reveal any evidence of its use as a mortar pestle so that the possibility still exists that it could have been one of the projectiles fired by a slingshot at the moated site, as this was reputed to be one of the most potent weapons of the Irish against the Anglo-Norman invader.[57] Again, without a proper scientific excavation it would be impossible to verify this possibility. It is possible that the object comes from a well-built stone structure (8 by 5 m) which was noted in the north-west corner of the platform in 1973. This site would have been quite a problem to capture, having 8 m-wide moats as well as stone revetted internal banks. There were also traces of associated earthworks to the immediate east of the main site but again their identification will have to await further archaeological excavation.

In the case of moated sites the extensive field surveys of the surviving earthworks now need to be complemented by a research programme of excavation to test the theories for their origins, distribution pattern, major functions and exact chronology which are almost entirely based upon an examination of the relict sites and upon the limited documentary sources. They can be recognized in the landscape as rectangular earthworks, from about 500 to 4,000 sq m in area, with raised corners where the internal banks have had the benefit of two amounts of upcast from the digging of the surrounding moats, which are usually from 2 to 10 m in width with a 'U'-shaped profile. In south-east Ireland they were found to be concentrated in lowland areas below 200 m OD where the soil was fertile.[58] Because the moats of these sites were most often filled with water in antiquity an attempt was made by Barry to try and identify their original source of water. However, because of the change in the water table since medieval times and the consequent effect this had on the pattern of streams and springs only 43 per cent of the known sites were close to identifiable adequate water sources.[59] The importance of water for these moats, whether as a barrier against an aggressor, for drinking, fire-fighting among the wooden buildings of their interiors, or for sewage disposal, is emphasized by the fact that many of them were located beside a river or streams.

Finally, it is necessary to examine why there is so little mention of these sites in the contemporary manorial documents, when over 750 rectangular earthworks have survived into the landscape of the last century. It has been suggested by C. A. Empey that the answer may lie in the date of the inception of these settlement forms into the Anglo-Norman colony and the way in which the manorial sources were compiled. In a fascinating examination of the settlement history of the cantred of Knocktopher, Co. Kilkenny, in the middle ages he concluded that because there was not one reference to the six surviving sites in the area in any of the documents, even in the detailed extent of 1312 which actually gave a picture of the barony in c.1200 when the original fiefs were granted, they belonged to the secondary colonization of the area on the slightly less productive soils. Additionally because there are very few moated sites associated with medieval parish churches in Ireland, unlike the situation in England, he concluded that they were probably built after the parochial system was established, and thus he assigns them to the period 1225 to 1325.[60] This conclusion based upon negative documentary evidence fits in almost exactly with the archaeological evidence and with the one piece of direct documentary evidence in the account roll for Old Ross in Co. Wexford. What succeeded the moated sites as the major type of defensive rural settlement form in the late fourteenth and fifteenth centuries will be examined in chapter 7.

If, as has been noted above, deserted medieval villages are difficult to identify in any numbers in Ireland then the unmoated manor houses which are usually to be found with them, or indeed the undefended isolated Anglo-Norman farms in the countryside, will be almost impossible to detect archaeologically. However, it is likely that the number of sites in the latter category will be very small because of the general lawlessness of the colony. Perhaps the only safe locations for undefended manor-houses or farms would be close to nucleated settlements. How these sites could be identified, other than by an excavation following on the location of stray finds of medieval date, remains problematic. Perhaps the surviving manorial documents might enable the historian to locate the general vicinity of the manor house as well as giving some descriptive detail about it. One such detailed description is to be found in the 1312 extent for Knocktopher, Co. Kilkenny,[61] where many buildings are described, probably clustered around the motte which was probably built before 1200. A castle (castrum) is mentioned in which there was a hall, a residence and a chapel. It is unlikely that these buildings would have fitted on top of the motte (levelled in 1973) so that it is probable that there was also an associated bailey of which no trace remains. In the more heavily Normanized areas, especially in the south-east, the available documentary evidence would indicate that by the early thirteenth century conditions were so stable that the mottes were hardly ever used, except in cases of attack upon a particular settlement.[62] That there was also a bailey at Knocktopher is further reinforced by the rest of the description of the principal buildings of the manor. Thus there was a kitchen within an outer gate; it was common practice at the time to separate the kitchen from the hall because of the fire risk in wooden buildings. Outside this exterior gate there was a small building and a bretasche, which could either refer to the buildings on the motte itself or, as Empey has suggested, to some kind of wooden blockhouse or barbican to defend the approaches to the castle at its most vulnerable point.[63] There were also agricultural buildings necessary on a farm such as a wooden barn and a byre. Inside the courtyard (curia) there was a stone hall (probably the chief dwelling house of the manor) and various other buildings in poor repair. Finally, there was a dovecote with no doves in it, three fruit and vegetable gardens and two mills.

Other early-fourteenth-century extents, such as the 1304 example for Cloncurry in Co. Kildare, also present a similar picture of the buildings in the manor-house complex.[64] Again in this extent stress is put upon the sorry state of the structures which may have been an accurate reflection of their true condition or, more likely, an attempt to play down their full value to their tenant-in-chief. As these were the manors where a motte castle probably formed a focus for building development it is a pity that none of these sites have been excavated to see whether the remains of the associated buildings can still be exposed. But where the centre of a manor or sub-manor was not marked by an earthwork such as a motte or a moated site it is a very much more difficult exercise for the archaeologist to exactly locate the manor-house complex. Undefended manor houses of this type would be virtually impossible to identify in the landscape, although examples which were located within now-deserted medieval nucleated settlements may be identified through excavation, such as happened with the early medieval manor house at Wharram Percy in Yorkshire.

However, as with the two possible moated sites which came to light only as a result of the excavations by UCC along the route of the Dublin–Cork natural gas pipeline, one such unmoated medieval house was also located. The finds from this house at Castledermot, Co. Kildare, and its environs, which included an area of gravel flooring and several pits, were sherds of imported thirteenth-century pottery, local cooking wares, iron slag, a large number of animal bones and an iron key.[65] These are the type of artefacts that are often found in association with medieval manor houses in Britain, and this structure could well be interpreted as a manor house. Along with the possible medieval grange excavated at Jerpoint Church these are the only two undefended medieval manor-house sites recently excavated in Ireland. Otherwise, apart from buried traces of some unenclosed sites, which can be identified either from the air or by using site prospecting equipment, the only way in which these sites can be located is by chance. And obviously, as is also the case in England, the construction of lengthy pipelines or the building of motorways produce large numbers of previously unknown sites, some of which are medieval in date.

Medieval crafts and industries

If our general knowledge of all types of medieval rural settlement sites is limited then it is hardly surprising that our information on the crafts and industries that were found in medieval Ireland both within and outside the towns is somewhat restricted. Perhaps the best starting point for any such enquiry would be from an examination of the available documentary evidence, and especially the manorial sources which often confirm the kinds of industries you would expect to find in any pre-industrial rural community. Thus to return again to the manorial account rolls for the manor of Old Ross in the late thirteenth century we learn that there was a smith employed at the moated site of Ballyconnor. Other industries that were mentioned included carpentry, with a reference to a carpenter's shop, cobbling (there are several mentions of prices paid for shoes), milling (there are at least two mills noted in the accounts), and brewing. Despite detailed references to these types of establishments in other manorial documents there is, as yet, very little archaeological evidence for these structures at rural sites in Ireland. However some urban sites, notably in Dublin, have uncovered the workshops of some of these crafts and industries for the early medieval period. But where both rural and urban archaeological sites are invaluable is in providing many examples of the types of artefacts that were produced by these workshops.

In any brief survey of the archaeological evidence for crafts and industries in medieval Ireland it is impossible to describe and analyse adequately the many thousands of artefacts which were located by Ó Ríordáin and Wallace of the NMI in the Dublin excavations over the last quarter of a century. Because this section of the book, along with most of the rest of the volume, is heavily dependent on published material it can only offer a glimpse of the wealth, diversity and range of the artefacts recovered from the Dublin sites. Any definitive analysis will have to await the publication by the NMI in association with the RIA of a series of monographs entitled *Medieval Dublin: the National Museum of Ireland Excavation 1962–81*, scheduled to begin in the summer of 1987. These will deal with both the Hiberno-Norse and Anglo-Norman periods in the city's history, and will examine major structures, such as the houses and their plots of land, as well as their artefacts and the environmental evidence.

At the vast majority of excavated medieval sites the most common type of artefact recovered is often medieval pottery, either imported or indigenous. However, when evidence for its actual production is examined for Ireland only two kilns of the period have been found, both in Ulster, with a possible third site near Adare Castle in Co. Limerick. Thus it is very difficult to know the origin and chronology of the many examples of indigenous medieval pottery made in imitation of English and Continental imported wares, and our current knowledge about these imports is much better than about the Irish wares of the period.

As noted earlier in this book the pre-Norman period was mainly aceramic, apart from fairly undistinguished souterrain ware which seems to have been concentrated in the north-east of Ireland. This type of pottery originally acquired its name because the earliest examples were usually found in association with souterrains, but examples have been found in other types of site.[66] It is totally different from the medieval types, comprising poorly fired cooking pots probably made in open fires rather than in kilns, coil-built with little or no decoration. McNeill has suggested that these pots were probably made by itinerant potters who worked in much the same way as the itinerant metalworkers of Early Christian Ireland.[67]

Into this environment came the Anglo-Normans in the 1170s, probably bringing with them the latest examples of their jugs from the Bristol Channel and other south-west English types. As in so many other areas of our knowledge of medieval Ireland there is a dearth of many late-twelfth-century examples of this pottery from excavation sites apart from several Dublin sites.[68] One rural exception to this was the finding of a Paffrath ladle at Ballyfounder, Co. Down, by Waterman in a later layer containing decorated glazed jugs on a ringfort heightened by the Anglo-Normans. This association would suggest that the ladle was not deposited until the middle of the thirteenth century, which would indicate its survival over at least a century.[69] According to McNeill no jug sherd of English provenance in Ireland can be securely dated to before 1225, and he further suggests that the change-over from 'twelfth'- to 'thirteenth'-century wares probably occurred closer to 1170 than to 1225. It is difficult, he writes, to argue this convincingly from English evidence because of the lack of building activity there during the reign of Richard I (1189–99) and in the minority of Henry III (1216–27).[70] It is well to bear McNeill's observations in mind when the imported wares from the major medieval sites are discussed below because again and again the suggested dating evidence is 'thirteenth to early fourteenth centuries'.

If we first of all examine the evidence for these imported wares it immediately becomes clear that the two major sources of supply, not surprisingly, were England, especially from the western areas, and eastern France. However, the proportion of material from these two major pottery sources tends to vary from site to site and this may reflect a particular site's geographical location in relation to Britain and the Continent. Although at Wood Quay in Dublin over half of the medieval pottery sherds found during the excavation were of Dublin manufacture, the majority of the exports were from western Britain, and especially from the Ham Green kilns near Bristol. Most of the imported glazed jugs originated from Saintonge near Bordeaux, and from north-western France. Not only was pottery used for tableware and for storage of wine and water, but as floor- and roof-tiles, finials for chimneys, curfews and even candlesticks.[71]

Conversely, the sites in Ulster have produced pottery mainly from the Cheshire kilns of Audlem and Ashton, and from their offshoot at Rhuddlan. Other thirteenth-century potters at Carrickfergus and the Lecale area produced very similar pots which causes great identification problems. Other types of imported wares mainly originate from south-west Scotland and Carlisle so it looks as though Ulster's major sources for imported pottery were largely from north-west England and Scotland. There was very little trade in the products of south-western England such as the Ham Green kilns which supplied so much pottery to the southern half of Ireland in the late thirteenth and early fourteenth centuries. Also, the number of high quality green-glazed jugs from France is thought to make up only about 10 per cent of the pots found on sites in Ulster and the later polychrome ware is also very rare there.[72] Again, this compares with about 25 per cent of the pottery found in the medieval layers of the Dublin city excavations originating from France.[73]

This leads us on to an examination of the imported wares found in southern sites apart from Dublin. On most sites along the eastern seaboard and in Leinster generally the output of the kiln complex at Ham Green is a dominant factor. Indeed, it has been remarked that more sherds of Ham Green ware have been located in Ireland than in England, surely a testimony both to the importance of Bristol in Irish trade and the export success of the product in the middle ages. Major sites such as those in the city of Cork, Trim Castle, Co. Meath, and Kells Priory, Co. Kilkenny, all produced substantial amounts of Ham Green ware among their pottery finds. Although it was the high quality glazed jugs which were usually found, some sites such as Lady Lane in Waterford have also produced examples of coarse cooking pottery from Ham Green.[74] Other sites such as Shop Street, Drogheda, Co. Louth, also produced evidence for Gloucester ware as well as many sherds of highly decorated Chester ware.[75] During the

Cork city excavations in the 1970s Twohig stated that 80 per cent of his pottery was imported into the city in the middle ages, of which half came from Ham Green and the other half from the prolific kilns at Saintonge near Bordeaux in south western France, then part of the Angevin Empire which was still under the control of the English crown.[76] In recent years further research on medieval pottery in Ireland has tended to show, however, that much more of it was produced indigenously than was hitherto realized, and this may well also apply to Cork.[77]

These glazed jugs were the luxury end of the market and thus were probably used at table to hold water or wine. French jugs were usually tall and thin, while British examples were squatter and more globular in shape. Later French polychrome ware from the Saintonge region, with body decorations in the form of birds and shields, for example, were thought to have been imported into Ireland between 1280 and 1310 and have thus been employed by archaeologists such as Sweetman to help construct a chronology of site occupation at the moated site at Rigsdale, Co. Cork.[78] Sherds of these very fine imported jugs are found both on sites which were occupied by the topmost strata of Anglo-Norman society, such as the castles of Ferns and Trim, and in the major urban centres such as Cork, Drogheda and Dublin.[79] However, in the last few years some sherds of this polychrome ware have been located in mid-fourteenth-century horizons in both Britain and Ireland which has led to a gradual extension of its chronology to around 1330.[80] Green-glazed Saintonge pottery jug sherds have also been found in greater numbers than the polychrome variety in many urban sites such as Cork, Drogheda, Dublin and Limerick as well as in the castles of Adare, Ferns, Limerick and Trim.[81]

Other French imports include less fine ware from north-western France, which was found on the Dublin city excavations along with some examples from the Rouen–Paris–Beauvais area.[82] Although the north-western French wares were found in fairly large quantities in Dublin, only a few sherds have been located in other sites such as Trim and Drogheda.[83] Generally speaking, Saintonge imports tend to outnumber all other types from France. However, there were also imports of late medieval pottery from other European countries such as the Rhenish skillets, painted Mediterranean wares, Dutch vessels and archaic majollica, mainly from the Dublin city excavations.[84]

If we now re-examine the dating for the first imports of English jugs into Ireland it is interesting to note that there is new evidence to suggest a slightly earlier date for their inception. For instance, in his excavation at Lady Lane in Waterford Moore dated the probable construction of the city wall to the early thirteenth century as the Ham Green pottery found in association with it cannot currently be dated any earlier than 1220. However, if the start of this pottery type could be pulled back a generation or so it would mean that the wall was already built by 1170 and this would square with the description of the city by Giraldus Cambrensis when it was captured by the Anglo-Normans.[85] This wall can only be dated with any precision by historical means because of the lack of chronological accuracy regarding the dating of the main artefacts of the period.

There has also been confirmation for this earlier dating of English glazed jugs in both Ulster and Dublin. For Ulster, McNeill has collated all the available evidence for English pottery found during excavations of early medieval sites, mostly mottes, in the earldom and has concluded that a significant proportion of the glazed jugs must, in fact, date to the period 1175 to 1225. His hypothesis has recently been strongly buttressed by Lynn locating sherds of Ham Green pottery under the motte at Rathmullan which would indicate that they were deposited there before 1200.[86] In addition, during the Wood Quay excavation in Dublin some sherds of Ham Green ware were found in the redeposited rubbish banked against the rear of the earliest quayside, which has been dendrochronologically dated to c.1210. And as this material was probably redeposited it must have been slightly earlier than the quay itself,[87] although it must be remembered that this date only relates to the felling of the trees preparatory to the erection of the quay.

Moving on to locally made medieval pottery there is currently a major problem relating to the important Leinster wares which are to be found on virtually all medieval sites in the eastern half of the country, namely a total lack of kiln sites for the production of this pottery. To date, the only two certain medieval kilns are both located in Ulster, at Downpatrick, Co. Down, and Carrickfergus, Co. Antrim (the latter only discovered in the 1970s).[88] A quantity of fourteenth-century pottery wasters was located by Sweetman during his excavation at Adare Castle, Co. Limerick, in the 1970s which indicated to him that there was probably a kiln in the vicinity.[89] This interpretation was reinforced by the finding of a quantity of other pottery wasters within the walled grounds of Adare Manor by M. J. O'Kelly and A. MacDonald of UCC.[90]

The glazed jugs produced by the Downpatrick kiln are probably in the contemporary English tradition of pottery manufacture and have been found in medieval levels in sites in Lecale, Co. Down, such as Clough, Ballynarry and Lismahon.[91] Until quite recently it was thought on stylistic grounds that the pottery was being produced only for a short period of time from the end of the thirteenth to the beginning of the fourteenth century.[92] Of course this pottery could be from a yet undiscovered second kiln at Downpatrick, but the discovery of a kiln at Carrickfergus by Delaney which produced simple jugs, cooking pots and pipkins, and which has also been dated to the first half of the thirteenth century, gives added support to the suggestion that the pottery from the Downpatrick kiln has hitherto been dated much too late.[93] This earlier dating for the Carrickfergus kiln is secure as along with its last firing load there was numismatic evidence to show that it was in use before 1250.[94]

McNeill has argued that there must have been a third kiln in Ulster supplying the jugs found at sites such as Greencastle, Co. Down,

Muckamore Abbey, Co. Antrim and Armagh Friary. It must also be remembered that the indigenous souterrain ware, coil-built cooking pots, also continued in use in east Ulster probably through the first quarter of the thirteenth century until Irish potters started to produce the everted-rim cooking pots so typical of England. The earliest everted-rim pottery to be found in Ulster came from the castle at Dundrum, which suggested that as early as around 1200 the influence of English styles was changing the indigenous souterrain ware pottery into everted-rim forms. It is this Anglo-Norman ware which was to dominate the cooking pots of Ulster right up to the sixteenth century, an indicator of the conservatism in this aspect of medieval society.[95]

Elsewhere in Ireland the major sites in the eastern half of the island have all produced more pottery of local manufacture than imported wares. Despite the abundance of locally produced wares of the thirteenth and early fourteenth centuries, mainly in the form of jugs, storage jars and cooking pots, no medieval pottery kiln has yet been located in either Dublin or its environs. K. J. Barton has identified three basic Dublin wares from this period. The 'A' group largely comprises jugs and was strongly influenced by the products of the Ham Green 'B' kiln near Bristol. The 'B' wares were broadly contemporary with the 'A' group but were more commonly large cooking vessels with fewer examples of jugs. The Dublin 'C' wares were cooking vessels of simple crude appearance with large quartz grits in their fabric. There was also the development of new features and vessel forms primarily among the Dublin 'A'-ware jugs in the early fourteenth century in imitation of the fine wares from France and western England which were probably flooding into the port.[96]

Some of the pottery at Trim Castle was comparable to Dublin medieval wares and some of the jugs and cooking pots were similar in form to Downpatrick pots, although they were probably all made in Trim or its environs.[96] The jugs were of late-thirteenth- to early-fourteenth-century date, and there was a relatively small number of hand-made cooking pots which were of the same date. In the fourteenth-century filling of the west gatehouse of Trim Castle Sweetman located a very uniform class of pottery jugs with various glazes which he called 'Trim ware' (fig. 23).[97] At Ferns Castle Sweetman also found glazed jugs of Irish types, some being similar to his fourteenth-century 'Trim ware'. He also located sherds of local crude ware and cooking pots in the castle's fosse, none of which were turned on a fast wheel.[98] At his Drogheda excavation the locally made jugs were comparable to those from Trim, while the cooking vessels were very close to examples from Ferns Castle and the wheel-turned examples were again similar to some found at Trim.[99] Closer to Dublin, the church site at Kilteel, Co. Kildare, produced some forty sherds of unglazed cooking ware, and the bulk of these were of the local north Leinster type with a buff surface, a black core and quartz and mica grits.[100]

Another important industry for which there exists some archaeological

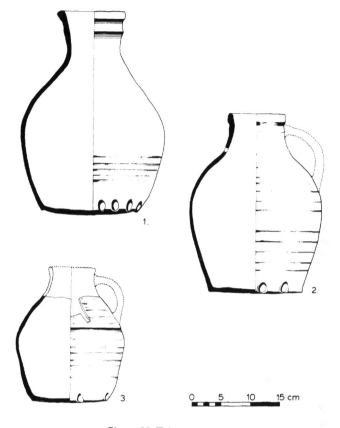

Figure 23 Trim ware pottery

evidence is that of the production of floor tiles. With the exception of pieces from the excavations at Dublin, Carrickfergus Castle, Co. Antrim, Trim Castle, Co. Meath, and Shop Street, Drogheda, Co. Louth, all the known examples of medieval tiles in Ireland are from religious houses.[101] Not surprisingly, given their success in Ireland, most of the tiles are to be found in Cistercian foundations, although the many inlaid and line-impressed tiles found during the excavation of Kells Priory, Co. Kilkenny, revealed that the Augustinians were also used to this type of floor covering. Urban houses of the friars in Carrickfergus, Limerick and Drogheda also possessed tile pavements. Usually the pavements were confined to the sanctuary of the church or other important areas of a religious house such as the prior's residence. Some of the earliest tile pavements, according to Fanning who is preparing a published corpus of them with E. Eames, may well have been put into the two cathedrals of Christ Church and St Patrick's in Dublin by the middle of the thirteenth century.[102] His distribution map (fig. 24) also reveals that 'tile pavements were almost exclusively laid down in the religious houses located in the Norman-held areas of Leinster, Ulster and Munster'.[103] The most westerly location for these tiles was from the excavation of the Dominican priory in Limerick, which was essentially an Anglo-Norman town at the time.

As the closest parallels for some of the earliest two-coloured tiles in

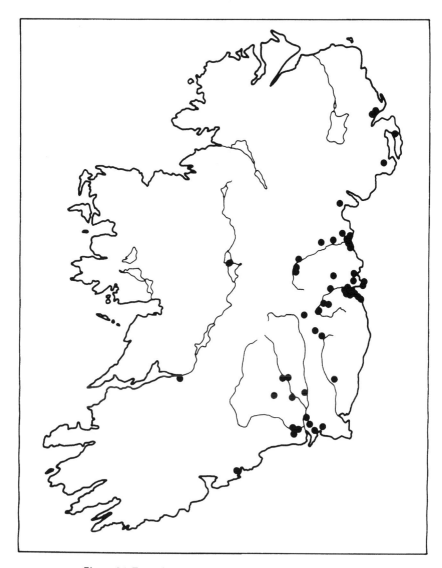

Figure 24 Distribution map of medieval pavement-tiles

Ireland are to be found in south-west England and Wales they were probably imported through ports such as Bristol, much in the same way that Dundry stone from the quarry close to that port was exported to adorn major contemporary Anglo-Norman buildings. By the fifteenth century, when line-impressed tiles were in fashion, the closest analogies, according to Fanning, are to be found in North Wales and the Chester region.[104] The first tile kiln of probable medieval date in Ireland has also recently been discovered in Drogheda by K. Campbell.[105] This has dramatically confirmed the tentative evidence of the finding of waster material in the town on earlier occasions which led Fanning to postulate the probable existence of such a kiln in Drogheda. He has also suggested, given the tile fabrics and the presence of wasters at both Kells Priory and Duiske Abbey, as well as wasters at St Canice's, that another kiln could possibly be located in the Kilkenny area.[106] It will be interesting to see whether this, too, will be confirmed by future archaeological enquiry.

Roof tiles have also been recovered on several medieval sites, including several examples from Dublin. At Ferns Castle, where fourteen fragments were located, two of them were paralleled with examples found by G. Beresford in his excavation of a medieval manor at Penhallam in Cornwall. These coxcomb ridge tiles are similar to those found at Tintagel and Launceston castles, both in Cornwall. Generally these roof-tiles would be dated to the thirteenth or early fourteenth centuries, especially as their green glaze and fabric is so close to the pottery of the period.[107] Other green-glazed medieval ridge tiles of thirteenth-century date were found in excavations at Duiske Abbey at Graignamanagh, Co. Kilkenny, Kells Priory, Co. Kilkenny (where complete examples were recovered), Mellifont Abbey, Co. Louth, Swords Castle, Co. Dublin, and Kilteel Church in Co. Kildare.[108] Fourteenth-century examples were located in Swords Castle and Kilteel as well.[109] At this stage it is not possible to say whether these tiles were made locally or were imported from England.

Although there has as yet been only limited success in locating pottery and tile kilns in Ireland, several grain-drying kilns have been excavated at medieval sites in different parts of the island. It is not surprising, given the generally damp climatic conditions of Ireland, especially in the medieval period, that these kilns were a necessity wherever grain was being prepared for the production of bread. At the Early Christian and medieval monastic site at Tullylish, Co. Down, a large triple-flued circular kiln was located (fig. 25).[110] Other examples have been found both in urban locations, such as on South Quay in Drogheda, and in rural sites such as a possible moated site at Kilferagh, Co. Kilkenny, and near two medieval mud-walled houses discovered at Bourchier's Castle, Co. Limerick.[111]

Perhaps one of the most important industries of medieval Ireland was the production of woollen cloth, supported by sheep-rearing which was a major component of medieval agriculture, especially on the lands of the great Cistercian houses. However, the only type of surviving archaeological

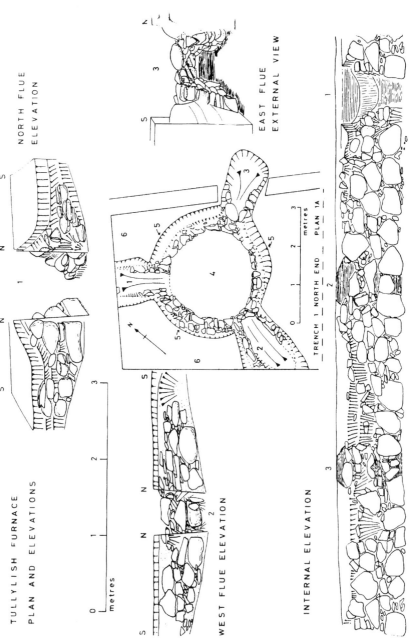

Figure 25 Plan and elevation of Tullylish grain-drying kiln, Co. Down

evidence we have for the important exports of wool-fell from Ireland, which figure very prominently in the medieval customs returns, are the large iron sheep-shearing shears found at sites such as the two medieval houses at Caherguillamore, Co. Limerick, Trim Castle and several sites in Dublin.[112] But when we analyse the archaeological evidence for the actual production of woollen cloth or indeed for the manufacture of linen cloth in the middle ages in Ireland, we find that it is limited.

Among the artefacts that do survive are the spindle-whorls used in the spinning process which are found both in urban sites such as in High Street, Dublin, where they were made out of bone, and rural sites like the moated site at Rigsdale, Co. Cork, where they were of stone.[113] In Dublin several wooden beetles and spindles made out of a copper alloy have been located, as well as iron shears and a variety of needles in bone and bronze. At the High Street site, again, weaving tablets and a weaver's sword made out of yew were found in late Viking levels.[114] In Dublin and Cork bone pin beaters, which were used to adjust individual threads in the weft of the cloth, were found in the excavations showing that weaving was a widespread craft in Anglo-Norman towns.[115] However, there is no certain archaeological evidence in Ireland for either the thickening or fulling process or, indeed, for the final dyeing of the cloth.

Some pieces of textile have survived, mainly on waterlogged sites in Dublin. At Wood Quay a dyed woollen garment was located,[116] while at High Street small pieces of gold braid were found along with fragments of other textiles in early medieval horizons.[117] Fragments of cloth, including silk, from a thirteenth-century context were also recovered by O'Ríordáin from his Winetavern Street excavation in Dublin.[118] More exotic textiles have also been found, such as the two pieces of silk associated with a leather scabbard located at the base of the east fosse at Ferns Castle. These pieces were dated to the late thirteenth or early fourteenth centuries as they were found with pottery sherds of that date.[119] However, so few fragments of cloth have been found in excavations that our knowledge of the styles of medieval dress is still largely dependent upon manuscript illustrations, and upon (largely aristocratic) tombstones and brasses such as are to be found in St Canice's Cathedral in Kilkenny; these have been the subject of a classic study and catalogue by Bradley.[120]

The reverse is true of the leather-making industry which was of great importance to medieval man, not only for his footwear, but also for scabbards, belts, purses, gloves and other personal adornments. The main raw material was, of course, cattle hide although goat and pig skins were also used. Indeed, one of Ireland's major exports in the middle ages was hides, which were mainly sent to Flanders, the Low Countries, Gascony and Tuscany.[121] Again, for the sheer volume and range of articles made out of leather the medieval levels of the excavations in Dublin cannot be bettered. Part of the High Street site had an abundance of worked leather from the late twelfth and early thirteenth centuries. The majority of the leather consisted of soles which were either worn, damaged, or holed and which had therefore been discarded. According to O'Ríordáin the shoe uppers were cut away from the worn soles and reused to make smaller pieces of footwear. Most of the leather was from cattle-hides but some were made out of goat skins. The concentration of so much leather obviously suggests that this area was the cobblers' quarters over much of the medieval period.[122] Indeed the Dublin excavations also produced many examples of decorated knife sheaths, leather belts, wrist straps, children's boots, and a stamped leather book cover from France, as well as cobblers' tools which included punches, and awls with lathe-turned wooden handles.[123] The excavation by Lynch of the OPW in the moat area around the Corke Tower at Dublin Castle also located many more soles and other pieces of medieval footwear in the waterlogged conditions in the moat.[124]

Other urban sites have also produced large quantities of worked leather, notably Drogheda where Sweetman found among the many scraps of leather two almost complete shoes, thirty-four soles, fourteen uppers, eight belt fragments, two small pieces of sheaths and other smaller worked pieces (fig. 26).[125] This concentration of leather in one medieval layer of the site was remarkable because of the limited area which was investigated. The fact that twenty out of the twenty-four shoes which had their front piece intact had pointed toes reinforces the current archaeological picture in the rest of Europe that these were common throughout the medieval period and were not confined to the later middle ages as was once thought.[126]

In Cork the excavations of part of the medieval city walls parallel to Grand Parade produced sizeable pieces of three leather shoes along with several smaller pieces of soles, welts, thongs and uppers. One was of 'turnshoe' type of the late twelfth to early thirteenth centuries. The other two were welted shoes of the mid-sixteenth century. At the earlier excavations by Twohig of the site of the College of Holy Trinity, Christchurch, large numbers of leather scraps, sheaths and shoe pieces were found in the area behind the medieval street frontage, indicating that leather working was practised here in the middle ages.[127] Other medieval urban sites which produced substantial numbers of leather scraps and shoes include those found in the Irish Quarter excavation at Carrickfergus.[128]

At most of the urban sites which have produced evidence of leathercraft there have also been the material remains of metalworking. Again there is a wealth of artefacts from the Dublin excavation which stress the importance of metalworking in the city centre in the medieval period. Evidence for this industry included crucible fragments, moulds, hammers and drill-bits, as well as some of the products of the workshops such as fish hooks, knives, shears, needles, iron pins, barrel padlocks and keys. Bronzeworking in particular was important in Dublin in the eleventh and twelfth centuries, especially in the Christ Church Place site. In particular the city was probably producing bronze pins on a large scale, both the earlier ringed variety and the simpler stick or cloak pins which were produced up until

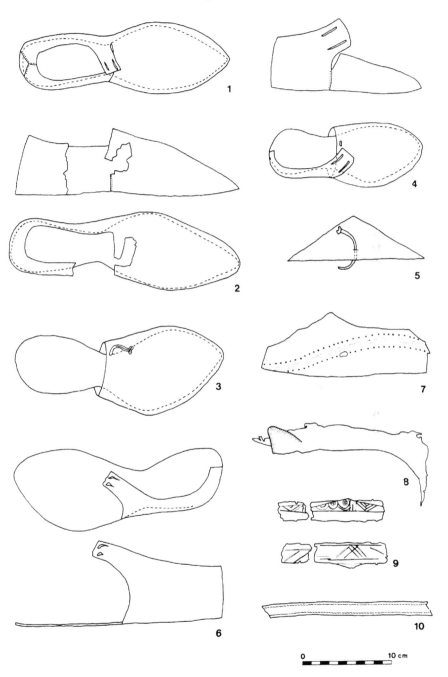

Figure 26 Medieval shoes from Drogheda, Co. Louth

the fourteenth century. Most of these latter pins were plain headed but some had elaborately carved or chiselled heads, one being in the shape of a horse's head. Other personal ornaments such as bronze and silver annular brooches, finger-rings and bronze buckles which were found in the Dublin excavations were also probably made in the locality. Bronze tweezers, some with exquisitely chiselled designs, were also found.[129]

There are also historical references to commercially exploitable iron-ore deposits in Ireland although they are not explicit as to where these could be found. For instance, in 1289 Nicholas de Clere was granted a mandate 'to make a profit of the king's mine of silver, copper, lead, iron or other metal reported to be recently discovered in Ireland'.[130] Whether this was a speculative grant or not we cannot be sure although silver was definitely mined from the thirteenth century onwards at Knockaunderrig, Co. Tipperary.[131] There is also the tradition that the prosperity of the now deserted medieval town of Clonmines in south Co. Wexford was largely dependent on the nearby silver and lead mines which were worked up until the sixteenth century.[132] These may be the mines referred to in the statutes of the Irish Parliament in 1457 which granted to a 'William Willeston of Dublin, Merchant, who with certain miners in England and France . . . knows certain mines in Co. Wexford' the right to work them for twenty years.[133] We also know from other contemporary sources that fifteenth-century Ireland was considered to have substantial reserves of gold and silver.[134]

It is debatable as to how much iron ore was produced in Ireland because the existing documentary sources are full of references to the large imports of iron from Brittany, the Iberian peninsula and England.[135] Indeed, 'Spanish iron' was a notable commodity in medieval Ireland and was specifically mentioned in several murage charters, such as one for Callan, Co. Kilkenny, in 1403.[136] The importance of iron to the economy of Irish ports generally can be seen in the protest by the burgesses of Drogheda in 1364 at being compelled by the 1325 Ordinance of the Staple to trade their hides, wool and cloth with the port of Calais because there was no iron to be found there.[137]

In pre-Norman Ireland there had been a long and famous tradition of high-quality metalworking in both rural sites such as at the ringfort at Garryduff, Co. Cork,[138] and in the Hiberno-Norse ports such as Dublin where crucible fragments, slag, vitreous matter and stone ingot moulds indicated intensive iron- and bronze-working at both High Street and Christ Church Place in the eleventh and twelfth centuries.[139] This fine metalworking continued beyond the Anglo-Norman invasion as is revealed by parts of the shrine of the Book of Dimna which date from the middle of the twelfth century. Unfortunately, there is a lack of surviving high quality metalwork from the second half of the twelfth century until the Gaelic resurgence of the fourteenth and fifteenth centuries when many relics and shrines were restored.[140]

In Ulster, according to McNeill, the Anglo-Normans changed the pattern of iron production as they centralized it and put it onto a full industrial footing, often within urban areas.[141] He cited as an example of this trend the two large iron-smelting furnaces in an industrial area to the immediate south of the motte at Coney Island, Co. Armagh, set up by the Archbishop of Armagh to exploit the Lough Neagh bog ores. But if the available evidence for medieval iron-smelting in Ireland generally is examined, there is little evidence at present to suggest that this industry was concentrated on large-scale industrial sites, especially as a ready source of coal or charcoal would have been a necessity. It would seem rather that most settlements had facilities with just enough capacity to satisfy their individual needs. Some rural sites have produced large quantities of iron slag such as the 16 kg found by Waterman at Lismahon motte, Co. Down. He also found traces of a timber-framed workshop associated with three small oval pits, one of which was probably a furnace, along with carbonized hazelwood to supply the necessary charcoal. These were all related to the first phases of site occupation in the late twelfth and thirteenth centuries.[142]

At Bourchier's Castle, Co. Limerick, Cleary uncovered an ironworking complex close to the remains of two thirteenth- and early-fourteenth-century houses, but although hearths, pits, a slate-covered drain, stone foundations and postholes were identified neither furnaces nor smelting pits were found. However, the large quantity of iron slag (over 11 kg) and the many iron objects such as knives, nails and a jew's harp strongly indicated that ironworking was carried out nearby. As these features were stratigraphically later than a yard enclosure of the early fourteenth century, ironworking probably continued here from the middle-fourteenth until the seventeenth centuries.[143] At Ballyman, Co. Dublin, another fourteenth-century ironworking area was excavated adjacent to the early medieval church there. Again, although an iron jew's harp, knives, spikes and a pin were found the actual smelting area was not located, although the type of slag recovered indicated that it had been smelted in small bowl-type furnaces.[144] The early medieval monastic site at Tullylish, Co. Down, also produced considerable evidence for metalworking.[145]

In urban sites, apart from the considerable evidence from late Viking and early Anglo-Norman horizons in Dublin, ironworking remains have been found in Carrickfergus and Cork. At Market Place in Carrickfergus Delaney discovered iron slag in large amounts, including furnace bottoms, from a cobbled area at the lowest levels of the excavation. Later research showed that the smelting was based on local iron ores from Co. Antrim. The products from this ironworking included four thirteenth- or fourteenth-century knife blades with their stamped maker's marks and two jew's harps.[146] The excavations on South Main Street, Cork, recovered crucibles, slag and furnace bottoms which were associated with iron and bronze craftsmen who produced small articles of dress such as buckles and strap-fittings and embellishments for horse harnesses, all integral parts of everyday life in medieval Ireland.[147] Of course, one of the main industries which was dependent on metal production was the minting of coins but our evidence for this is mainly historical.[148]

Another craft which was practised in many medieval households was the production of small personal objects out of bone, antler tines and the horns of goats and sheep. Again, Dublin is famous for its bone combs which were probably made in districts such as High Street and Christ Church Place where over 600 examples were found. These broadly date from the late tenth to the twelfth centuries and were made from red deer antler. They have been classified by M. Reynolds of the NMI. She divided them into nine classes, with the few surviving pre-ninth-century examples being small, highly decorated bone combs which were inherently weak. Then in the ninth century strong, well polished antler combs were introduced into Ireland, followed in the twelfth century by strong horn or wooden combs.[149] The comb-making workshops were identified by the large quantities of antler waste and the numbers of partially finished component parts of these combs which were concentrated in specific areas on the two sites.[150] Very few deer bones were found among the countless animal bones from the Dublin excavations, indicating that the combs were not by-products of venison consumption by the city's inhabitants. Rather, the existence of natural ruptures on most of the discarded antler burrs reveals that they had probably been collected in the neighbouring forests after they had been shed by the deer.[151]

Along with these single- or double-sided combs decorated with dot-and-circle, chevrons and hatching patterns there were many other small objects made from bones of animals butchered in the city and from the discarded antler tines. For instance, one thirteenth-century knife handle from Wood Quay was carved in the shape of a crowned figure clasping a chain or cloak strings with its right hand.[152] In the earlier Hiberno-Norse period many bone trial or motif pieces[153] were uncovered in Dublin, often with interlace or geometric designs carved upon them. These carvings range from roughly scratched sketches to completed designs in full relief. While their exact purpose has never been completely explained it is probable that the finished designs served as patterns for bronzeworkers or silversmiths practising their trade in Dublin. These trial pieces have also been located on rural sites dating to the Early Christian period such as the thirty roughly-executed slate examples found by Lynn at Gransha, Co. Down, an artificially heightened and defended hillock.[154]

When we come to examine the evidence for a craft that must have been of prime importance to medieval Ireland, that of carpentry, the lack of surviving wooden buildings is at once apparent. The difference in the survival rates of medieval structures between England and Ireland is nowhere more strikingly illustrated than with wooden buildings as there are many of them surviving in England, albeit many in modified form. The only known wooden construction of medieval date to have survived in Ireland to the present day is the fifteenth-century roof of Dunsoghley tower house in north Co. Dublin, the timbers for which came from trees regenerating in the late fourteenth century.[155]

In spite of this total lack of upstanding wooden buildings much is known about medieval woodworking techniques, mainly due to the waterlogged conditions of the Dublin archaeological sites. Murray has comprehensively studied the remains of the wooden buildings of the early medieval period on four of the Dublin sites. The buildings fall into three major categories: small dwellings, larger more substantial dwellings and ancillary buildings such as latrines and sheds. From the middle of the tenth century to the early twelfth the basic four-post plan of these mainly post-and-wattle structures remained virtually unchanged. With the coming of the Anglo-Normans at the end of the twelfth century there was a gradual change to heavier timber-framed buildings of oak rather than ash, as can be seen at High Street (fig. 27). Other examples include the large squared timbers of the heavy thirteenth-century cagework warehouses located by Wallace at Wood Quay. Here the large squared timbers had mortices in their upper surfaces to hold the upright posts with the gaps between them probably filled in with wattle screens. As the thirteenth century progressed an increasing number of town houses were probably being constructed partly or wholly of stone, as is evidenced by the floor-, roof- and ridge-tiles, as well as chimney pots from stone-supported roofs found during the Dublin excavations. For example, the remains of a mortared stone building of late-thirteenth- to early-fourteenth-century date were excavated at Christ Church Place, Dublin.[156]

The sequential development of the medieval quays at Wood Quay has also been precisely dated by the use of dendrochronological techniques by Baillie of QUB.[157] According to Wallace the carpentry techniques used in these thirteenth-century wooden revetments were broadly the same as those practised by their Scandinavian predecessors. There seems to have been a reliance on the axe and the adze rather than on the saw; and pegs and radially cut boards were in general use. The differences were in the wood employed, oak rather than ash, and in the use of larger squared building beams and mortice and tenon joints. This general continuity of carpentry techniques from the Viking to the Norman period was due in large measure, according to Wallace, to the fact that these invaders 'had little impact on the technical repertoire of the native craftsmen who had mastered locally available raw materials as well as the limitations of tools and the requirements of the environment and who were probably retained and patronised by each successive wave of newcomers'.[158]

The Wood Quay site also produced many reused ships timbers in the medieval revetments. These dated to the eleventh and thirteenth centuries, and among the parts of thirteenth-century ships to have been found were frames, a bulkhead, stems, a keel, a beamknee, and two large Y-shaped

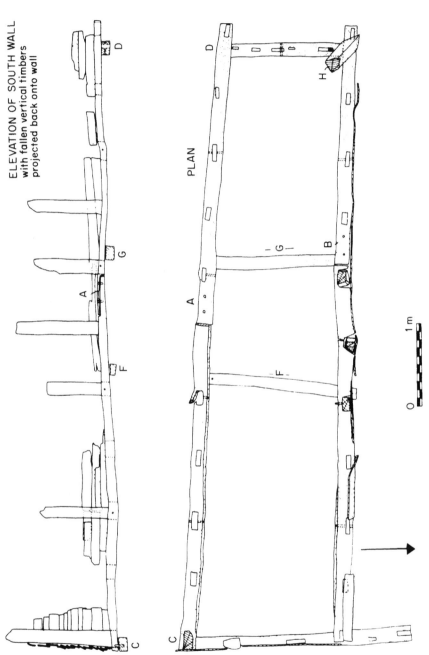

ELEVATION OF SOUTH WALL
with fallen vertical timbers
projected back onto wall

PLAN

0   1 m

Figure 27 Medieval timber-framed structure from High Street, Dublin

timbers which may have been mast crutches. Baillie was able to establish by dendrochronological analysis that the wood was of Irish origin so the boats were probably constructed in Dublin.[159]

Some carpentry tools have also been located on excavations, mainly in Dublin where a saw, axes, chisels, punches, awls, boring bits and gimlets have been found. A woodworker's plane from an eleventh-century level was also located at Christ Church Place. Other sites which produced medieval carpentry tools included Trim Castle where a small axe of late-thirteenth- to early-fourteenth-century date was suggested by the excavator to have been used for trimming or light woodworking.[160] An iron adze of about the same date was also located at Rigsdale moated site in Co. Cork.[161]

Wooden bowls and mugs have been found on several urban and rural excavations including, of course, Dublin, Adare and Trim Castles and Kilmagoura moated site.[162] Other artefacts which were produced on lathes and found in the Dublin excavations ranged from plates and ladles to gaming pieces.[163] The craft of the cooper also survived with staves and hoops found in the medieval levels of Dublin, and an ash stave was also located at Ferns Castle.[164] It is scarcely surprising that so many remains of barrels were found in Dublin as all the major east coast ports shared in the wine trade from Gascony and, to a lesser extent, from the Iberian peninsula.[165] Wine from France was also re-exported to both England and Scotland via ports such as Waterford in the fourteenth century.[166] One of the main reasons that there is so much documentary evidence on the wine trade of medieval Ireland is directly related to the fact that it carried such a high import duty as a luxury which was not 'itself so vital that a higher price or a more restricted supply would have dire consequences upon the medieval Irish economy'.[167] Although most wine imported into Ireland was consumed as an alcoholic beverage by large sections of the population, it was also used for ecclesiastical purposes during mass, and old wine was very useful as a preservative.[168]

The other material used for large buildings such as castles and religious houses was stone, and Ireland had a long and famous indigenous tradition of stoneworking on ecclesiastical structures and sculptural crosses in the pre-Norman period.[169] Thus there must have also been a flourishing indigenous quarrying industry in the Anglo-Norman era, which was the case for Ulster where McNeill found no evidence for the import of stone in the middle ages.[170] Thus Carrickfergus Castle was constructed using local red sandstone as well as white limestone from Cultra, Co. Down, across Belfast Lough. At Dundrum Castle local calcareous tufa and sandstone from Scrabo Hill were used.[171] Over much of south-eastern Ireland, on the other hand, imported stone played an important part in the dressing of many Anglo-Norman buildings. One such example was the abbey of Mellifont where along with the local slate for the rubble walling and the sandstone from Co. Meath, limestone was imported both from Caen in Normandy and from the Dundry quarries near Bristol. This limestone was used from the thirteenth century until the later middle ages when local sandstone was again employed at Mellifont.[172] It would not have been too difficult to have brought the stone in from England and the Continent down the River Boyne from the thriving port of Drogheda. Other important Anglo-Norman structures which employed Dundry stone included Christ Church Cathedral in Dublin which also used black marble shafts made out of stone from the Isle of Purbeck in Dorset.[173] According to Stalley the extent to which Dundry stone was utilized in buildings in both Britain and Ireland is well illustrated by an incident in 1251 when the royal bailiffs seized stones which were awaiting shipment to St Thomas' Abbey in Dublin from the port of Bristol as they were needed to repair the local castle.[174]

Other Anglo-Norman buildings in eastern Ireland utilized local stone such as the Co. Meath sandstone used in the rounded window arches on the lower portion of the keep of Trim Castle, while the rest of the keep's walls were constructed out of roughly coursed local limestone.[175] In the west the Augustinian priory at Clontuskert was built out of grey limestone from around Ballinasloe, Co. Galway.[176] The city wall of Dublin at Wood Quay was constructed out of a rubble fill within mortared stone facings of local limestone,[177] similar to the wall at Grand Parade in Cork which was constructed almost entirely of limestone with a very small amount of red sandstone. Its construction method was also similar to that of Dublin's wall as it had two well-built facings and a rubble core all held together by 'a strong lime and sand mortar'.[178] At Lady Lane in Waterford the medieval city wall was mainly composed of shale blocks but there was a much larger number of red sandstone stones mixed in with them in the gate tower.[179] Finally, the excavations at Charlotte's Quay, Limerick, showed that the city wall there was also made up of heavily mortared limestone rubble faced with cut limestone blocks.[180]

These constructions in both wood and stone meant a great deal of employment for skilled carpenters and masons. Many of them came over from England to practise their skills both for the Crown and for the greater nobility and they have been extensively studied by Stalley.[181] One such mason called Nicholas of Coventry was active in Dublin in the first half of the thirteenth century, while another craftsman from Worcestershire was employed on St Canice's Cathedral in Kilkenny.[182] Other master craftsmen from England have also been studied by Stalley, especially William de Prene, who during his short career was appointed 'Carpenter of the King's Houses and Castles in Ireland' in 1284. Six years later in 1290 he was promoted to 'Keeper of the King's Works in Ireland', but his downfall came about in 1292 when he was found guilty of theft, embezzlement and 'faulty work' which had caused the collapse of the bridge at Limerick with eighty deaths. As a felon he was stripped of his position and succeeded by Adam de Claverle in 1293.[183]

Although the Crown and the greater Anglo-Norman nobility would probably have favoured English craftsmen, and this is borne out by the surviving records, there was also a flourishing school of Irish masons and carpenters. These native craftsmen were obviously active at Cistercian monasteries such as Boyle, Co. Roscommon, and the Augustinian abbey at Ballintubber, Co. Mayo; both of which were far outside the influence of the Anglo-Norman lordship. It is known, for instance, that at Boyle in 1230 the death of a Donnsleibhe Ó hInmhainén, 'a holy monk and chief master of the carpenters', was recorded.[184] It is significant to record that the Ó hInmhainéns were an important family of craftsmen in pre-Norman times as they are named as such on the shrine of St Patrick's Bell which is dated to between 1094 and 1105.[185] There must also have been a professional master mason employed at the abbey as well, although his name does not survive into the written record. Nevertheless, the sculptural mastery of the stonework on five churches in Connacht, including Boyle, all indicate a sculptor and his companions who were virtually artistic representatives of the O'Connors.

Finally, several ecclesiastical sites have produced small fragments of medieval painted window glass such as Mellifont Abbey, Co. Louth, Kells Priory, Co. Kilkenny, Clontuskert Priory, Co. Galway and Duiske Abbey, Co. Kilkenny.[186] At Duiske, for instance, the painting consisted of floral designs with cross-hatching done in red paint.[187] Painted window glass of the medieval period has also been found at Dublin and Trim Castles.[188] Because of the lack of extensive archaeological evidence it is not possible to know whether any of this glass was made locally or whether it was imported into the country. However, there is a very small number of known imported glass artefacts such as the thirteenth-century Syro-Frankish enamelled glass beaker found at Winetavern Street, Dublin.[189] On balance it is possible that some glass was made in Ireland in the middle ages but that finer products were probably imported from abroad, especially from continental Europe.[190]

In summary, what this section on medieval craft and industry in Ireland has revealed is the almost total lack of knowledge about the technology or the way in which major classes of medieval artefacts were made. And some important crafts such as the production and illumination of manuscripts are not pertinent to archaeological avenues of enquiry. The only industry which has had the benefit of major archaeological investigation has been that of the pottery trade. Nevertheless, outside Ulster, not one medieval pottery kiln has yet been located (apart from a possible site at Adare, Co. Limerick) and so our knowledge about the probable origin of the extensive local manufacture of jugs and cooking pots is still rudimentary. This is, therefore, an important gap in our knowledge about medieval technological development and an obvious area for much more historical and archaeological research. Even by comparison with our nearest neighbour, England, where Clarke recently remarked on 'a peculiar lack of interest' in the subject, Ireland is currently far behind in any attempt to elucidate this 'most important aspect of medieval life'.[191]

5 The growth
of medieval towns

It was stated at the beginning of this book that possibly the first sign that
the Irish public as a whole was becoming interested in its medieval past
was the controversy generated over the decision by Dublin Corporation in
the late 1970s to go ahead with their development of the Wood Quay site
on the south side of the River Liffey as a new Civic Centre. This was
despite the many archaeological structures and artefacts dating from the
tenth to the fourteenth centuries which had been partially investigated on
the site by a team led by Patrick Wallace of the National Museum. These
excavations, although amongst the largest in Ireland, were only the culmi-
nation of a long series of urban investigations in the heart of the historic
city of Dublin, first by the OPW and latterly by the NMI. Indeed, it is still
true to say that urban archaeology in the Republic of Ireland has, up to
now, been almost exclusively confined to Dublin, Drogheda, Cork,
Galway, Kilkenny, Limerick, Waterford and Wexford.[1] However, the core
of the late medieval and Plantation town of Carrickfergus, Co. Antrim,
was investigated by Thomas Delaney of the Ulster Museum in a series of
excavations from 1972 to 1979, and, more recently, there have been several
excavations in Drogheda, Co. Louth, another major northern port in the
middle ages.

From the above list of Irish cities and towns which have been
investigated archaeologically it is apparent that all of them are ports, and
while it is true that most of the major medieval cities were ports there are
many important inland examples, such as Kilkenny, which is only just
being archaeologically examined. Kilkenny is lucky in that, unlike many
of its contemporaries, it still preserves much of its medieval character,
dominated by its cathedral dedicated to St Canice and its large castle,
much altered over the centuries, and by the remains of other churches and
monasteries of the medieval period. Its medieval street plan is also well
preserved and in Parliament Street there is a very fine stone-built house
erected in 1594 for John Rothe (pl. 13). It will also be among the first urban
centres to be published in the *Irish Historic Towns Atlas* under the aus-
pices of the RIA.

Plate 13 The outer courtyard of Rothe House, Kilkenny

Indeed, as mentioned in chapter 4, it was the Anglo-Normans who effectively planted a proper network of towns and cities throughout all of Ireland, except for the western fringes which remained under Irish control during the period. This concentration of boroughs within the 'heartland' of the Anglo-Norman colony is apparent from an inspection of Graham's distribution map for Ireland which plots a total of around 300 examples (fig. 28). It would appear that the most heavily urbanized counties were Louth, followed by Kildare and Dublin. This distribution should only be regarded as a provisional statement as research is still uncovering documentary evidence, mainly in the form of charters, to indicate the existence of more boroughs in Anglo-Norman Ireland. Also there is the problem that many of the smaller boroughs were really only villages that were given borough status to attract settlers to them. There have been several attempts to try to define precisely what is meant by the word 'town' in the medieval Irish context,[2] but a combination of the lack of archaeological research and the small number of surviving medieval documents relating to the foundation of urban settlements makes it unlikely that this problem of definition will be ever satisfactorily resolved.

Perhaps the best approach is to take the pragmatic view that if there is doubt about a particular nucleated settlement it should be regarded as a 'rural borough' unless it can be shown to have had economic specialization within its boundaries, as well as evidence of involvement in more than purely local trade. Thus in this chapter we will be examining the archaeological evidence for those settlements which were truly urban in the modern social or economic sense of the word. It must be stressed that any general conclusions about the layout, economic and social conditions and the chronological development of urban settlements in medieval Ireland can only be of a tentative nature until a much wider geographical spread of sites has been investigated. It may be thought initially that these major centres of Anglo-Norman population would be among the best documented aspects of the medieval period. There is, comparatively speaking, a wealth of documents surviving for cities such as Dublin, but for the lesser towns there is often little detailed information. For instance, McNeill has stressed the absence of even a reference to markets or charters granting the right to hold them in any of Ulster's boroughs.[3]

Medieval Dublin

If we examine Dublin separately from the other towns, because of its unique position as the centre for the Anglo-Norman administration, it soon becomes clear that the archaeologist has much more to offer the historian than just filling out details of those aspects of medieval urban life that are mentioned in the documentary sources. What the excavations have revealed is the continuity of property boundaries, the expansion of the wharves and warehouses of the city onto the River Liffey, some of the

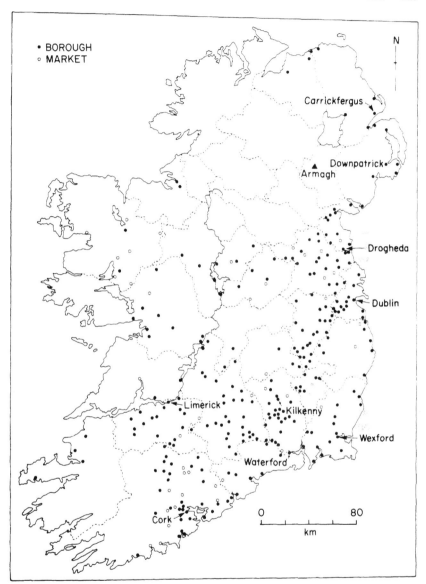

Figure 28 Distribution map of medieval boroughs and markets

industries that were important to the economic well-being of the city, and
the structural history of ordinary urban dwellings which are definitely not
to be found delineated in the documents. In many cases the medieval
written sources concentrate upon the principal buildings of the city such as
the castle and the cathedral or upon the leading citizens, usually from a

fiscal point of view. Like many classes of medieval documents they only refer to that small section of the population that was literate, almost invariably those of seigneurial or ecclesiastical rank. This is also the case with the surviving manorial extents and surveys which only deal with the major holders of land and property and tell us nothing about those people who held land from them or, indeed, of the families of these landowners.

As has been already shown in chapter 1, the development of the Hiberno-Norse city centred around the Christ Church Cathedral area. The Anglo-Norman invasion of 1169 does not seem, archaeologically speaking, to have caused any cataclysmic change in either the structures or the artefacts exposed by the excavations there. This may, in part, be due to the strong links between Hiberno-Norse Dublin and the major ports along the west coast of Britain, especially Bristol, during the two centuries before the Conquest. It has been pointed out by Stephenson that one interpretation of Henry II's charter of 1171–2 is that there was probably a colony of Bristol merchants resident in the city *before* 1169.[4] This suggestion is hardly surprising given the geographical propinquity of Bristol to the east coast of Leinster, and especially to the major Hiberno-Norse port of Dublin.

One great drawback which results from the geographical clustering of all the excavations around Christ Church Cathedral is that we still know nothing archaeologically of the growth of the outlying suburbs of the city during the middle ages. Thus all our knowledge is of the core of the city alone, and so it is not yet possible to chart the expansion of Dublin throughout the period accurately.

If first of all we examine the evidence produced from the houses and plots in Dublin we find that the archaeologist has been able to supply much information on their main constructional features, the internal living arrangements, the furniture, and even on the trades carried out in some of them. Again, the site with most surviving constructional evidence for houses was Wood Quay where Wallace noted a striking continuity both in house plots and property boundaries from the tenth to the thirteenth centuries. Thus, at the level of everyday urban life the events of 1169 did not seem to make any appreciable material difference except that the standard of woodworking of the houses generally declined after the Anglo-Norman invasion.

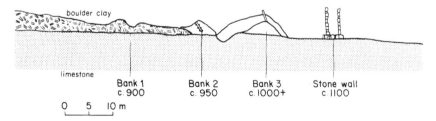

Figure 29 Section of the medieval waterfront at Wood Quay, Dublin

The internal arrangements of these structures also remained broadly similar to those of the Hiberno-Norse period, with many houses being divided up into two or three areas or rooms, usually marked by light wickerwork partitions. The bedroom could often be identified by the wooden benches along one wall, the living area was usually where most of the small finds were located, and the kitchen area had traces of a hearth or oven. The specialized workshops were often identified by waste material such as bone blanks for the ubiquitous bone combs, or leather pieces for the cobblers left out in the plot or buried in pits, which the waterlogged levels of most of the excavated sites had preserved. Sometimes the tools themselves survived such as the weaver's sword of yew, the stone loom weights, the spindle whorls, also of stone, and the broken and discarded casts of metalworkers.

Wallace was also able to demonstrate by archaeological evidence that at Wood Quay the stone city wall was erected around AD 1100.[5] It was made up of a rubble fill with mortared stone facings, c.1.5 m wide and originally possibly 3.5 m high. South of this wall were the eleventh- and twelfth-century houses which were rectangular in plan, on average around 7 by 4 m, with central hearths and brushwood bedding along the side walls. Most of the property boundaries were trapezoidal in shape, unequal in area, with their narrowest end fronting onto the quayside.

From the end of the twelfth century until the start of the fourteenth a series of waterfronts was erected on reclaimed land on the south bank of the River Liffey because the silting up of this broad river made it impossible for heavily laden cargo boats to unload their contents along the existing quays (fig. 29). Indeed, throughout most of the middle ages Dalkey, along the coast to the south of the city, was used as an out-port for Dublin. Thus this real loss of revenues as a result of the gradual silting up of the river caused the citizens of the city to extend their waterfront at least five times in the medieval period at Wood Quay.[6] The first attempt was marked by the building of a bank some 25 m north of the city wall with a post-and-wattle fence acting as its core. Up to 3 m north of this the first wooden revetment was erected in c.1210, constructed of squared oak posts behind which were horizontal planks held in place by the refuse of the city which piled up against it, and braced in the front. Six identifiable units probably

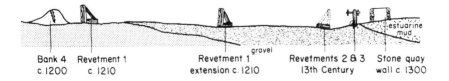

Bank 4   Revetment 1   Revetment 1   Revetments 2 & 3   Stone quay
c.1200   c.1210   extension c.1210   13th Century   wall c.1300

Figure 29 (cont.)

demarcated divisions of ownership. There is one gap in the line and about 20 m north of this there was positioned another revetment similar to the main one, except that the timber cladding was made up of re-used ships' timbers. Later on in the thirteenth century a further timber revetment was put up 12 m further out into the bed of the river, this time back-braced. Then the final wooden revetment was built in the same century just north of the previous one, made up of uprights, boards, and principal base-plates with back-bracing again. All of these waterfronts were precisely dated to within a decade by dendrochronological analysis by Michael Baillie of QUB.[7]

According to Wallace these revetments were probably constructed for three major reasons: they provided the facing for the vertical dockside to protect the reclaimed land against estuarine deposition; they increased the draught of water for shipping (although the existence of front braces on two revetments obviously meant that the boats did not dock directly against them); and the reclaimed land behind these lines of revetments provided space for warehouses and other mercantile buildings that were needed to service the expansion in external trade in the city in the early middle ages. Crisscrossing the whole site were lines of drains all running north–south at right angles to the city wall. Two of them were replaced by stone-lined examples in the later thirteenth century and these seemed to have been in use up until the mid-eighteenth century. Plank-lined cesspits were also found dotted over the area, a reminder of the lack of a sewage system for the medieval city.[8]

Both from the historical written record and also from the survival, albeit often in a greatly modified form, of some of the major medieval buildings we can gain some idea of the standard of living of the wealthy minority of the population. The stone castle, probably built in about 1204, has already been dealt with in chapter 3 but we know from the chronicle of Roger of Hoveden that Henry II entertained the Irish chiefs in the winter of 1171–2 in a post-and-wattle palace possibly built by indigenous craftsmen just outside the walls of the city.[9]

We also know from Giraldus Cambrensis, and from the archaeological evidence of Wood Quay, that a city wall was already in existence when the Anglo-Normans captured the city in 1170 although we cannot be sure of its twelfth-century circuit. What is virtually certain is that the Anglo-Normans did not lose any time in strengthening and repairing parts of the defensive perimeter against any possible later attempt by the Irish to retake the city. In the thirteenth century the original circuit was dramatically increased northwards to encompass ground recently reclaimed from the Liffey. There was probably extensive suburban development including important establishments such as the Hospital of St John the Baptist which was probably founded in the 1180s. In a deed of 1200 this hospital is described as being 'at the Newgate'. Given the propitious trading climate of the early middle ages there is little doubt that the walls were extended alongside the south bank of the Liffey by the first half of the fourteenth century (fig. 5).

Apart from the castle and the city walls the only other medieval structures to remain fairly intact are ecclesiastical. This includes the two cathedrals, Christ Church and St Patrick's, both extensively modified in the nineteenth century, as well as only one of the many medieval parish churches of the city, that of St Audoen's. Here the original early-thirteenth-century nave survives, along with a Transitional west door of *c*.1200 in date, and a fifteenth-century chapel dedicated to St Anne. Other parish churches and religious houses of post-medieval fabric stand on the sites of their medieval predecessors, such as St Michan's on the north side of the river and St Werburgh's close to Dublin Castle. There is also the very fine vaulted chapter house, built in about 1190, of St Mary's Cistercian Abbey, a National Monument which should be more widely known. The only church to have been archaeologically investigated, apart from the attempt to find the Scandinavian church of St Olave along Fishamble Street during the Wood Quay excavations, was that of St Michael le Pole to the south of the Castle. The excavation took two months in 1981 and was funded by the site developers prior to their construction work.[10] The archaeologists found evidence of occupation before the twelfth century represented by postholes, pits, gullies and animal bones, as well as seven burials (including one lintel grave). The remains of the church along with a masonry support for a possible round tower to the south side of the entrance all indicated that it dated to the early part of the twelfth century. Medieval pottery sherds from the late-thirteenth to early-fourteenth centuries were found in all the cuttings as well as fragments of a line-impressed tile. In 1993 two of the thirteenth-century towers of the city wall, Geneval's Tower and Isolde's Tower, have also been uncovered by archaeological excavations and will be preserved for posterity.

Thousands of artefacts of Anglo-Norman date have also been recovered on all the excavation sites in Dublin. By far the largest category has been sherds of pottery, both local and imported, which have been discussed in chapter 4, as have all the other major classes of artefacts recovered from the twelfth- to fourteenth-century levels in the Dublin excavations.[11]

There were also a few objects recovered from the Anglo-Norman levels of the Dublin excavations that had definite historical associations. These included several *ampullae* (pilgrims' flasks) of pewter, three of them depicting St Thomas à Becket who was probably the most famous martyr in the living memory of the citizens of medieval Dublin, as well as bronze pilgrim badges from places such as Rome. These were probably worn by pilgrims to show that they had visited the shrine at Canterbury, possibly the medieval equivalent to the wearing of sweatshirts overprinted with holiday resorts in our more materialistic society. A lead seal or *bulla* of Pope Innocent III (1198–1216) and a lead seal matrix of an Adam Burestone were both found at High Street (pl. 14).[12]

Everyday life in medieval Dublin is also reflected by the vast quantity of animal, bird and fish bones, the scientific examination of which has

Plate 14 A modern wax impression from a lead seal matrix (diameter 67mm)
of Adam Burestone, High Street, Dublin

provided clues to the probable diet of the inhabitants. The survival of
shellfish has shown that cockles and mussels were most common, with
oysters becoming more popular throughout the medieval period. Our
knowledge of the medieval citizens' diet has also been strengthened by
analyses of seeds and other botanical material from sealed archaeological
horizons in pits and other locations. These revealed that they ate
strawberries, apples, cherries, plums, sloes, blackberries, rowan berries,
and hazel nuts. In the thirteenth-century levels fig seeds were located,
which is not very surprising as figs are mentioned in many medieval
documents. It would also appear that the seeds of goosefoot and other
weeds such as black bindweed, knotgrass and pale persicaria were also
used as food in medieval Dublin.[13] Samples of insect remains were also
taken from these thirteenth-century levels to try to reconstruct the urban
environment of the time.[14]

The scientific analyses of these samples, along with radiocarbon and
dendrochronological dating which can give the archaeologist a more
precise date for structures and horizons, all combine to enable the scholar to
reconstruct the daily life of that large section of the city's population which
did not leave a trace on the documentary record. And close co-operation
between historian and archaeologist in the future should reveal even more
information of the everyday workings of this, the most important of
medieval Irish towns. For instance, the contemporary sources are full of the
problems of fire in its crowded environment, such as the Great Fire of June

1304 which is thought to have devastated the area around Bridge Street and the nearby quays.[15] However, the areas so far archaeologically examined have not produced evidence for such large-scale fires which must often have wrecked the largely wooden structures of the city.

And, as mentioned earlier, future excavations outside the core of the historic city would help chart the growth of the suburbs outside the walls as the population grew throughout the early middle eages. If we are to believe Friar John Clyn the mortality rate in Dublin caused by the Black Death (1348–50) was as high as 14,000,[16] which if we take the usually accepted estimate of mortality from the Black Death, c.33 per cent,[17] would give us an overall population of the city of around 42,000 inhabitants in the mid-fourteenth century. Although this figure is probably much too high the archaeologist would still need to cast his net much wider in order to chart the limits of the city in the later middle ages, although we know that in places like Grangegorman, Co. Dublin, now firmly within the north-western suburbs of the urban area, there was a great harvest of grain in 1337.[18] It would, therefore, appear that the city's expansion was mainly in the south-east with some development to the immediate north of the River Liffey above Christ Church. Some excavations have taken place in the western suburbs of the city which have revealed traces of the first Anglo-Norman defensive ditch, along with waste from a thirteenth-century bronze workshop.

Other urban excavations

Perhaps the urban area to have received most archaeological attention in comparison to its size in a sustained programme of work has been the northern port of Carrickfergus, Co. Antrim, which probably developed around the powerful castle erected there by John de Courcy in the late twelfth century to control access to Belfast Lough. Indeed the excavations which have taken place there over a period of eight years have produced no evidence of any occupation before the twelfth century. One of the most significant findings has been the realization that in the modern Market Place and High Street areas property boundaries have shown a very high degree of continuity from the middle ages to the present time. Unluckily, there has been a lack of dateable artefacts from sealed archaeological horizons in these areas so that the historical development of these plots has not been securely dated.[19] The excavations also failed to produce substantial remains of medieval structures so that very little can be said about the general socio-economic conditions of the medieval burgesses of this important northern port. This is particularly frustrating to the archaeologist when so much has come to light in the city of Dublin and, to a lesser extent, in towns such as Cork, Waterford and Drogheda. However, what the excavations have shown from the wide variety of imported pottery located there is that the port traded mainly with north-west England and Scotland as well as internally in Ireland. The quality and range of the medieval numismatic evidence also reinforces the ideas of some scholars about the importance of the town as a trading centre, while medieval brooches and a thirteenth-century gold finger-ring with an amethyst reveal the high standard of living enjoyed by some, at least, of its inhabitants. The excavation of the large site at Joymount on the north-east side of the town revealed a 17-m length of the town's thirteenth-century defences which comprised an earthen bank revetted by a wooden palisade inside a ditch c.4 cm wide. On the same site fragmentary parts of the eastern end of a medieval friary were located along with sixty-eight burials from its cemetery as well as medieval floor-tiles and painted window-glass, which were probably also from the friary.[20]

Coming south again, Cork has probably enjoyed the most attention from urban archaeologists in recent years of any city apart from Dublin. The medieval city developed on two islands, between the north and south channels of the River Lee and the main streets which ran in a north–south direction linked these two islands with the help of timber bridges. The city was enclosed by a stone wall in the thirteenth century and several excavations have taken place along its length.

The first excavations in medieval Cork were co-ordinated by Dermot Twohig, then of UCC, in the mid-1970s, with his two major sites being Skiddy's Castle on north island and the Holy Trinity–Christchurch area on the south island. Medieval pottery finds from the first site revealed that it probably had not been occupied until before the mid-thirteenth century and in 1445 a tower-house was built on the site by one John Skiddy, after which the area was named. Interestingly enough Skiddy's Castle was built upon a timber raft which was tied into the underlying peat by a number of pointed stakes. As was also the case at both Dublin and Carrickfergus it was found that there was a continuity in the location of lane-ways and property boundaries on this site from the early thirteenth century until the present day.[21] The second site not surprisingly produced stone foundations of the Holy Trinity–Christchurch College which was built in 1482 with vertically driven stakes, similar to those at Skiddy's Castle, beneath them. Along the street frontage timber-framed and post-and-wattle houses were constructed in the early middle ages until they were replaced by stone examples in the early fourteenth century. A short length of the town wall and a semi-circular flanking tower, possibly 'Hopewell Castle', were also excavated. The medieval street frontage along South Main Street where the College of Holy Trinity–Christchurch was located produced finds which ranged in date from around 1200 to 1400. As at most medieval urban sites, the largest category of finds was of pottery sherds, 80 per cent of the medieval types being imported wares from the Saintonge region of France and from the Ham Green kilns near Bristol. Other finds included worked leather fragments, worked wood, metal objects, crucible fragments, slag and furnace bottoms, bone combs, antler gaming pieces, stone net-sinkers, whetstones and quernstones.[22]

Another portion of the town wall was excavated in 1980 on Grand Parade[23] and was found to be up to 2 m in height with a battered outer face, from 2.35 to 4 m thick, made up of limestone blocks with a small proportion of red sandstone. Unlike Skiddy's Castle the wall had no oak raft as a foundation but was sited on top of a layer of gravel with the great thickness of its base providing it with some constructional stability. The majority of finds were of pottery sherds, the earliest being thirteenth-century in date, such as fourteen sherds of Saintonge strap handles as well as several examples of medieval native Irish ware. As the water table here was located only 1 m below ground level, pieces of leather survived which could be reconstructed into at least two shoes of twelfth- to early-thirteenth-century date. Late medieval sherds of pottery predominated, along with glass fragments of the seventeenth to eighteenth centuries, wood and flint, and clay pipe pieces. These later artefacts all illustrate the continuity of settlement and trading functions in Cork after the thirteenth century.

Despite these excavations and the survival of portions of the wall, little is known of its length or of the gates and towers that date from the medieval period. Although details exist from the thirteenth century of several grants to pay for the fortification of the city these do not provide enough detailed information to answer these questions from the historical sources alone.

The same problem is found, to a limited extent, in Waterford where an excellent map has been produced by the Corporation showing the city's walls (fig. 7). Although six complete towers still survive along the wall their construction dates are not certain. Indeed a recent excavation at Lady Lane uncovered a possible medieval postern gate as well as producing even more problems in accurately tracing the line of the medieval wall in the area.

The city was obviously of great importance to the Anglo-Norman kings as is attested by the fine series of Royal charters granted to its burgesses. The earliest surviving charter was that of King John in 1215, in which he granted liberties and free customs to the burgesses similar to those enjoyed in Dublin. The grant of these charters is also a sure reflection of the military and strategic importance of the city to the Anglo-Norman lordship of Ireland.

During the reign of John the city walls which, if we are to believe the writings of Giraldus,[24] were pre-Norman in origin, were greatly extended westwards and southwards from their original 8-ha triangular-shaped area. The construction and maintenance of the medieval extension to the walls of some 13 ha in area were paid for by regular murage grants to the city throughout the thirteenth century, the first surviving one dating to 1224. That Waterford was expanding dramatically throughout the thirteenth century was also reflected in the surviving customs returns on wool, wool-fells and hides from 1275 to 1333. In these Waterford was in second place after New Ross in Co. Wexford, paying over 24 per cent of the total customs paid in Ireland over these years.[25] Between them the almost contiguous ports of Waterford and New Ross probably carried over half of Ireland's assessable external trade at the time.

It is therefore surprising that such an important Norse and medieval settlement in Ireland should not have been investigated archaeologically before the 1980s. One of the major reasons for this may have been due to the lack of large-scale redevelopment of its centre until recently. In fact the first excavation by Michael Moore of the OPW[26] took place at the end of 1982 and continued into the following year at the site for a new school between Spring Garden Alley and Lady Lane. It was known that the possibly pre-Norman city wall ran through this site and that St Martin's Tower, which marked the southern apex of the original city walls, was probably located there as well (fig. 7). Indeed the OS 6-inch map for this part of the city records that it is the site of 'St Martin's Castle', and the parish boundary circles around two small drum-shaped towers which were incorporated into the later St Martin's Orphanage which had been on the site until it was cleared in the last few years.

The excavated portion of the city wall, up to 2 m thick with a slight external batter, ran behind the two gate towers and is possibly pre-Norman in date because it is similar, in some respects, to the Hiberno-Norse wall at Wood Quay in Dublin.[27] However, the evidence from pottery sherds would indicate that 'the wall was built at a time when green-glazed pottery was in plentiful supply and this suggests a date closer to 1200 than to 1170'.[28] Because of complex rebuilding it was very difficult to date securely the foundations of the only medieval gateway so far discovered in Waterford which was erected on this site at the apex of the city's defences (pl. 15). However the drum shape of the two towers is comparable to other thirteenth-century gate towers found in towns such as Drogheda in Co. Louth (see pl. 16, p. 136). Both towers were supported on oak rafts held in place by vertical posts on top of the waterlogged subsoil of the area, similar to those found at Skiddy's Castle in Cork. (It is hoped that a precise date for these rafts will be provided from dendrochronological analysis by Baillie at QUB.) A road was laid through the gateway and a stone-walled house was also erected in the north-east corner of the site. This house, with dimensions of 6 by c.5 m with a central hearth, has been dated from Ham Green and Saintonge pottery sherds to the middle of the thirteenth century.[29]

The excavation also revealed that the thirteenth-century extension of the wall was not joined on to the possible Hiberno-Norse circuit here at St Martin's Castle, as is shown in nearly every map of the city, but was constructed as a separate entity. There was some difficulty in locating the return of this pre-Norman city wall from St Martin's Castle northwards to the long-destroyed Turgesius's Tower on the quay. It is probable that much of its length here was destroyed by the building of the later orphanage.[30] Two short lengths of it were eventually located, and underneath the second one there appeared in the waterlogged deposits of an earlier defensive

Plate 15 The base of St Martin's Gate, Waterford

ditch a possible eleventh- or twelfth-century post-and-wattle sub-rectangular building.[31]

The discovery of this structure should make scholars look afresh at Giraldus's famous description of the capture of Waterford by the Anglo-Normans in 1170. It has often been wondered why the Anglo-Normans were able to find a house jutting out over the city wall, held up by a beam, which they cut, causing the house to collapse and thus breaching the wall.[32] Obviously the settlement was expanding so much in this period that the wall was built on top of dwelling houses – much as was done by the Normans in England after 1066 at cities such as York where we learn from the *Domesday Book* of the large number of houses destroyed to make way for their motte castle. It is possible then that one of these evicted Waterford householders had built a new house using the wall for a support.

The artefacts which were found were similar to those from Dublin except that in Waterford pottery sherds make up a higher percentage of the total. There are examples of eleventh-century Andennes ware, sherds of late-thirteenth- to early-fourteenth-century Ham Green pottery from near Bristol, and of jugs from south-western France which probably contained wine imports. The coarse ware ranged from pre-Norman types similar to those found at Wood Quay, Dublin, to others from a twelfth- to thirteenth-century context, which were similar to sherds found during the excavation of other medieval east coast ports.[33] A bone handle of a medieval knife and an early medieval bone comb with metal teeth were among the other small finds.

Although much has been accomplished in elucidating Waterford's Viking and medieval past more archaeological research needs to be completed on such questions as the full extent of the city and its walls in the decades following the reign of King John in the thirteenth century. Another crucially important area, archaeologically speaking, is the quayside on the south bank of the River Suir, where it has been estimated that at least sixty vessels could anchor.[34] From the documents we already know about the importance of wool exports to the city and in 1300 there is also evidence of Waterford's importance as an entrepôt as the majority of 3,000 hogsheads of wine was re-exported through the city from Anjou to the armies of Edward I in Scotland.[35] Excavations centred on Arundel Square between 1986 and 1992 have uncovered many structures and over 200,000 artefacts dating from the tenth to the seventeenth century. Altogether one-fifth of the medieval town has now been completely excavated, including the medieval parish church of St Peter and its associated graveyard. Over 80 wooden houses, similar to those found in the Dublin excavations and dating from the middle of the eleventh century, were also uncovered. Six cellared structures of the same period were also found, as were large timber structures of the twelfth and early thirteenth centuries.[36]

The south-east coast port of Wexford has also had some small archaeological excavations but these were not able to throw any more light on the origins, development or early decline in its economic life in the middle ages. Again, like most of the ports along the eastern seaboard, its beginnings probably owe much to the Norse who founded a trading settlement there in the ninth to tenth centuries. It was the first town to fall to the Anglo-Normans and prospered up until the end of the thirteenth century. Indeed, it had by then expanded so much that a new circuit of walls with five gates had to be erected to enclose its new bounds. But then we learn of 128½ waste tenements in the town in 1298,[37] which fits in well with the picture of decline portrayed by an inquisition of 1326 which described the poor repair of its castle and associated buildings, as well as recording that the number of waste burgages had risen to 221½.[38] The customs returns were also in decline probably because of the close proximity and competition of the prosperous ports of New Ross and Waterford, and because its harbour was slowly silting up.

The first of the four small excavations in Wexford was carried out by A. B. O'Ríordáin in 1970 for the NMI, prior to the expansion of White's Hotel, on a very small area in Main Street where he found on the old ground surface a coin of John (c.1210) and a few sherds of late medieval pottery.[39] Then Fanning for the OPW excavated part of St Selskar's Augustinian abbey in 1973 which exposed some of its medieval foundations in the course of a conservation programme. A few sherds of sgraffito and Buckley ware and some fragments of carved stone were the only finds located in this thirteenth-century structure.[40] Then Wallace examined another site on Oyster Lane in 1974 which was so small that he was only able to excavate part of the medieval properties revealed there.[41] All the structural features were in alignment with each other and only diverged some 40° from the present line of the street. He was unable to find any evidence for the Norse period because sealed under the first two occupation layers, which were broadly dated to the thirteenth and fourteenth centuries, was a natural sand layer. In these first two layers he located floorboards, joists, property boundaries and stone-lined drains in association with imported and local medieval pottery sherds. The latest occupation layer was dated to the seventeenth century.

Two years later, in 1976, as a result of damage to the town wall in Abbey Street, Mary Cahill and Michael Ryan of the NMI undertook a short investigation of the place where the wall had been breached.[42] This was not part of the original circuit of the wall, which could well have been started in pre-Norman times if Giraldus Cambrensis is to be believed.[43] It was probably part of an extension of the town's defences which, unhappily, cannot be exactly dated by reference to the surviving documentation. The consensus of opinion among local historians is that this extension cannot be earlier than the fourteenth century and may even have been constructed in the following century, after the Parliament of 1463 had granted 'a common share' towards the maintenance of the town walls. The archaeologists were also unable to give a date for the construction of the wall in Abbey Street because of the disturbance of archaeological levels, and no trace was located of an outer fosse, for which there is seventeenth-century evidence. Finds from the excavation were limited to a few sherds of late-medieval and post-medieval pottery, two fragments of roofing slate and some skeletal material.

It is a pity that all the excavations in Wexford up until the present have been of too small a scale to give any real indication of the town's economic life in the early middle ages or, indeed, to chart its early decline in the late thirteenth century. It is also interesting to note that no archaeological evidence of Norse settlement has been uncovered. Wexford would be an ideal candidate for further larger-scale archaeological investigations to try and elucidate its layout and the economic and social conditions of its inhabitants, as well as the scale and pattern of its internal and external trade, as it was one of the smaller east coast ports of medieval Ireland. It would be extremely valuable to learn whether its pottery imports conformed to the broad patterns established by the Dublin and Waterford excavations, or whether Wexford's continental trading partners were different.

The final medieval port on the east coast to have been fairly extensively excavated is Drogheda in Co. Louth, the most important port in the northern part of Ireland, which paid the fourth largest amount of customs on the wool staple between 1276 and 1333.[44] Many of the archaeological finds have been the result of road improvement in the town and the construction of two new bridges across the River Boyne. However, there was no programme of excavation prior to the first phase of the construction of the new ring road, and the likelihood is that several archaeologically significant horizons were cut through as members of the Co. Louth Archaeological and Historical Society found considerable quantities of medieval pottery, mainly Saintonge ware, as well as a medieval gaming piece along the road's route.[45] Then in 1976 O'Floinn of the NMI found over 500 sherds of pottery, mainly of thirteenth- to fourteenth-century date, in the spoil heap of a trench which straddled the south-west part of the town wall. About 80 per cent of it was locally made, the rest being mainly imported French wares with a few sherds of Ham Green ware and one or two sherds from Chester.[46] The pipe trench itself revealed the existence of a 1.5 m-depth of archaeological stratigraphy.

In 1981, prior to the construction of a new bridge across the River Boyne replacing the old St Mary's bridge, Sweetman for the OPW undertook a limited excavation on the north side of the river.[47] The reason this side was chosen for investigation was because the proposed northern abutment of the new bridge was close to the possible site of the medieval chapel of St Saviour, as well as being just west of Bothe Street, the oldest known street on that side of the medieval town. In the small area under excavation, approximately 15 by 11.5 m, there were very few structures of medieval date, namely two small pits and an alignment of wooden posts which suggested that they were either part of a wharf or a revetment. Dendro-chronological analysis of these timbers all gave dates of around 1200 which would indicate that the wharf was probably constructed at the start of the thirteenth century. There was also a narrow wall, around 50 cm wide, at the western end of the cutting, part of which had been constructed at the end of the thirteenth century.

The range and quality of the 5,000 small finds which were recovered from the site, over half of which were sherds of medieval pottery, make them one of the first major published collections of artefacts from an Irish medieval urban context. Just under a half of these pottery sherds were of indigenous manufacture, with another fifth coming from France, mainly from the Saintonge area, and the remaining 329 sherds from Chester, the Ham Green kilns, and Gloucester. It is interesting to compare these figures with those provided by O'Floinn. The greater proportion of imported French wares in the 1981 excavation is possibly explained by the location of the site, both within the compass of the city walls and also perhaps on the very quayside from which they were landed.

Other medieval finds included line-impressed and inlaid decorated pavement-tiles of thirteenth- to fifteenth-century date, a large quantity of leather, ten pieces of bronze including part of a horse harness, nails, lead and glass objects. A study of a small sample of the animal bones which survived on the site also revealed a high incidence of sheep, possibly from the extensive flocks of the large estates of land farmed by the important Cistercian abbey of Mellifont nearby. Next in importance in the diet of the medieval inhabitants of Drogheda was cattle, followed by pig, with a few horse bones and even fewer bones of wild animals. As all these bones were derived from a deliberate infilling of the disused quayside in the latter half of the thirteenth century they can be regarded as a random sample as they seem to have come from several different sources, presumably from within the town itself.

Another interesting feature of this small site is the lack of any occupation or, indeed, any activity on this part of the quayside throughout the fifteenth and sixteenth centuries. Whether this was the result of the contraction of the occupied area caused by the Black Death and its aftermath, or other localized reasons, will really only be answered by further excavation in the port. In the seventeenth century a stone quayside, a cobbled laneway and steps were constructed there and the large quantity of post-medieval pottery, clay pipes, floor-tiles, and metal finds all point to a dramatic revival of the port's trade, especially with England and primarily through the port of Bristol.

More recently, in 1982, substantial remains of the medieval Hospital of St James were excavated by Kieran Campbell on behalf of the Corporation of Drogheda.[48] During this investigation up to 12 m of the town wall was revealed together with a lime kiln which was associated with its construction. Outside of the wall the inner edge of a rock-cut ditch which contained waterlogged medieval deposits was also uncovered.

Apart from the archaeological evidence there also exists a considerable collection, in an Irish context, of historical documents relating to Drogheda. Much of this has been examined by John Bradley, currently under contract to the OPW to produce an urban archaeological survey for Ireland. In a valuable article[49] he stated that although the Vikings are recorded as having been on the River Boyne there is no evidence to suggest that they established a permanent settlement anywhere near the site of Drogheda. Both Bradley and Graham[50] agree that the 1194 charter given by Walter de Lacy to all his burgesses living on the south side of the river at Drogheda in Meath would suggest that he founded a borough here both because it was the lowest narrow bridging point of the then navigable river which would help its economic development, and also because of its strategic location dominating one of the most important river systems in Ireland. Until 1412 there were separate towns on either side of the river, probably as a result of the Boyne being chosen as the boundary between the two dioceses of Armagh and Meath. Drogheda in Louth, on the north bank of the river, was according to Bradley also probably in existence before the end of the twelfth century with St Peter's Church being founded before 1186 on the north side and with the principal street axis established before 1215. Indeed the urban settlement on the north bank is much the larger of the two, probably because on this side there is a larger expanse of level ground suitable for house construction.

Bradley has also extensively investigated the economic development and prosperity of Drogheda from the written sources and it is interesting to see how it ties in with the archaeological evidence, mainly the sherds of jugs which were imported from southern France full of wine from the English dependencies there, in the thirteenth and early fourteenth centuries. The records also reveal that Drogheda functioned as an entrepôt, with the wine being shipped on to the English army in Scotland, or up into Ulster. Other imports were iron and salt although it is not now possible to gauge how important they were in the total range of imports that came into the port. Not surprisingly, the majority of Drogheda's exports were agricultural products derived from the rich Meath and South Louth hinterland which were sent to the Royal armies in Scotland, Wales and Gascony, as well as to the ports of Chester, Southampton, Dieppe and those of Flanders (fig. 30). These farm goods were also the basic commodity traded in Drogheda's market, and there is also evidence of a thriving trade in corn and wine with other ports on the east coast, such as Waterford, Cork, Kilkenny, Wexford, Kinsale and Youghal.

The continuity of property boundaries in many cities in both England and Ireland has been shown archaeologically. Bradley was able to suggest that for Drogheda the plot pattern of individual holdings within the historic core, found on the first edition of the OS town plans (c.1840), is most likely a survival of the medieval pattern.[51] He was also able to illustrate this conservatism by locating fifteen medieval properties around Bothe Street in Drogheda in Louth from research into some surviving late medieval deeds and charters of the area.

Drogheda is also lucky in that despite the effects of the bloody siege of 1649 several medieval structures still survive. These range from Millmount motte on the south side of the river, probably erected by Hugh de Lacy before 1186, and some elements of the medieval churches of the town, to part of the town wall near Millmount, the arch of the Butter Gate and the barbican of St Laurence's Gate, the finest one still extant in the entire country (pl. 16). It is a great pity that the surviving portions of the town wall are not extensive enough to give scholars an idea of the probable chronology of the various parts of the wall, especially as there are at least thirteen murage grants surviving for the town between 1234 and 1424.[52] Further archaeological excavations along the probable line of the wall may produce some foundation remains which might help to date its construction and, as Bradley suggested, an investigation of the port area to the east of the bridge would be valuable in determining its layout. An analysis of the medieval artefacts recovered during the excavations should also illustrate the extent of the suggested shift in Drogheda's trading pattern to Iceland and Portugal in the later middle ages. There are other indications of the continuing prosperity of the town in the fifteenth century, such as the construction of several church towers, and it would be helpful if the exact nature of this prosperity could be determined by excavation.

The only port to have been archaeologically investigated on the west coast is Limerick on the mouth of the River Shannon. Up until 1981 all the excavations were small-scale, including Sweetman's investigation of the

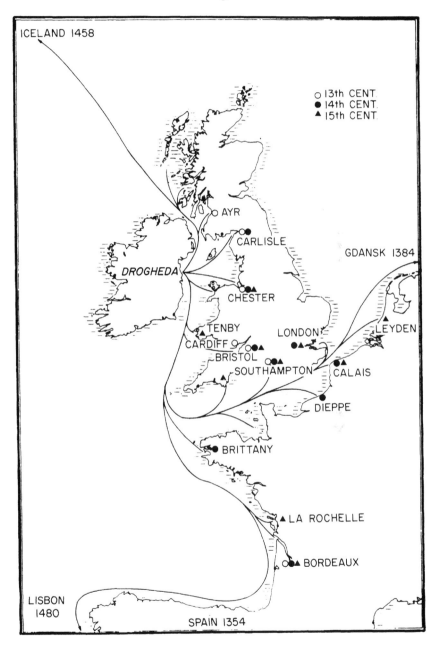

Figure 30 Map of the overseas trade of Drogheda, thirteenth to fifteenth centuries

Plate 16 St Laurence's Gate, Drogheda

castle which has been examined in chapter 3. In 1975 Elizabeth Shee of UCC excavated part of the church and the adjoining cemetery of the Dominican priory in advance of road construction.[53] Finds from the site included sherds of thirteenth- to fourteenth-century green-glazed south-western French ware, some late medieval wares from Germany and France, North Devon sgraffito ware and gravel-tempered ware, a silver Edward I penny, medieval floor-tiles, and a shale bracelet.

In 1981 Ann Lynch of the OPW directed the excavation of a large site at Charlotte's Quay prior to the erection of Government offices.[54] Most of the archaeological strata of the site had been destroyed or disturbed by a gasworks and by housing developments. Nothing survived of St Michael's Church, founded c.1200, or of any other medieval buildings known to be in the area. However, the foundations of the West Watergate, which consisted of two roughly D-shaped towers flanking a cobbled passage 2.6 m wide, were excavated. A probable fifteenth-century wall was also located outside and parallel to the town wall, constructed to divert the waters of the Abbey River closer to the Watergate. Sections of the town wall, probably built between 1310 and 1495, did survive, the most substantial portion being 26 m long, with an average height of 2.7 m. The 'site of castle' shown on later maps of the city could not be located, nor was there any evidence of the structures of the late medieval waterfront there. Because of all the later disturbances on the site there were very few finds, and most of them could not be securely stratified.

The largest excavation, to date, in this historic city produced neither much structural evidence nor many artefacts because of the damage done by later buildings on the site, a common problem in urban areas. However, over the next few years the building of a ring road and new bridge is to be undertaken, and part of its proposed route will take it through the medieval core of the city. For much of its course the new road surfaces will not be significantly lower than the present ground level and, hopefully, damage to archaeological horizons should be kept to a minimum. Nevertheless, the Corporation is employing an archaeological team to do test excavations in areas where there are archaeological structures and where the ground level will be extensively cut into.[55] Thus the immediate future should prove to be both informative and exciting for our understanding of the historical development of this important western port.

Finally, in the north there have been excavations in Armagh and Downpatrick. Of these the most concentrated have been the investigations by C. J. Lynn of the DoE (NI) on several sites on Scotch Street during large-scale redevelopment of the area.[56] They centred on an attempt to excavate part of a threatened Early Christian and medieval ecclesiastical site, *Teampall na Fearta Martar*, according to legend the first church founded by St Patrick and also the supposed place of his burial and that of his sister, Lupita. Medieval occupation levels were also located in sites on Castle Street, Thomas Street and Abbey Street.[57] Lynn also excavated the

Franciscan Friary church in Armagh but found that all the medieval levels had been destroyed.[58] Excavations on several redevelopment sites at 46–56 Scotch Street in 1984 produced Early Christian occupation evidence and some traces of an Augustinian nunnery.[59] And at Downpatrick the excavations have been mainly concentrated around the prehistoric hillfort although medieval levels have been located in the city, along with the important thirteenth-century pottery kiln.[60]

In the broader European context urban archaeology is still in its infancy with only one city, Dublin, having any really protracted programme of excavations and even there the area which has been investigated is still estimated at being under 10 per cent of the area enclosed by the city walls. Secondly, all the excavations that have taken place in urban centres in Ireland to date have not conclusively helped to elucidate the origins of these places, and there has yet to be an excavation of any of the suburbs that grew up in these towns in the middle ages. It is also salutary to note that substantial monographs on the Dublin, Cork and Carrickfergus excavations have yet to appear.

However, perhaps the most unsatisfactory aspect of urban excavations in Ireland has been the fact that, for the most part, they have been 'reactive' in that they have taken place in an emergency situation with developers pressing to get onto a particular site. Hopefully, one of the results of the current Urban Survey by Bradley will be that areas within towns which are at risk from redevelopers will be identified well in advance of any building work so that a proper excavation programme can be mounted. What is needed presently in Ireland is the formulation of both a national and a regional plan for future urban archaeology so that known important sites can be adequately protected and all historic areas within cities can, at least, be sampled archaeologically. There have also been some recent hopeful developments at sites such as St Michael le Pole in Dubin where the developer has met the basic cost of an exploratory excavation, as happens in several enlightened countries on the continent of Europe. This should happen more in the future when the findings of the Urban Survey are communicated to local authorities and their planning offices. This survey should also help to educate both local authorities and their communities about the importance of their urban archaeological heritage and assist greatly in its future presentation and preservation.

6 The archaeology of the medieval church

There are many problems associated with any investigation and analysis of the archaeology of the medieval church in Ireland. One major difficulty is the lack of archaeological excavation of any but a very small number of medieval ecclesiastical sites. One of the reasons for this lies in the continuing use of the graveyards around the church buildings which would make exploration a very difficult task. And, unlike in England, the churches or abbeys themselves are usually in ruins so that burials have also taken place inside them in post-medieval times. There have, therefore, been very few excavations of the many medieval parish church remains that are to be found all over Ireland. The situation regarding medieval religious houses is a little better, although many of the excavations here have concentrated upon the church and claustral areas so that our knowledge of the out-buildings and the lay brothers' range is almost non-existent. Thus our understanding of the socio-economic impact of these religious foundations upon medieval life generally has not yet been substantially advanced by archaeology. Another problem has been that these excavations have often treated the site in isolation from the surrounding patterns of settlement.

Historically, the development of the medieval church in Ireland was different from the situation in England. Because of the predominance of monasteries in the Early Christian church, which I discussed in chapter 2, it was not until the early twelfth century that Ireland was divided up into proper territorial dioceses. The 1140s also saw the establishment of houses of the major continental orders, and most notably of the Cistercians whose arrival was greatly helped by the friendship that existed between St Malachy of Armagh and St Bernard of Clairvaux, arguably the greatest medieval Cistercian. But all the indications are that the organization of the church into parishes in most parts of Ireland had not really developed before 1200 or even later.[1] The Anglo-Norman invasion also gave a new impetus to the foundation of these new monastic houses as well as the setting up of houses of the powerful military orders, the Knights

Hospitallers and the Templars. Then in the thirteenth century the mendicant orders of friars also established their houses in Ireland. In the fifteenth century there was a second spate of building friaries, especially Franciscan, in the Gaelic areas of the south and west. The dissolution of the monasteries in 1536–40 by Henry VIII spelled the end of the medieval church although many of the religious houses, especially those in the isolated parts of the country under Gaelic control, continued in clandestine use until Cromwell's campaign in the middle of the seventeenth century.

The archaeological study of the parish church in medieval Ireland is still in its infancy although much more progress is currently being made as a result of the many archaeological surveys which have commenced over the last decade or so. For instance, at least twenty-three standing remains of medieval churches have been located in Co. Louth by the Archaeological Survey of Ireland, with between thirty and forty in Co. Meath and another twelve in Co. Monaghan.[2] The majority of surviving examples date to the fifteenth century with a few being of an earlier period. There are also several instances of pre-Norman churches being extended in the middle ages to serve as parish churches such as happened at St Doulagh's, Co. Dublin, Dysert O'Dea, Co. Clare, and Inismacsaint, Co. Fermanagh. It is also clear that parish communities often used the churches of the numerous religious houses. This practice is confirmed in the documents of the dissolution of the monasteries in 1541 where the naves of many Cistercian abbeys were described as having been the parish church from time immemorial.

The vast majority of medieval parish churches with standing remains are very simple in plan with almost no decoration. Their main architectural features such as mouldings, window tracery or even the shape of the doors and windows themselves, from which a rough chronology can be established, will often not be found *in situ* because of later disturbances or the destruction of many of these sites. Changes in the ground plans as they expanded or contracted over the centuries can provide a relative chronology, as can be seen at Kilcash, Co. Tipperary, and St Nicholas in Dundalk, Co. Louth. The type of stone can also provide a general indicator of chronology, with sandstone mouldings and a west doorway suggesting a twelfth- or thirteenth-century date, and hammered limestone mouldings and opposing north–south doors in the nave being a feature of later medieval churches.

One such example of these simple medieval parish church remains which still dot the Irish countryside is that of St Fintan at Sutton, Co. Dublin (pl. 17). In plan it is little more than a tiny box with no structural division between nave and chancel, and is 6.7 m long and 3.8 m wide. With its western doorway and fragments of sandstone window tracery it is probably of twelfth-century date. There was probably an earlier church here from the seventh century but no trace of it remains today. Thus an archaeological excavation here might be able to locate this earlier church, if it existed, as well as finding the original floor level and some remains of the roof of the

Plate 17 St Fintan's Church, Sutton, Co. Dublin

twelfth-century church. If enough dateable artefacts and sealed horizons were found in association with the church a more secure chronology for its use might be established, especially as there are no known references to it in the surviving sixteenth-century documents.

However, in the major Anglo-Norman towns new churches were built and some were as large as any cathedral erected in Ireland during the middle ages. One of the largest was the church of St Mary in New Ross, Co. Wexford, founded probably by William Marshal, Earl of Pembroke (d. 1219), and his wife Isabel in around 1210. It was cruciform in plan and was 47.5 m long and 41 m wide across its transepts. The nave which was originally aisled is now occupied by a nineteenth-century Church of Ireland church. In the east gable there are three very fine lancet windows, and other lancet windows are also to be found in the church.[3] Today the church and its graveyard are rich in medieval tombs and other stone carvings of the period. It is not really surprising that the parish church of the port which topped the thirteenth-century customs returns for wool, wool-fell and hides, and which was probably founded by the chief representative of one of the most powerful families in England, should have been constructed on such a grand scale.

Other important parish churches include St Multose in Kinsale and St Mary's, Youghal, Co. Cork, St Nicholas, Carrickfergus, Co. Antrim, and Gowran, Thomastown and Callan all in Co. Kilkenny. An indication of their size and stability is the fact that all of them are still in use. The church of St Multose in Kinsale was probably founded in the early thirteenth century and consists of an aisled nave and chancel as well as a north transept. An almost unique feature here is a tower in the north-west corner which is contemporary with the church. The other important medieval parish church in Co. Cork, St Mary's in Youghal, has a cruciform plan with an aisled nave and a short aisle in the north transept. It was dated by Leask to the middle of the thirteenth century.[4] Finally, the church of St Nicholas in Carrickfergus, cruciform in plan with nave aisles and a hypothetical length of 56.7 m was probably started around the year 1200 and McNeill has cogently argued for Cistercian influence in both its plan and elevation.[5]

There has been a small number of excavations of medieval parish churches recently. In Ulster, Waterman excavated Banagher Church, 3.2 km from Dungiven, Co. Derry, which was traditionally founded by St Muiredach O'Heney in the early thirteenth century and continued in use until the seventeenth century. The nave was dated from the early to mid-twelfth century and the chancel was added in the early thirteenth century. The east end appears to have been extensively remodelled in the fifteenth century to provide a small sacristy behind the altar. To the south-west of the chancel is a small mortuary house, traditionally the burial place of St Muiredach; while the foundations outside the cemetery gate are probably the remains of priests' tower houses,[6] similar to the one beside St Mary's Abbey at Howth, Co. Dublin (pl. 18). In Dublin, excavations by M. McMahon of the Dublin Archaeological Society in 1982 on the church and graveyard at Artaine South on the north-side of the modern city uncovered the ground plan of a single-cell structure measuring 11 m by 5.36 m internally, with north and south doorways. The door jambs of the north door indicated a thirteenth- to fourteenth-century date for the foundation of the church, which must have remained in use until the early sixteenth century because of the discovery of a large quantity of glazed floor-tiles of that date in disturbed levels in and around the church.[7] There was also the excavation in 1981 which revealed the early-twelfth-century church of St Michael le Pole and possibly the base of a round tower south-west of Dublin Castle. Finds there suggested that the church was in use throughout the middle ages and on into the post-medieval period.[8]

If we now turn to a very brief examination of the cathedrals of medieval

Ireland (as no modern excavations have taken place at any of them) it soon becomes apparent that none of them are any larger than the bigger parish churches of medieval England. This is probably a result of the relative poverty of Anglo-Norman Ireland and the large numbers of cathedrals built in a relatively smaller country. In Armagh and Downpatrick the cathedrals were rebuilt in the Anglo-Norman period but both have been substantially remodelled in recent times.[9] Perhaps the finest of all the early medieval

Plate 18 Priests' house, Howth, Co. Dublin

cathedrals is Christ Church in Dublin which, with its near neighbour St Patrick's, mainly dates to the first half of the thirteenth century. The choir was constructed a little earlier and is in Late Romanesque style while the nave is Early Gothic. The cathedral was probably completed around 1240 but underwent a considerable amount of restoration in the nineteenth century. R. A. Stalley has proved that the decorated capitals of the cathedrals reveal that masons from western England were employed in its construction.[10] St Patrick's, the largest medieval cathedral in Ireland, was constructed from about 1220 until 1254, apart from the lady chapel which was not finished until 1270. Although its design is close to the nave of Christ Church there are also fundamental differences. According to Stalley, 'The interior is more spacious and there is a greater feeling of harmony, for unlike Christ Church there were no prolonged halts in building operations to cause a fundamental break in style.'[11] However, like its neighbour, it has suffered from massive Victorian restoration.

Of the other medieval cathedrals in Ireland many have been greatly altered over the succeeding centuries. One of the best preserved, and arguably one of the most typical of thirteenth-century Anglo-Norman cathedrals in Ireland, is that of St Canice's in Kilkenny. It has a rectangular plan with a wooden roof and tall lancet windows and was probably completed some time around the middle of that century.[12] It is, however, the ruined cathedrals that are more promising to the archaeologist, and it would be valuable to compare, for example, the stone vaulted cathedral of Newtown Trim – founded in c.1206 on the banks of the River Boyne 1.6 km from Trim Castle – with either Ardfert on the coast of Co. Kerry or Cashel in Co. Tipperary, which although nominally within the lordship always had an Irishman as Archbishop in the thirteenth century.[13] It is a pity that the medieval cathedral at Waterford was demolished in 1773 because of the danger of falling masonry. Now its site is covered by an eighteenth-century Church of Ireland cathedral within which there is, however, a scale model of its predecessor. From this and other evidence it would appear that it had some of the sophistication of the Dublin cathedrals although it would have been smaller in scale and probably less ornate.

Where archaeology has made some impact on our understanding of the growth and development of ecclesiastical sites it is as a result of the excavation of the houses of the religious orders of the twelfth and thirteenth centuries. That these excavations have very often been limited both in their scope and in the area investigated has been the result of their being secondary to the needs of the architects of state archaeological organizations who wished to present the major features of these monasteries to the public. Thus there has yet to be a research-oriented excavation here on a medieval religious house comparable to that undertaken at Bordesley Abbey in Worcestershire in England.[14] It was the Cistercian order, introduced into Ireland at Mellifont, Co. Louth, in 1142, which was to have the greatest influence on both the religious and economic aspects of life in medieval Ireland. Stalley has identified thirty-three successful houses of the order which survived until the Reformation[15] and five have been excavated, usually on a small scale, over the last few years.

Cistercian monasteries were usually sited in remote places with a nearby source of running water for domestic water supply, drainage and fishing. The highest building, the church, was built to the north of the cloister which then had both shelter from the wind and the maximum amount of sunshine. Usually on the eastern side of the cloisters were the chapter house, the parlour, the monks' refectory and above it their dormitory which was usually linked to the church by night stairs, such as still survive at Dunbrody, Co. Wexford. On the western side of the cloisters were the quarters of the lay brothers, usually comprising a refectory and cellars with their dormitory and the garderobes (toilets) above. Often very little remains of this western range as they were not as solidly constructed as the monks' buildings. Finally, as the abbey was expected to be self-sufficient, there was also an outer court containing the guest-quarters, school, granary, brewery, bakery and gatehouse. Only at Dunbrody and Mellifont are there the remains of gatehouses, while at Inch in Co. Down there are traces of a bakery. Thus it is to the latter two areas of the abbeys that archaeologists could expect to make most contribution to any elucidation of their layout and in an assessment of their importance to the daily life of the monastic community and beyond.

However, as stated above, because of the overriding needs of the architectural sections of the various state bodies these areas are usually neglected. Thus the first modern excavation of a Cistercian abbey, that of Mellifont by de Paor in 1954–5, was restricted to the buildings immediately surrounding the cloisters as it was carried out in association with conservation work on the monument. Earlier investigation had uncovered most of the layout of the monastic complex but the finds, their archaeological context and the general stratigraphy of the site were not adequately recorded. De Paor's excavation, despite his enforced absences from it on other official business, did locate the crypt at the west end of the church, a passage running between the cloisters and the lay-brothers' quarters as well as evidence for a serious fire in the early fourteenth century which necessitated the rebuilding of much of the church. Finds from the excavation included a useful corpus of medieval pottery and floor-tiles as well as a hoard of medieval silver pennies from the crypt, and a silver chalice and paten from the chancel of the church.[16] Then in 1980 Stalley produced a comprehensive architectural study of the abbey (fig. 31) which stressed the close relationship between the first abbey church at Mellifont (1142–57) and its Burgundian forerunners such as Fontenay. He also closely examined the later phases of construction there in the Early English and Decorated periods of architecture. In this study he convincingly redated the chapter house a century or so earlier to the beginning of the thirteenth century by a close examination of its capitals. Finally, he examined all the

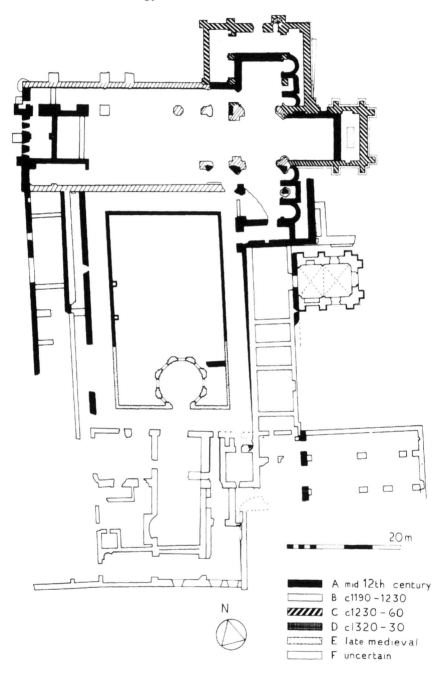

N

A   mid 12th century
B   c1190 –1230
C   c1230 – 60
D   c1320 – 30
E   late medieval
F   uncertain

20m

Figure 31 Plan of Mellifont Abbey, Co. Louth

carved and moulded stones preserved on the site together with a hitherto unknown collection of medieval floor-tiles. This enabled him to understand far more details about the remodelling of the church, both in the middle of the thirteenth century and in the years around 1320. Also the discovery of decorative features, hitherto unknown at Mellifont, revealed the magnitude of the architectural influence exercised by the abbey over its Irish daughter houses. The dressed stone was usually sandstone, probably quarried somewhere in Co. Meath, except in the mid-thirteenth century when it was a yellow oolitic limestone, probably imported from Caen in Normandy. Dundry stone from a quarry near to the important port of Bristol was also used to some extent at that time, although in the later middle ages local sandstone was again employed.[17]

Perhaps the most attractive building to survive was the lavabo, or wash-house, which Stalley dated to around 1210, and which has only one other known parallel in Ireland, at Dunbrody, where its plan was circular. As Stalley remarked the presence of such a building indicates the wealth of the particular abbey as smaller abbeys only had basins in the cloister walk. Portions of the lead piping of the water supply system were also found in the cloisters. At Grey Abbey in Co. Down one of the main drains still survives, and during the excavation of Tintern Abbey, Co. Wexford, Lynch located part of the complex water supply of the Cistercians, the main drain to the south east of the cloister. She found that the drain, fed by natural springs, was constructed from the middle to the end of the thirteenth century and continued in use until the late fourteenth century when it was backfilled with rubble. Its excavation was of great value to archaeology as pieces of worked wood as well as waterlogged seeds were found in its sediment, along with a large quantity of medieval pottery, lead tokens, roofing slates and glazed ridge tiles.[18]

The final feature to be added to Mellifont in the later middle ages was the tower erected above the crossing of the church, although all that remains of it are the enlarged piers and internal buttresses that were necessary to support its weight. Altogether, at least seven Irish Cistercian abbeys had towers erected over the crossing, usually in the fifteenth century. According to Stalley the best parallel for what the Mellifont tower would have looked like is to be found at Jerpoint, Co. Kilkenny, where it rises almost to a height of 26 m (pl. 19). No totally satisfactory explanation has yet been put forward as to the main purpose of these constructions in the later middle ages. According to Stalley, 'Bells may have been the official motive for erecting the towers, but it is likely that status, prestige and defence were equally important factors.'[19]

All further excavations of Cistercian houses, except possibly that undertaken by ÓhEochaidh for the OPW in 1967–70 of the mainly fifteenth-century abbey of Holy Cross, Co. Tipperary, for which there is no published report, have been of a smaller scale than at Mellifont. In 1977 Bradley and Manning were able to excavate portions of a mid- to late-

Plate 19 Jerpoint Abbey, Co. Kilkenny, with its fifteenth-century tower

thirteenth-century tiled pavement, some of which was *in situ*, in the north transept of the church of Duiske Abbey, Co. Kilkenny. But apart from these tiles little else was discovered of medieval church furnishings.[20] The abbey was founded from Stanley in Wiltshire at the beginning of the thirteenth century but apart from its church, which has recently been restored, it is very difficult to identify the other component parts of this large monastery as they have been completely encroached upon by the modern village of Graiguenamanagh. An interim plan was, however, published as an appendix to the excavation report.[21]

Further south, Lynch excavated for the OPW for two seasons (1982–3) at Tintern, Co. Wexford, a Cistercian abbey founded *c*.1200 from its namesake in Wales. Again as this was in advance of conservation work the excavation concentrated upon the church and the cloister area. Unluckily, as a result of the church being cleared out after the dissolution of the monasteries and then used as a local cemetery no medieval features survived within either the nave or the chancel. The excavation failed to elucidate the full plan of the church as the north aisle and transept were not located. However, several metres of the foundations of the eastern cloister arcade wall were found in association with thirteenth-century pottery. The fifteenth-century tower above the church crossing, and the nave and chancel were then converted to residential use in the sixteenth century.[22]

As well as these excavations, the cloister area and parts of the transept of Knockmoy, Co. Galway, founded in 1190 by King Cathal Crovdearg O'Connor, have been excavated by Sweetman. It is most famous for the now barely visible fifteenth-century frescoes on the north wall of the chancel. The excavation revealed the base of the fifteenth-century cloister as well as the south transept, although no medieval small finds were recovered and there were very few pieces of cut stone from the cloisters. It is also interesting to note that the floors were mortar rather than tiles, confirming yet again that tiled floors were only found east of the River Shannon.[23] There was also a small 'trial' excavation undertaken by Lynch of the OPW of the Cistercian foundation at Boyle, Co. Roscommon, a daughter house of Mellifont, founded in 1161.[24] According to Stalley, 'The architecture . . . is equally fine (as the decorative carving) and the majesty of the south arcade is unparalleled elsewhere in the country'.[25] Although the abbey was predominately a Gaelic settlement Stalley has suggested that the master mason employed at Christ Church, Dublin, also worked here.[26] Further archaeological excavations here would be of great value in order to see whether the development of an Irish house was fundamentally different to an Anglo-Norman foundation such as Tintern.

Before we leave our examination of the archaeology of the medieval Cistercian abbeys in Ireland some mention must be made of the richest foundation, that of St Mary's on the north side of the River Liffey in Dublin. Only the beautiful vaulted chapter house of about 1190 and a passage to the south of it survive as the rest of the abbey has been built over. In 1886 many of the medieval floor-tiles of the church were located during an excavation. This area is likely to be redeveloped in the near future and it is planned that a trial excavation takes place before any building work commences. The finds and structures revealed by any such excavation will be of great interest as this was one of the very few urban Cistercian houses, and was also used as a meeting-place for the King's Council in the middle ages.

The other early medieval religious order in Ireland which has attracted the attention of archaeologists is that of the Augustinian canons. Again, the introduction of this reformed order to Ireland owed much to the great St Malachy who visited their house at Arrouaise in France in 1139. He realized that their rule, based on the writings of St Augustine of Hippo, was most suitable in his aim to reform the Irish monasteries. Unlike the monolithic Cistercian order each abbey could add its own liturgical usages to the Rule and they were largely independent of each other. Thus some were founded in isolated spots, and were almost indistinguishable from those of the Cistercians, while other houses of the canons served cathedrals such as Christ Church, Dublin. This also meant that there was no single plan for their layout and no standard architectural scheme. According to Stalley the Augustinians had the largest number of religious houses in medieval Ireland, although only thirty survive, of which eight are large in size.[27] Indeed one of the largest priories in medieval Ireland, Athassel in Co.

Tipperary, belongs to this order. It was founded by William de Burgo at the end of the twelfth century and was dedicated to St Edmund. As well as the church and cloister buildings, which are of thirteenth-century date, and the remains of the crossing tower, there are also portions of the outer wall that originally surrounded the priory. The main entrance was through a large gatehouse, in front of which is a bridge over a now silted up stream. This stream which links up with the nearby River Suir, according to Stalley, probably functioned both as another defensive barrier to the exposed western side of the priory and as a leet for a water mill.[28] An excavation here might be able to throw some light on the more ephemeral buildings which would have occupied the outer court of the priory, as well as locating, to its north, the town which was burnt by the Irish at least twice in the fourteenth century. Traces of these earthworks can be seen in aerial photographs of the abbey (pl. 20).

Of the Augustinian priories that have been investigated two, Clontuskert in Co. Galway and Kells in Co. Kilkenny, have been excavated by Fanning on behalf of the OPW in association with conservation work on them. These

Plate 20 Aerial photograph of Athassel Abbey, Co. Tipperary, showing its associated earthworks

two particular priories make an interesting comparison as Clontuskert was a Gaelic foundation whereas Kells was Anglo-Norman. Although a full report has been published on Clontuskert[29] only interim reports have as yet been produced on Kells, although Empey has recently published an account of the historical development of the community there.[30] The Augustinian priory of St Mary at Clontuskert was probably founded in the latter half of the twelfth century, reputedly on the site of a pre-Norman Celtic monastery dedicated to St Baetan. However, during the excavation no structures or finds could be assigned to this period, despite an almost complete investigation of the later monastic site. A survey of the earthworks around the priory did not reveal any definite sign of either a substantial enclosing bank or the monastic *vallum* normally associated with such early monasteries. However, it is possible that this was located at Crossconnell which is some distance from the priory.

The medieval remains of Clontuskert Priory were, nevertheless, considerable. The original plan was of a long undivided church which dated from the late twelfth to early thirteenth centuries. This became the chancel of the later church when a nave was added in the late fourteenth to early fifteenth centuries. Its final addition was a north transept which was constructed in either the late fifteenth or early sixteenth century. Despite the destruction of the archaeological levels by later burials the complete ground-plan of the claustral range was uncovered. Many small finds were recovered, including some late-thirteenth-century coins and pieces of a green-glazed French barrel costrel. Bronze objects of medieval date included a decorated cheek piece, a stirrup and a small enamelled clasp. There were also several iron objects which were mostly household implements and mainly medieval in date. It is instructive to note the relative paucity of medieval pottery compared with religious houses in the east, such as Mellifont and Kells. However, another western Augustinian abbey at Ballintubber, Co. Mayo, excavated by O'hEochaide for the OPW, also yielded little pottery. Fanning also commented upon the absence both of Ham Green wares and hand-made cooking pots, 'which are commonly found on medieval monastic sites in the eastern counties'.[31] Clontuskert also lacked decorative floor-tiles as well as roofing slate and roofing-tiles which are found in medieval monasteries of Leinster, such as Graiguenamanagh and Mellifont. He concluded, therefore, that the finds 'reflect the cultural differences which existed in early medieval times between the Irish foundations of the West and the great Anglo-Norman or, indeed, Irish houses of the Pale and surrounding areas'.[32]

Another puzzling feature of the small finds of Clontuskert, which will be explored on a broader scale in chapter 7, was the lack of examples from the fifteenth century when the historical record reveals that the priory was flourishing under the patronage of the O'Kellys. There is no doubt that it was extensively rebuilt after the disastrous fire of 1404, as is attested by the extant carvings. Nevertheless, the majority of finds date from when the priory was reoccupied after the dissolution of the monasteries. These late medieval finds of the late sixteenth and early seventeenth centuries indicated to Fanning that the site was continuously occupied, perhaps even in a monastic way, throughout the reign of Elizabeth I.[33]

Kells Priory, Co. Kilkenny, which Fanning excavated from 1972 to 1975, was founded at the end of the twelfth century by Geoffrey de Marisco who brought over four Augustinian canons from Bodmin in Cornwall to colonize it. Most of the existing buildings, however, date from the fourteenth and fifteenth centuries. This large monastic complex (fig. 32) with its defensive perimeter walls and towers is divided into two courts by another wall and a central gateway. The northerly court contains the nave and chancel church and the claustral buildings, and this was where

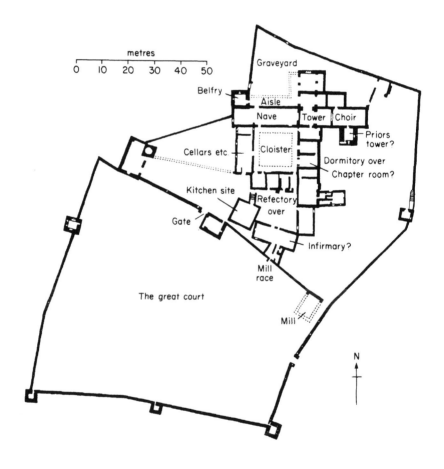

Figure 32 Plan of Kells Priory, Co. Kilkenny

Fanning's excavations were concentrated. The church has some similarities to the one at Athassel, with a tower on the north-west corner and a lady chapel to the north-east. A tower was also added over the crossing in the fifteenth century. In the larger southern court, the prior's vill, the walls are pierced by five tower-houses, probably constructed in the third quarter of the fifteenth century.[34]

Despite the later reuse of the church as a cemetery, Fanning was able to locate a few pieces of the original floor as well as some medieval wall plaster. He found that the western portion of the nave was extended, possibly when the west domestic range was completed in the fourteenth century. He also found the remains of a light partition wall in the nave's centre dating to the later middle ages. In the nave aisle and in the nave of the north transept, more than 2,000 fragments of decorated medieval floor-tiles were found, although none *in situ*. This revealed that tile pavements of mosaic, line-impressed, stamped and plain tiles had probably been common in both the church and in the claustral range. Fanning found parallels to the decorative patterns, such as floral patterns, the lion rampant and geometric designs, on the line-impressed tiles in the Cistercian houses of Mellifont and Jerpoint. Sherds of medieval and later pottery and medieval painted window-glass were also found.[35]

In the cloister area the foundations of the arcade walls were revealed as well as cloister buttress bases on each side and at the four angles. Traces of the original floor of the ambulatory (the walking area of the cloister) consisted in some places of pebble cobbling and elsewhere of a substantial mortar floor. Many fragments of the cloister arcade were excavated, mainly of limestone. From an examination of these fragments and other pieces found in the western aisle of the transept the form of the cloister arcade has been established and they are in the process of reconstruction by the OPW. Stylistically they can be dated to the early fourteenth century, and this has been reinforced by associated small finds such as a reckoning counter of Edward I and an annular brooch of the same date. The west room of the south range and the earlier deposits under the collapsed vaulting of the north-west tower all revealed medieval pottery of English, French and local provenance, as well as a number of coins and bronzes.[36]

Further excavation of the north transept and aisles revealed three probable building phases. In the first a short transept with side chapels was erected in the twelfth century, followed in the late thirteenth to early fourteenth centuries by the construction of an eastern aisle and by the lengthening of the transept. Then in the sixteenth century this east aisle was blocked and a western aisle constructed. In the lady chapel an early wall footing was exposed which Fanning suggested may have been part of a small side chapel which belonged to the early transept plan. In the area below the later altar in the lady chapel some fragments of medieval floor were found *in situ*. In the choir many more fragments of inlaid tiles, mostly fifteenth-century in date, were found and some of them had been reused as liners for a series of sixteenth-century graves which had been inserted into the eastern end of the choir. Finally, a watergate was excavated along the broken length of the enclosure wall which was parallel to the King's river.[37]

In the seventeenth century the claustral area was extensively cobbled as it was used as a stabling area by the later secular owners of the priory, who were probably living in the refurbished north-west tower.[38] This throws a new light on the fact that although the monastery was suppressed in 1540 and granted to James, Earl of Ormond, priors continued to be elected until the Cromwellian period, although by this time the title may have been essentially secular.

As mentioned above, the other Augustinian abbey to have been excavated to any great extent in the Republic was Ballintubber, Co. Mayo. The excavations took place in the 1960s in conjunction with restoration of the church for liturgical uses. It was founded in 1216 by Cathal Crovdearg O'Connor, probably on the site of an earlier monastery. The church itself is aisleless, but has transepts as well as a vaulted chancel and chapels. Stalley has demonstrated that both the layout and some of the major design features of the abbey are derived from nearby Cistercian houses, which demonstrates the importance of that order's architecture in medieval Ireland. Not only is the rib vault above its choir similar to that at Knockmoy, but also to Corcomroe in Co. Clare. The round-headed windows in the east end of Ballintubber correspond very closely to those at Knockmoy, while the many similarities between the carved capitals at Ballintubber and Boyle has indicated to Stalley that the same sculptor was employed at both places.[39] The monastery was dissolved in 1542 and subsequently leased to secular tenants until 1653 when the Augustinians appear to have taken over again. In 1653 its domestic ranges were largely destroyed by Cromwell's troops, but the church remained intact until it was finally restored in 1966.

Several Augustinian houses have been excavated in the north over the last few years, although the majority of investigations have been small-scale because of the particular constraints in operation on them. Perhaps the site which has undergone most investigation is that of the priory at Dungiven, Co. Derry. Here, on a promontory high above the River Roe, lies the pre-Norman monastery associated with St Nechtan which was refounded in the twelfth century by the Augustinians under the patronage of the O'Cahan family who later erected a castle on the site. After the dissolution it was remodelled in the early seventeenth century by Sir Edward Doddington to create a large house and bawn, and the church was also refurbished. The surviving church has a mid-twelfth-century nave and an originally stone vaulted chancel of the thirteenth century which Hamlin has described as 'the most accomplished piece of church architecture of its date in mid Ulster'.[40] On the south wall of the chancel is a fine fifteenth-century O'Cahan tomb.

Excavations during the years 1968–70 by E. A. T. Harper for the then

Historic Monuments Branch, Ministry of Finance (NI), in association with conservation work, concentrated on the west end. They revealed that there was possibly an earlier church on the site which pre-dated the twelfth century and that the existing church was extended at the west end in the medieval period. This extension was probably blocked off from the nave and the original west end restored but that this extension continued in use after the dissolution of the monasteries, probably for secular purposes. Further additions of a secular nature were also made at this west end. Finally, the existence of medieval structures along the south side was established which would imply that this priory had a conventual lay-out.[41] Later excavation by A. D. Bratt in 1975 for the Historic Monuments and Buildings Branch, DoE (NI), showed that both the tower in the south-west corner of the nave and the standing west wall were inserted into the Romanesque nave, probably in the fifteenth century.[42]

At Muckamore, some 2.4 km south east of Antrim town, C. J. Lynn of the Historic Monuments Branch, Ministry of Finance (NI), did a small excavation in 1973-4 on the supposed site of an Augustinian priory which had been preceded by an Early Christian foundation. Although the layout of the cuttings was severely restricted by the curve of a 4 m-high garden wall and by the edge of the proposed roadway the two opposite corners of the cloister and adjacent buildings were located, which allowed Lynn to estimate roughly the size and the layout of the monastic buildings. He was therefore able to estimate the size of the church, which was on the north side of the cloisters, as being probably more than 25 m in length and aisleless, although he could not determine its width with any precision. The cloister garth was 14 by 21 m, its ambulatory was 2.2 m wide and the cloister arcade wall survived to a height of 90 cm in places. Part of the interior of the most northerly building of the east range was uncovered, as well as a garderobe building at the south-west corner of the west range. In the silt of a stream which flowed under this last building Lynn found pottery and bronze and iron objects as well as coins. Fifteen of the coins, which dated to the fourteenth century, were found in a well-defined level at the top of the silt and therefore gave a terminal date for these deposits. He also concluded that the buildings were erected after 1185 as a John de Courcy coin was found in a shallow feature running under the west cloister arcade wall.[43]

This excavation has demonstrated that where there are no surviving remains and where the documentary record is not helpful the chronology of site occupation as well as the dimensions of the principal buildings can still be recovered. Obviously, a larger excavation of the abbey could reveal its complete layout and provide more information about its socio-economic development.

Because of proposed road widening and realignment there were two seasons of excavation on the northern side of the ruined church of the Augustinian Abbey at Movilla, Co. Down. In 1980 M. J. Yates carried out a trial excavation on the site and this was followed in 1981 by a slightly larger investigation by R. Ivens, both on behalf of the Historic Monuments and Buildings Branch, DoE (NI). Before the excavation it was known that this was the site of an important and influential Early Christian monastery which was refounded, together with Bangor and Saul, as an Augustinian house. The long narrow church which is at the edge of a large graveyard is mostly thirteenth-century in date, apart from the west gable which was rebuilt in the fifteenth century and provided with a decorated window. It was also probably a centre for the production of thirteenth-century foliate coffin lids as it was close to the Scrabo sandstone source, and it was also an important landowner in the region in the middle ages. The abbey was dissolved either in 1541 or in 1542–3, but Hamlin was unable to find out what the buildings were used for then except for a 1744 reference to a graveyard.[44]

Of the two trenches opened by Yates only one of them produced a considerable depth of occupation levels dating back to the Early Christian period but when Ivens extended the excavated area he found little in the way of archaeological stratigraphy. However, he found some evidence for intermittent occupation on the site from the later Mesolithic to the Bronze Age. No substantial occupation of the area occurred until the last centuries of the first millennium AD when the many finds of crucibles and slag indicated a bronzeworking industry. This would suggest that this was a peripheral part of the early monastery, exactly where Hamlin argued the later abbey would have been located.[45] It was not until the thirteenth century that a large stone structure was erected which was probably of more than one storey. Ivens has suggested that the ground floor was probably used as a combined byre and store and workshop.[46] The fact that the majority of medieval glazed pottery of the thirteenth century was associated with this building or its midden heap possibly indicated that its occupant was of higher status than the earlier users of the site. The diet, however, remained broadly the same as it had been in Early Christian times according to the surviving animal bones. Thus cow was the most important component followed by sheep or goat and pig. A large gully which may have been a thirteenth-century property boundary linked to the last building contained several types of stone roof slate. At the end of the thirteenth century or early in the following century the large stone building was allowed to fall into disuse and was eventually demolished. It was also probable that the church was in decay at this period as Ivens found painted glass and lead closing strips in the same horizon.

During the thirteenth and fourteenth centuries the area to the west of the building was left open and two or three wells were dug there. However, occupation of adjacent areas obviously continued as the sizeable midden heap to the north of the stone building continued in use and even spilled over the ruins of the building itself. But the site does not seem to have been occupied after the fourteenth century although a small area of rough paving overlying the midden could have been related to renewed building activity at the church in the fifteenth century.[47]

It is interesting that these excavations at Movilla investigated an area outside the usual claustral range of buildings and yet produced a building contemporary with the church. As I have noted (p. 139) it is not sufficient just to examine the cloister ranges of buildings as the monastic complex obviously encompassed a much larger area. And it is these peripheral areas which are so much in need of archaeological investigation because they often do not feature to any great extent in the surviving documents. It is only by larger-scale excavations of these outer areas of the religious houses that we may gain some idea of their socio-economic importance in the everyday life of medieval Ireland.

There has also been the excavation of the east range of the Augustinian priory of St Mary on Devenish island, Co. Fermanagh, which overlooks the early monastic remains. However, although there is one late reference which indicates that a priory was here before 1130 all the visible remains date to the middle of the fifteenth century and, therefore, discussion of this site will be included in the following chapter.[48]

Finally, there was a limited excavation carried out by Fanning of the OPW in 1973 of the Augustinian priory of SS Peter and Paul (known locally as St Selskar's Abbey) in Wexford town. It was probably founded in the late twelfth century by the local Roche family and comprises a double nave and a fourteenth-century square central tower. He excavated the church down to its original floor levels and discovered underneath the base of the westernmost pier of the nave aisle the moulded door jamb of the original thirteenth-century aisleless nave. He uncovered the foundation of the eastern respond and some form of rood screen at this junction of the nave and chancel. He also excavated the belfry tower down to its original floor levels and found a few sherds of sgraffito and Buckley wares as well as some fragments of carved stone.[49]

It is instructive to examine some of the reasons for the greater number of Augustinian foundations in medieval Ireland in comparison with the equally successful Cistercians. This point has been examined in some detail recently by Empey in an article on the history of the Augustinian priory of Kells, Co. Kilkenny.[50] Unlike the Cistercians, the houses of Augustinian canons could be as small as their patron wished and could also be set up in a town or by a castle. Once a priory was established their secular patron could become closely involved in its affairs as the Augustinians lacked the Cistercians' centralized structure of control. They also appealed greatly to the tenants of the great Anglo-Norman lords as they were allowed to accept ecclesiastical revenues from the many churches and tithes held by these Anglo-Normans. Empey also makes the suggestion that Augustinian canons may have taken part in parochial work in Ireland, just when new parishes were evolving on manors, as they were not covered by the ban of the Fourth Lateran Council.[51] Although the evidence for this is not yet conclusive it would go some way towards explaining their popularity in Ireland.

The unreformed Benedictine order was really only introduced on a large scale into Ireland in the twelfth and thirteenth centuries. Altogether it has been calculated that up to nine houses were set up by the Anglo-Normans, while there was also one pre-Norman foundation.[52] Archaeologically very little is known about this order in Ireland as only the abbey at Fore, Co. Westmeath, has extensive remains. It was founded about 1200 by one of the de Lacys, close to an earlier monastery. The simple nave and chancel church was constructed about 1200, with a transitional triple-light east window. The surviving claustral buildings are of fifteenth-century date but incorporate fragments of the original thirteenth-century ranges on the ground floor. There are also the fragmentary remains of a gateway, mill and *columbarium* (dovecote). In the fifteenth century the abbey was fortified by the addition of towers to the church, similar in some respects to those at Kells. In Ulster there are the remains of a thirteenth-century Benedictine church incorporated into Downpatrick Cathedral, and at the early monastery at Nendrum, Co. Down, a chancel which was added to the church dates from the late twelfth century when a Benedictine cell was established there.

Later in the thirteenth century the arrival of the mendicant friars in Ireland made a great impact upon the settlement pattern of religious houses. The Dominicans arrived in Ireland in 1224 and soon set about establishing houses in the towns and cities where they could best minister to the needs of the local communities. The other great mendicant order, the Franciscans, came to Ireland in 1231–2. Despite later urban development some of their houses have survived in a better state of preservation than equivalent houses in Britain and on the Continent. The early churches of the friars were very simple in plan and austere in architectural features. However, by the early fourteenth century both orders were constructing large and impressive churches. The most striking feature of their churches in Ireland was a central tower which marked off the choir area for the friars from the nave which was for the populace. In the more successful friaries it was often necessary for an aisle to be added to the nave to accommodate a growing congregation, and sometimes a transept, which had to be added on the side away from the cloister. The finest medieval friaries to survive in Ireland usually date from the extraordinary revival which took place in the fifteenth century, mainly in the Gaelic areas of the west. This phenomenon will be examined in more detail in chapter 7.

The only Dominican priory church of medieval date to have been excavated in the recent past was St Saviour's in Limerick city. It was probably founded in 1227 by the King of Thomond, Donnchadh O'Brien who was buried there in 1241. It was re-edified by James, sixth Earl of Desmond, who was also buried in the priory. The excavation in 1975 in advance of proposed road construction across the site was directed by E. Shee of the Department of Archaeology, UCC. Very little survives above ground level of the priory – only the north wall of the church and a number of carved stones. Examination of the church wall revealed that the gable ends of two buildings were set at right angles to the north wall, and the line of a possible cloister was also identified. Investigations in the interior of the church failed to find its south wall and led Shee to suggest that there was probably a south transept in the nave. Three medieval slab-built graves were found in the lowest levels of the church and in an area to the north of the church ten more east–west inhumations were found as well as two walls parallel with the church. She also located the sills of two blocked-up doorways on the north side of the church. Finds included thirteenth- to fourteenth-century green-glazed ware from south-western France, some later medieval wares from France and England, German and English stonewares, sgraffito ware from North Devon and gravel-tempered ware, as well as an Edward I silver penny and part of a shale bracelet.[53]

As this limited rescue excavation was unable to elucidate the claustral buildings of the priory at Limerick it would, perhaps, be useful to examine briefly the upstanding remains of arguably the finest Dominican house in medieval Ireland at Kilmallock, Co. Limerick. It lies just outside the medieval walled town of Kilmallock on the River Loobagh and was probably founded in 1291. The choir of the church probably dates from about that period. On its south side it has six magnificent windows which have now lost most of their tracery and its east window is made up of five gracefully graduated lancets. The central tower was probably started soon after the choir but was heightened later. The nave has a south aisle, and a transept was also added in the first half of the fourteenth century. The well preserved cloister buildings date to the fourteenth century, but their layout is totally different from that of the Cistercians, as is the plan of the church.[54]

There is little more archaeological information available on the Franciscan order in Ireland. By 1331 there were thirty-two houses in the country, most of them established in the larger Anglo-Norman towns and only a few founded by Gaelic Irish families. Of course, this pattern was to change dramatically from the latter half of the fourteenth century as the Irish Franciscan province reflected more and more the divisions in the country between Irish and Anglo-Irish. One of the more important Gaelic foundations was at Armagh, probably founded in 1263–4 by Archbishop Patrick O'Scannail, which was excavated in the 1960s and 1970s. It enjoyed the support of prominent patrons such as MacDonnell Galloglagh and the O'Neills and played an active and important part in the religious and political life of that city throughout the middle ages until its suppression in 1542. It would seem, however, that some kind of religious life continued after this event although it was closely involved in the warfare of the latter half of the sixteenth century and was in ruins by c.1601. Lynn's excavation in the 1970s concentrated upon the thirteenth-century church, which at 49.8 m long is the longest known friary church in Ireland. At its west end there are the remains of two arches that opened into a south aisle which no longer exists (fig. 33). There was no sign of a transept having been added, although some projecting stones in the wall and part of a rubble pier base in the middle of the church indicated an inserted belfry tower. According to Lynn future excavation in the area to the immediate north of the church might be very valuable in revealing the first thirteenth-century claustral range of an Irish friary, as earlier excavations by Harper revealed the presence of substantial medieval foundations there.[55]

The majority of small finds from the friary were either late medieval or post-medieval in date. Most of the pottery sherds located were of everted-rim cooking ware recovered from disturbed grave fill; only three sherds of glazed pottery were found, probably dating to the thirteenth and fourteenth centuries. The coarse cooking pottery could not be closely dated as better stratified groups of the same type range from the early thirteenth century at Dundrum Castle, Co. Down, to the middle of the sixteenth century at Carrickfergus, Co. Antrim. Other finds included post-medieval coins apart from an Edward I silver penny which was unhappily unstratified, ninety pieces of coloured glass dated generally on English parallels to the fifteenth century and a bronze mount and some pistol balls, probably dating to the warfare of the late sixteenth century in the area.[56] It was a pity that the finds came from recently disturbed contexts but they broadly illustrate the known history of the friary and, as Lynn notes, 'the church survives as a useful illustration of friary architecture and reminds us of the great influence of friars generally in medieval Irish society'.[57]

Apart from Armagh the only other houses of the Franciscan Order in Ulster were in Downpatrick, Carrickfergus and Cavan and nothing remains of these above ground level. However, during Delaney's excavations at Carrickfergus possible traces of the Franciscan friary were found on the Joymount site. These included a possible stone precinct wall of the friary as well as short lengths of three parallel stone walls and some cobbling which were interpreted as forming part of the east end of the friary. Associated with these walls was a medieval cemetery which included the skeletons of women and children. Most of the finds were medieval, such as decorated floor-tiles, painted window glass and thirteenth- and fourteenth-century pottery.[58]

Further south the friary in Kilkenny, founded by Richard the Marshal in c.1232, has also been excavated. All that remains above ground are the ruined choir, which was extended in the 1320s, and a mid-fourteenth-century tower. A chapel or sacristy and some remnants of the domestic buildings are located to the south of the church. Unluckily, no report has yet been published on the excavations of the nave and choir which took place in 1969 under the direction of Ó hEochaidh for the OPW. This friary is historically important as the Anglo-Irish annalist of the fourteenth century, Friar John Clyn, was a member of its community. Generally speaking, Franciscan churches usually took a long time to be completed as they were often short of financial support in their early years, mainly

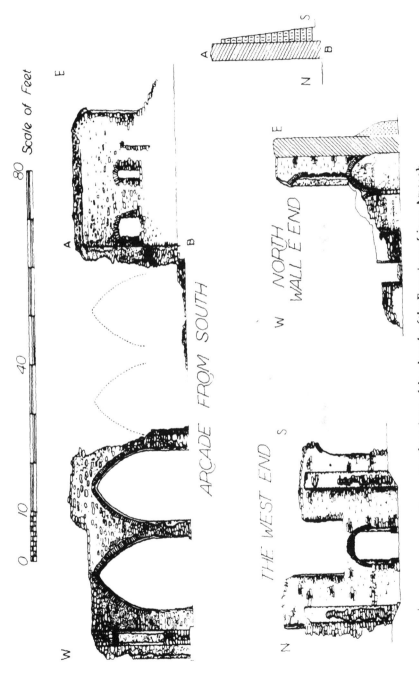

Figure 33 Elevations of the church of the Franciscan friary, Armagh

because of their strict interpretation of the rule of poverty. It was probably the granting of royal alms in 1245 that spurred on the building of the choir at Kilkenny.

In 1984 A. Lynch of the OPW carried out a small excavation in advance of conservation work at Moor Abbey, Co. Tipperary. The friary was founded by Donchad Cairbreach O'Brien, King of Thomond early in the thirteenth century. As has so often been the case no medieval features were found inside the fifteenth-century church because of widespread disturbance caused by post-dissolution burials and modern drains. Parts of the cloister foundations were also uncovered. Stone-lined postholes, some with wooden posts *in situ*, were interpreted as the remains of scaffolding posts erected during the construction of the church.[59] Other early Franciscan friaries that suggest the initial poverty of the order in Ireland include Castledermot, Co. Kildare, founded in 1302 and the 'French Church' in Waterford, founded in about 1240. Other houses were, however, more richly endowed, such as that at Ardfert, Co. Kerry, founded in the 1260s, and Ennis, Co. Clare, founded shortly before his death in 1242 by Donchad Cairbreach O'Brien.

The other major order of mendicant friars, the Carmelites, founded as many as twenty-four houses in Ireland from the 1260s onwards, but the only extensive remains still surviving are those of the thirteenth-century priory at Loughrea, Co. Galway, founded by Richard de Burgo. The tower and kitchen of the Carmelite friary of St Saviour founded in 1356 by James Butler, second Earl of Ormond, are also still to be found incorporated into the later Knocktopher House in Co. Kilkenny.[60] Smaller religious orders also set up houses in Ireland, such as the Premonstratensians at Tuam, Co. Galway, and Trinity Island in Lough Key, Co. Roscommon; the Gilbertines at Loughsewdy, Co. Westmeath; the Trinitarians at Adare, Co. Limerick; and the Victorine canons whose most important house was St Thomas's Abbey in Dublin. There are also the remains of some 14 medieval nunneries, mainly of Augustinian Canonesses or Cistercians.

The great medieval military orders also had establishments in Ireland – the Knights Templar were granted Clontarf, Co. Dublin, by Henry II in 1172, and the Hospitallers who were granted Kilmainham in Dublin by the Earl of Pembroke some time before 1176. Nothing now survives of either foundation although the Hospitallers' priory probably lies below the now magnificently restored seventeenth-century Royal Hospital for Old and Disabled Soldiers. At Kilteel, Co. Kildare, the Late Romanesque church and its lands passed to the Hospitallers sometime before 1212 although it is not clear whether a separate preceptory of the order existed there by that time as neither a foundation charter nor an original land grant survive. Traditionally it was thought that Maurice Fitzgerald, second Baron of Offaly, founded it before his death in 1257. Although it was an important house for the Hospitallers, and three general chapters of the order were held there in 1326, 1333 and 1334, little remains of it today apart from its fifteenth-century tower and gateway. It played an important role as a border fortress in the later middle ages as it was located on the south-west corner of the Pale.[61]

The Anglo-Normans also introduced other new orders into Ireland such as the Crutched Friars, who were in fact regular canons under the rule of St Augustine who ministered to the sick in their hospitals set up in many urban areas. Their first house was established in Dublin in 1188, and their thirteenth-century foundation of St John the Baptist at Newtown Trim, Co. Meath, was excavated by Sweetman of the OPW in 1984. He found the remains of a fifteenth-century rood screen marking off the choir from the nave, and a doorway in the gable end of the nave. He also located the remains of a tower leading to a room over the sacristy and part of the original domestic range to the north-east of the choir.[62] Other religious orders whose main aim was to tend the sick included the Hospitallers of St Thomas of Acon who had two houses in Ireland, and the Trinitarians who had only a single foundation. K. Campbell excavated the remains of the medieval Hospital of St James in Drogheda in 1982–3, the only example so far archaeologically investigated in Ireland. Although the thirteenth-century barrel-vaulted undercroft, measuring 17 by 6 m, was demolished to make way for a new road, he was able to excavate archaeological deposits up to 4 m in depth which gave a good stratigraphical sequence over five centuries. The medieval finds included sandstone architectural fragments, pottery, roof slates, ceramic ridge-tiles and part of a louver, an iron rowel spur and a bronze lock.[63]

It must be remembered that medieval religious houses did not only function as places of worship, but they were also centres of learning and provided the medieval equivalent of social welfare relief to the poorer sections of society as well as providing nursing care for the elderly and the sick among the population. Because of their number, their endowments and the people they employed, they played a vital part in the economic infrastructure of the Anglo-Norman colony. Since they were supposed to be economically self-sufficient the Cistercians in particular were in the forefront of agricultural techniques and organization in the middle ages. Their houses, especially those located on the good soils of the south-east, prospered from their agricultural undertakings. For instance, Duiske Abbey in Graiguenamanagh, Co. Kilkenny, like most other Cistercian houses in eastern Ireland, engaged in sheep farming. From charter evidence we know that the abbey supplied the Riccardi family of Lucca with £100 worth of wool from 1299–1303, along with another twelve small sacks of wool previously agreed.[64] Other important components of the abbey's income were cattle-rearing, milling and fisheries.[65] Unlike England it is extremely difficult to find any material remains of this agriculture, although Bradley has been successful in locating traces of the granges of Duiske Abbey, including the remains of a possible medieval barn in Annamult, Co. Kilkenny.[66]

Also (as discussed in chapter 4) the thirteenth-century stone building foundations excavated at Jerpoint Church, Co. Kilkenny, close to the Cistercian abbey of Jerpoint may well have been one of the farming granges which were a typical feature of the Cistercian system of agriculture in the middle ages. These granges became more and more necessary as the Cistercians acquired land and property in the thirteenth and fourteenth centuries. It has been estimated that, at its height, the order owned more than 500,000 acres in Ireland,[67] while the Rev. Fr Colmcille Conway has suggested that the total endowment of Mellifont was almost 50,000 statute acres.[68] The problem of farming such large areas was lessened by this system of granges which allowed the *conversi* (lay brothers) to live in buildings up to twenty miles from an abbey. In 1255 Pope Adrian IV allowed mass to be celebrated in these outlying granges which meant that the could be erected even further away from their original abbey. Granges were also set up by the Augustinians as has been shown by Bradley in his survey of one example at Duleek, Co. Meath.[69]

It would be instructive to compare medieval sheep-farming in a county like Leicestershire in England with the south-eastern counties of Kilkenny and Wexford, where much of it was controlled by the large Cistercian houses of the region which exported large amounts of wool to England and the continent. There it was used to supply the expanding cloth trade which was the mainstay of much of the economy of north-western Europe throughout the middle ages. Obviously, a co-ordinated programme of research utilizing historical documents would be extremely valuable in trying to trace more of these granges so that they could be investigated archaeologically in an attempt to elucidate further their importance to the agricultural economy of the major religious orders in Ireland. Indeed, the earthworks, often to be seen surrounding several monastic houses, have been rarely investigated to any degree. One exception was at Clontuskert where T. Fanning surveyed and outlined the complex of low banks, mainly to the north of the monastery itself.[70] They mostly enclosed areas resembling small fields of irregular plan, roughly square or D-shaped (fig. 34). A small excavation of one of these banks revealed that it was 40 cm high and 2 m wide, with small stones from successive field clearances acting as a facing on the northern slope. A very shallow fosse was also located but produced no finds. Fanning concluded that 'The overall impression is of a system of small fields or plots often referred to in medieval documents as orchards or messuages coeval with the medieval monastery and used for agricultural purposes by the monks or their tenants.'[71] He also noted that none of these earthworks were marked on any of the OS maps, except for an early pathway that linked the priory with the roadway.

The impact of the church upon the medieval building industry was considerable as it was a major patron of the expertise of masons, carpenters and other craftsmen. As Stalley has convincingly demonstrated, master

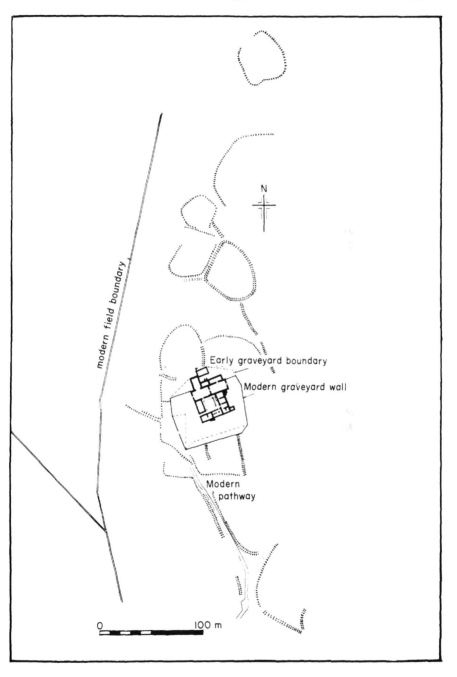

Figure 34 Plan of the fields associated with Clontuskert Priory, Co. Galway

masons were sometimes brought over from England to work on major churches such as St Canice's in Kilkenny. Not only was local stone used in church construction but there are also several examples of good quality stone being imported from western England, especially from the Dundry quarry near Bristol and even Caen stone from Normandy. It would be a useful exercise to try and quantify the importance of church architecture to the economic well-being of this industry. Without the stimulus provided by all the secular and religious organizations for new churches and residences throughout the middle ages there would not have been the same great developments in architectural techniques and styles. In most parts of Europe these developments can be traced from surviving building, but in Ireland these are often minimal so that archaeology can play a much larger part in any interpretation by the recovery of pieces of cut stone and other portions of the church fabric buried over the centuries.

We have seen in this chapter how the church dominated almost every aspect of life in medieval Ireland, be it religious, educational or socio-economic. The period from the twelfth to the sixteenth centuries saw fundamental change in the organization of the church. The twelfth century saw the introduction of the new continental religious orders which effectively sounded the death knell of the older Celtic monasteries. And with the end of this dominance of Early Christian monasticism the secular church was fully organized into dioceses and parishes over most of the country. The arrival of the Cistercians, in particular, brought about a carefully arranged layout of monastic buildings centred around an open space or cloisters with the church to the north, the chapter house to the east, and the domestic ranges to the south and west. By the middle of the thirteenth century it would appear that enough churches had been built to satisfy the religious needs of the community, and at the same time some of the earlier monastic zeal was beginning to wear a little thin. This state of affairs was rectified by the arrival of the mendicant friars who brought their message of hope to the towns and cities of the country and generally arrested the decline in religious life.

However, the Gaelic resurgence and the many socio-economic disasters of the fourteenth century seem to have led to a dramatic decline in church building, probably because more than enough existed for either a declining or a static population. It was not, therefore, until the following century that new churches were erected again, some with the patronage of great Anglo-Irish lords such as Ormond, Thomond and Kildare. Thus the Cistercians in Ormond-dominated Tipperary were able to refurbish extensively some of their older foundations such as Holy Cross and Kilcooly. It was also in the fifteenth century that there was a second great wave of friary construction, especially in the Gaelic west of the country. To this period date some of the finest Franciscan houses, such as at Ross Errilly, Co. Galway, and Quin, Co. Clare. This religious renewal, much of it attributable to the Observantine reform movement (a later medieval strict observance of the Franciscan rule), was foreshortened by Henry VIII in the years after 1536 when all the property and lands of the religious orders were appropriated by the Crown. Many ecclesiastical foundations, however, continued secretly after this time, especially in the west, but this was brought to an end after 1649 as a result of Cromwell's campaigns. These developments of the later middle ages will be examined in more detail in chapter 7.

Although this chapter has concentrated on the contribution made by recent excavations to our understanding of the layout and development of medieval churches and religious houses in Ireland, it has also revealed the limitations of this research. The random nature of many of these excavations, and the way in which they have often been subordinated to the needs of the architects in the state archaeological services, has meant that in general they have not been geared to solving particular problems.

Where archaeology has made some progress is in the elucidation of the nature of the fabric of the church, such as the floor types which were either of pounded earth, mortar, slabs or tiles. The present known distribution of medieval floor-tiles is particularly striking, being confined to the region east of the River Shannon. Whereas the tiny medieval parish church at Artaine South in Dublin was found to have been tiled[72] they were absent from major religious houses in the west such as Knockmoy and Clontuskert, both in Co. Galway.[73] That tiles were obviously in plentiful supply in medieval Dublin has been reinforced by the finding of several of them during the recent excavation near the site of St Saviour's Dominican priory.[74] Although economic reasons probably influenced the distribution of medieval tiles, other factors such as their availability and ease of transport obviously played their part, too. Excavations have yet to ascertain, either, the full extent of these tile pavements within the church itself and whether they were also to be found in other parts of religious houses, such as the chapter house or refectory.

It is also significant that the archaeological excavations at both Clontuskert Priory, Co. Galway, and Duiske Abbey, Graiguenamanagh, Co. Kilkenny, failed to locate any evidence for their roof coverings. This had led scholars such as Stalley to suggest that they were probably composed of lead which was removed when the monasteries were dissolved. He further argued that stone slates were probably the norm for most church roofs, although there is documentary evidence for the use of wooden shingles as well.[75] The internal decor has also been partially reconstructed by archaeology for Kells Priory, Co. Kilkenny, and Mellifont Abbey, Co. Louth, where slight traces of original wall plaster were located.[76]

Finally, the surviving environmental evidence, such as seeds, pollen and bone remains enable the archaeologist to reconstruct the diet of the inhabitants of the medieval religious houses as can be seen at Movilla, Co. Down,[77] and at Tintern, Co. Wexford, where Lynch found the bones of sheep or goat, otters, cats and many rats as well as waterlogged seeds in the filling of a deep stone-sided drain.[78]

7 The later middle ages: growth or decline?

As the reader has probably realized by this stage, the majority of structures and artefacts recovered from medieval sites in Ireland, as in the rest of western Europe, are broadly dated to the thirteenth and early fourteenth centuries. This is not surprising as this was the period of maximum economic growth in the middle ages which only slowed down later in the fourteenth century. For England some economic historians have suggested that this socio-economic 'downturn' may have begun as early as the end of the thirteenth century because over-population caused extensive soil exhaustion on the available cultivable land resources which thus put many of the poorer sections of society on or below a subsistence level of existence.[1] Or, more probably for the Anglo-Norman lordship of Ireland, it was the direct effect of the socio-economic catastrophes of that century, such as the years of the Great European Famine (1315–17) which coincided with the Bruce invasion and was soon followed by the Black Death (1348–50). Perhaps the economic decline of the late fourteenth and fifteenth centuries can be attributed to a combination of these factors, plus the increasing pressure put on the lordship by the Gaelic resurgence which ultimately led to proposals in the fifteenth century for the construction of linear earthen defences around the Anglo-Irish heartland, known as the 'Pale'.

There is also a school of thought which claims that this decline was more apparent than real; this has been cogently argued by A. R. Bridbury, for example, for urban life in late medieval England. He concluded that whereas some of the older established cities such as York were probably decaying, other smaller and possibly more resilient towns were either maintaining their previous levels of economic activity or were, in fact, showing definite signs of expansion.[2] To a certain extent, this case has also been argued by C. A. Empey for the major towns in the Butler lordship in Tipperary and Kilkenny, which sheltered behind their walls and prospered throughout the exigencies of the later middle ages.[3]

In the end, the general level of prosperity and economic well-being in late medieval Ireland cannot really be measured solely by reference to the surviving national and local medieval documents. Again, this is generally because of the non-survival of many classes of medieval sources which still exist for England and can be used there to provide some kind of evidence to measure the rise and fall of population, such as the fourteenth-century poll tax returns, and the long runs of manorial extents, surveys and accounts for various parts of the country. These documents can be utilized in order to quantify the economic performance of several feudal estates in England throughout the later middle ages. For Ireland the data base is insufficient either chronologically or regionally for any type of broad-based quantitative analysis to be undertaken. Thus, the available archaeological evidence for this period assumes an even greater importance in any attempt to answer the question about the general direction of society and the economy in these two centuries.

However, as stated at the beginning of this chapter, the archaeological evidence for the viability or otherwise of settlements in the later middle ages is based mainly on inferences drawn from negative evidence for any archaeological structures or finds for these two centuries. Given the small number of excavated medieval sites in the country in comparison to the probable total, it could fairly be argued (and often is by historical geographers) that the sample is too small to draw any valid conclusions from them. It is just possible, although unlikely, that all the sites so far excavated are typical of conditions in the later medieval lordship. That there were regional differences has already been shown, and this must be taken into account before any general overview is attempted. Nevertheless, medieval settlement sites have been excavated in most of the major geographical zones in Ireland, although again they are most heavily concentrated in the north-eastern corner of the island.

It is, nevertheless, important to examine the Anglo-Norman settlement pattern during the fourteenth and fifteenth centuries to see how far it reflects the decline of the lordship's fortunes as attested by the general political conditions of the period. Not only was the area of English control shrinking but this was accompanied by a consequent pressure on all its 'marcher' regions by a revitalized indigenous population. There was also a dramatic decline in the revenues of the Irish Exchequer, and three military expeditions had to be mounted from England during the later middle ages to try and retrieve the worsening situation in Ireland.[4]

Therefore, those rural settlements on the periphery of the colony, and especially those on more marginal agricultural land, would probably have been the first to go into decline or to have been entirely deserted. But, yet again, the full extent of this is obscured in Ireland because of the non-survival of documents and the lack of comprehensive archaeological investigations on rural medieval settlement sites. Along with the two moated sites in Co. Cork, Kilmagoura and Rigsdale, there are a few other medieval nucleated sites which seem to have been deserted in the early fourteenth century before the advent of the Black Death. And although the contemporary chroniclers are full of descriptions of the destruction and burning of major towns and ecclesiastical centres throughout the period of the Bruce invasion (1315–18) no mention is made of the smaller nucleated settlements that were probably destroyed as a result of the protracted campaigns throughout much of the country. Matters were made much worse by a run of poor harvests which caused widespread famine between 1315 and 1317 and recovery would have been difficult because of cattle murrains, pestilences and a general dearth of cereal crops throughout the 1320s and 1330s. Villages and rural boroughs which lay within the path of the Scottish army during these four troubled years must have been particularly at risk, for although larger urban conurbations could eventually recover from a burning these smaller marginal settlements would probably have gone under immediately.

It is valuable at this stage to investigate the socio-economic position of Anglo-Norman Ireland in the early fourteenth century, before all these traumas were to hit the colony. Although there were pressures from the indigenous population on various peripheral areas of the lordships these were still not widespread and there still seems to have been plenty of arable land available for the Anglo-Norman colonizers unlike the contemporary position in England.[5] Nevertheless, there is also evidence for the desertion of settlements in Ireland. The obvious conclusion is that the rise and fall of settlement is so complex that it cannot solely be attributed to population trends and must be the result of other factors like the internal migration of population such as that postulated by Denecke for German medieval villages.[6] This factor was also probably important in Anglo-Norman Ireland with the reduction of the area under the direct control of Dublin in the fourteenth and fifteenth centuries and the consequent decline and desertion of peripheral Anglo-Irish settlements.

That these processes were not confined to the later medieval period can be confirmed by the surviving thirteenth-century historical record. For instance, both Old Ross in Co. Wexford and Castletown in Co. Louth shared the same ultimate fate as they were early seigneurial *caputs* marked by mottes which went into decline when the focus of the local Anglo-Norman settlement shifted away from them in the course of the thirteenth century. The consensus of opinion suggests that the motte at Old Ross was erected by Isabel de Clare, the daughter of Strongbow, probably in the latter years of the twelfth century. There is also evidence of the existence of burgages here in 1307[7] but the settlement obviously went into decline with the foundation of the port of New Ross, only 8 km westwards. Either Isabel or William Marshal, her husband, founded this port before 1207, which grew into the most important international trading centre in south-east Ireland.[8] This was mainly due to its prime geographical position within the reach of the largest merchant vessels on the River Barrow, with a bridge linking it to the important city of Kilkenny, and surrounded as it was by an agriculturally prosperous hinterland.

The situation with Castletown was very similar; it was the *caput* of the de Verduns who were granted the area corresponding to the modern barony of Ferrard by King John soon after 1185. Again, Castletown may have had burgesses in the early thirteenth century as well as a church which is probably under the remains of the late medieval church to the north of the motte.[9] But as the 'Nova Villa' of Dundalk, less than 1 km east of the motte, developed as an important market centre and port on the major routeway linking Dublin with southern Ulster the original settlement at Castletown consequently went into decline. These are probably the two best known examples of decline in the early thirteenth century when the colony was generally expanding. But it must be stressed that their decline paralleled the rise of two other important urban centres which contributed greatly to the economic vitality of the lordship.

Later in the thirteenth century there were at least two other examples of decline caused by the economic power of over-mighty neighbours. The fate of Wexford which started to suffer at least as early as 1298 has already been discussed.[10] The same was probably true of Rosbergen, Co. Kilkenny, situated directly opposite New Ross on the Barrow river, which by 1307 found its burgesses paying well under half their usual rent 'because of the war'.[11] Whether this was a phrase employed to blame the Irish of the locality, such as the MacMurrough Kavanaghs, we shall probably never know. Nevertheless, these problems were obviously intensified by the growth of New Ross throughout the thirteenth century. Ferns in the north of Co. Wexford also had 49½ waste burgage plots out of 160 in 1298, probably as a result of the pressure put upon this isolated Anglo-Norman town by the MacMurrough Kavanaghs who eventually recovered it in 1360.[12] Thus in areas such as Co. Wexford the late thirteenth and early fourteenth centuries were seeing the encroachment of the indigenous people within the Anglo-Norman colony.

There are other examples of settlements that were probably deserted as a result of the Gaelic resurgence. These include the moated sites of Kilmagoura and Rigsdale, both in Co. Cork, which may have been abandoned in the face of the Desmond insurrection in the early fourteenth century.[13] The town of Athassel in Co. Tipperary on the banks of the River Suir, close by the largest Augustinian house in Ireland, was burnt in 1319 by John FitzThomas and then again in 1329 by Brian O'Brien along with Tipperary, which however survived.[14] Although St Joseph mentions that possible traces of the medieval town at Athassel can be traced in his low-level oblique aerial photographs nothing now remains of it at ground level[15] (pl. 20). This is, perhaps, indicative both of the efficacy of the two burnings and the insubstantial nature of the town's buildings. In most cases the only elements of a medieval nucleated settlement that survive to the present day are the castle or motte, and the church, here probably represented by the priory itself.

Other evidence of either desertion or total destruction of settlements that can be directly attributable to the Gaelic resurgence is very limited. It was the constant backdrop, so to speak, of all the other shorter term pestilences and famines, and thus made recovery for those Anglo-Norman settlements on the exposed frontier of the lordship very difficult, if not impossible. The general ebb and flow of Anglo-Norman control has been examined in detail by Empey for the Butler lordship in Tipperary and Kilkenny, and by Walton for the de Burgo lordship in Connacht, but there just does not seem to be the documentary evidence for charting the fates of individual settlements. Part of the problem lies in the nature of much of the surviving documentation: medieval central government records were usually concerned with fiscal and tenurial matters and do not necessarily give detailed information on particular localities; and the more localized manorial extents and surveys often do not contain very much more detailed information on particular settlement features.

Empey has shown that by the middle of the fourteenth century the Butlers had lost much of northern Co. Tipperary to the Irish. He argues that one of the major reasons for this was that whereas the Gaelic society of southern Co. Tipperary was completely destroyed by the Anglo-Normans it remained almost untouched in the north.[16] Thus this lack of absorption of the native population into Anglo-Norman society allowed them to organize against the Anglo-Norman settlers in the last decade of the thirteenth and the first decade of the fourteenth centuries. Empey then adds a cautionary note when he states that the Bruce invasion, followed by two disastrous Butler minorities, was the occasion but not the cause of the Gaelic reconquest.[17] He places this loss of territory by the Butlers to the Irish in its true contemporary perspective. Although, he estimates, the Butlers lost half of the approximate area of their lordship (around 750,000 acres) a large proportion of it, especially Ui Maine and some lands in Thomond, were never that valuable.[18] But the losses in northern Tipperary and elsewhere could not be made good very easily, so in order to maintain their position as one of the premier Anglo-Norman families the Butlers tightened their grip over the areas that still remained under their control.[19] Nevertheless, the effects of these losses on the total revenue of the lordship in the fourteenth and fifteenth centuries were drastic as they were reduced to a fraction of what they had been earlier.[20]

This decline in revenue was assessed in some detail by Empey for a few manors in northern Co. Tipperary. An inquisition post mortem of 1338 for the manor of Nenagh indicated that the value of its forty-nine identifiable tenements had fallen by almost 75 per cent from the previous century.[21] By 1345 the annual revenue of Thurles had also fallen, this time to about a quarter of its earlier value. He concluded that this had happened either because the lands lay waste or because of tenant resistance to payment of their rents.[22] Other manors of the region, such as Ardmayle and Moyaliff, were also gravely affected by the Irish 'wars', and the value of the manor of Caherconlish in Co. Limerick on the borders of Co. Tipperary had fallen to about one-third of its 1300 value thirty-eight years later.[23]

Empey further maintained that the Irish reconquest in the Butler lordship had run out of steam by the end of the fourteenth century largely because the Irish were unable to conquer areas where the Anglo-Normans were heavily settled. They did not have either the resources or the military capabilities to capture the well-fortified urban settlements of the Anglo-Normans. Important towns were, of course, successfully attacked by the Irish but they could neither occupy them for very long nor destroy them. Two examples of this were Carlow which was burned several times in the second half of the fourteenth century and Gowran, Co. Kilkenny, which was burned at the start of the following century.[24] But, especially in the area drained by the three great rivers of the Barrow, Nore and Suir, urban settlements such as New Ross, Kilkenny, Callan, Carrick, Clonmel, Fethard, Cashel and Waterford seem to have prospered throughout the later middle ages. Empey puts this down to the continuity of 'Anglo-Norman institutions' in the hinterlands of these towns which protected the traders and merchants who were vital to their economic well-being.[25] In Connacht, however, the situation was not so favourable for the survival of these institutions. In a recent doctoral thesis H. Walton has shown that even by the close of the thirteenth century Anglo-Norman settlement was in decline there. Even the powerfully protected Roscommon town was finally abandoned in 1360 after yet another burning by the Irish. In her work she also stressed the small size of these urban settlements in comparison with the rest of the lordship by showing that the fee farm of Roscommon, for instance, was only £12 per annum as against the 80 marks paid by Cork.[26]

It is again difficult to be sure which settlements were permanently affected by the campaigns of the Bruce wars although we know that many towns and the surrounding countryside in various regions of Ireland were burnt and pillaged. It is known, for instance, that Rory, son of Cathal Roe, plundered Sligo, Ballymote, Roscommon, Rinndown and Athlone in 1315, taking advantage of the dislocation caused by the Bruce invasion. But of all these settlements the only one now deserted is Rinndown in Co. Roscommon with only a very overgrown and ruined castle now surviving to mark this settlement. Although it is known that the castle was probably constructed in the early thirteenth century, possibly around 1227, by the Justiciar, Geoffrey de Marisco, very little is know about the town that grew up under the protection of its walls. The only remains of the town are the towered wall, a central gateway, an embanked ditch to its south, and at the western end of this ditch the remnants of a nave-and-chancel church. This church which stood just outside the walls of the town was probably erected by the Knights' Hospitallers. It is also known that the town was stormed by

Felim O'Connor in 1236, and that tolls were levied in 1251 for the construction of the wall around the town. However, there is silence about the town from then onwards until its final plunder in 1315, from which it probably never recovered.[27] Its size can only be guessed at by reference to the area in which it was probably located, between the defensive wall cutting of the peninsula into Lough Ree and the castle (fig. 35).

Other nucleated settlements which probably did not survive the twin onslaughts of the pillaging forays by Bruce's army and the effects of the famine were places like Fore in Co. Westmeath where another town had probably grown up beside the Benedictine priory of SS Taurin and Fechin which was founded about 1200 by one of the de Lacys. All that now remains of this town are the gates which were part of the medieval town's walls. However, in the nineteenth century there is documentary evidence surviving to show that a 'small village' still survived there although probably only a pale shadow of the size and extent of the original medieval nucleated settlement.[28]

During the following year, 1316, the Irish took full advantage of the confused situation caused by the Bruce invasion. The O'Byrnes and the O'Tooles plundered the coastal towns of Wicklow, while the Irish of the Imaile attacked the town of Tullow. In the Midlands the O'Mores raided Laois yet again, and the O'Hanlons besieged Dundalk.[29]

The problem in accurately assessing the impact of the Gaelic resurgence and the Bruce Invasion on Anglo-Norman settlement is that although the existence of several deserted villages and towns is known at the present day it is difficult, nevertheless, to pinpoint the exact reasons for these desertions without archaeological excavation or an adequate series of medieval documents. In Ireland we are still at the stage of data collection so that it is often impossible to make any value judgements as to the importance or otherwise of different historical factors, such as has been successfully undertaken by the Medieval Village Research Group in England.

When the effects of the Black Death (1348–50) are analysed, again, as was also found in England, it is notoriously difficult to prove desertion as a direct result of it because of the lack of sources. However, there is at least one site in Ireland, Kinsalebeg in Co. Waterford, which has been identified by Otway-Ruthven as a probable Black Death desertion. She was able precisely to date this desertion because in 1351 it was recorded that the burgages there which were assigned to Giles de Badlesmere's sister were all waste. This desertion would seem to have happened quite recently because an assignment of dower made in 1338 or 1339 gives no mention of any desertion.[30] But in many other cases the Black Death merely further weakened urban centres which had also probably suffered from the Great Famine and the Gaelic resurgence. Friar John Clyn wrote about the deaths of eight fellow friars in Kilkenny by March 1349.[31] Co. Cork seems to have been particularly badly hit as a 1351 list of burgesses in Youghal reveals that, out of ninety-one of them, thirty-nine were then represented by their

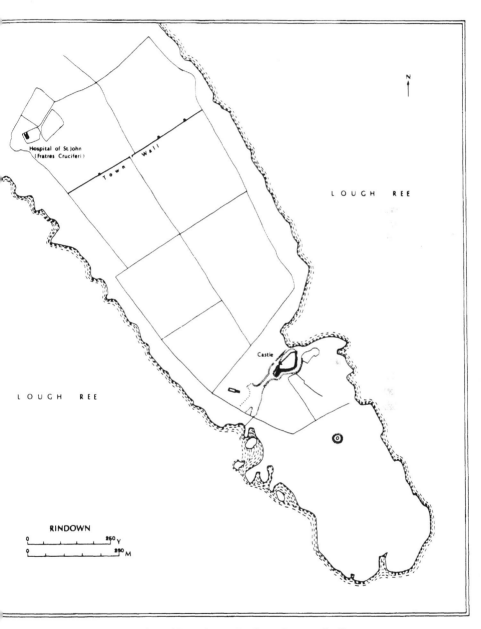

Figure 35 Plan of Rinndown Castle and town, Co. Roscommon

heirs, a strong indication of the high levels of mortality brought about by the plague.[32]

Another candidate for decline in the early fourteenth century was the settlement at Bunratty, Co. Clare, which had as many as 226 burgages in 1287. Like all important towns of the period it had extensive fortifications around it, which were studied by Westropp.[33] However, by the early fourteenth century many of the houses there were in ruinous condition. Again, it is not possible to identify the agent of desertion here but the settlement never recovered to anything like its original size as it is now only a small village clustered around a fine late medieval castle.

Throughout the fourteenth century in the surviving manorial documents there are indications of the very difficult conditions facing many settlements. For instance, in an undated extent of Imaal in Co. Wicklow (probably of the early fourteenth century) it is recorded that all the burgage lands of Donaghmore were in the hands of a single tenant. At another settlement also called Donaghmore, this time in Co. Cork, by the middle of the fourteenth century all the burgage lands were also in the hands of one tenant, a possible indication of population decline.[34]

These are, however, only glimpses of the effects of the Black Death on particular places where some documentary evidence has survived. For the vast majority of settlements the record is silent because, unlike the situation in England, long runs of medieval taxation records do not survive for the country whereby the economic well-being or otherwise of a particular place can be measured over time. The nearest Irish equivalent is Pope Nicholas IV's ecclesiastical taxation which can be used to assess the impact of the earlier fourteenth-century disasters such as the Great Famine and the Gaelic resurgence in those parts of the country where two returns survive. But there are many problems in using it to show the *general* level of wealth in early fourteenth-century Ireland.[35]

If English and continental evidence is taken as a broad indicator of the plague's effects on Anglo-Norman Ireland it would seem that the most densely populated regions of the colony, namely Counties Dublin, Kildare, Louth and Meath, fared the worst, especially in the crowded towns and cities of the eastern seaboard. In this context it is hardly surprising that probably the greatest Anglo-Irish chronicler, Clyn, wrote about the death of 14,000 people in Dublin from the Black Death,[36] yet the Irish annals are silent about its occurrence. It is probable that the indigenous population who were much more scattered throughout the countryside than their Anglo-Norman neighbours escaped the worst rigours of the epidemic, although this conclusion cannot be tested statistically.

Perhaps the Black Death's importance as a major determinant of late medieval population patterns has been overstated in the past. But where it is probably important is in its being the final causal factor for the desertion of settlements which had already been severely weakened by the other economic problems earlier in the century. As well as the famine years of

1315–17, there were also cattle murrains in 1321, 1324 and 1325. In 1327 there was a severe outbreak of smallpox, followed by influenza in 1328. In that same year, and in 1330–1 there were also major shortages of corn. And the Black Death in 1348–50 was followed by later outbreaks of the plague throughout the fourteenth century.[37] Indeed, it would seem that on some of the manors in Co. Dublin the outbreak in 1361 caused much higher mortality, especially to the aristocracy.[38] So the Black Death should be seen as part of the continuum of problems, both economic and social, which all but overwhelmed the colony in the fourteenth century. However, it was the occurrence of the plague in those first three consecutive years that allowed it to develop from the deadly bubonic to the even more deadly pneumonic variety and must have caused the decline and even the complete desertion of many marginal settlements.

Because of the lack of both documents and archaeological research the few deserted settlement sites so far identified by Glasscock, Graham, Meenan and other researchers within the Anglo-Norman colony have remained largely undated.[39] However, in Co. Laois, due initially to the research of Glasscock and latterly as a result of the recent publication of a model environmental history of the county by J. Feehan, the impact of the Black Death and the Gaelic resurgence on the medieval boroughs of that county can be broadly assessed. The borough for which most information survives, New Town Leys, was probably sited at the foot of the impressive rock of Dunamase on which are the battered remains of a once strong Anglo-Norman castle. Indeed the Ordnance Survey 6-inch map of 1839 calls the area to the west and south-west of the rock the 'site of ancient village'. According to Glasscock, although the ground is 'bumpy' no structures can now be identified there. It is known that there were 127 burgesses there in 1283,[40] a sizeable community in thirteenth-century Ireland, but there was obviously a dramatic drop in the early fourteenth century as only forty were recorded by 1324.[41] New Town Leys was attacked by the Irish from the nearby bogs soon after the Bruce invasion, the bells of its church were burnt and Lord John Bisset killed in its defence.[42] Thus the Black Death probably caused its final desertion, especially as it was only about one-third of its thirteenth-century size by the 1320s.

As an illustration of the problems of settlement identification in the county Feehan suggested that the Anglo-Norman town of 'Loughtyok' moved from its original location in Ballymaddock townland a mile or more to the south-east at Newtown townland soon after the Black Death.[43] But he is not totally sure of this because of the dual problems of identification of the original medieval place-names and the apparent lack of earthworks of such a town in the area. His uncertainty is made worse by the existence of a contiguous townland with the name 'Loughteeog' which is yet another possibility for the town's location.

The problems that Feehan has experienced in assessing the pattern of settlement in Anglo-Norman Laois is symptomatic of the country as a whole, especially as there have been very few areas that have enjoyed the attentions of a scholar of his calibre in attempting to explain the local medieval settlement history of a particular area. McNeill has also attempted to examine the fortunes of Anglo-Norman settlement in Ulster during the fourteenth century but he has obviously found it difficult to determine the effects of the Black Death with any precision because of the lack of documentation. He described the fortunes of those fifteen settlements which had the status of boroughs within the medieval earldom and showed that some of them, especially in the south of the country, never developed beyond being rural boroughs set up by a particular lord to attract settlers to the region.

Altogether seven out of this total were described by McNeill as 'rural boroughs' according to Glasscock's classification. Because these settlements were almost always at the bottom of the feudal hierarchy they often only feature obliquely in the surviving manorial documents. Thus these settlements are the most difficult cases when it comes to trying to trace their fortunes throughout the middle ages. All McNeill was able to deduce was that of two boroughs of the Bishop of Down only one of them, Kilclief, had burgesses paying rent in the escheator's account of 1305; while the other one, at Maghera, also in Co. Down, did not even appear in the document. Limavady in Co. Derry was given to James Stewart by Richard de Burgh in 1296, but by 1333 the inquisition of de Burgh's lands lists the mills, landholdings and court of the settlement but no burgages are mentioned.[44] McNeill suggested that they were only marginal settlements so it is hardly surprising that these were the kind of places which went under in the worsening socio-economic conditions of the time, especially in the Anglo-Norman lordship of Ulster which itself had a fairly precarious existence in the later middle ages.[45]

The other eight Ulster boroughs, which were probably of true urban character, all seemed to have survived the vicissitudes of the fourteenth century fairly well. The resilience of a port such as Coleraine, Co. Derry is illustrated in the patent rolls where it is recorded that one of its ships, the *Grace Dieu*, was trading in Gascony in 1317 during the Bruce invasion. According to McNeill another major reason for the economic well-being of the port was the erection of a bridge across the River Bann in 1248. And although it was broken down in 1315 during the Bruce war it was repaired by 1318.[46] Undoubtedly the most important borough was Carrickfergus, badly affected by the problems of the fourteenth century, although it probably remained a thriving trading centre right up to the post-medieval period. Carrickfergus traded mainly with north-west England and Scotland although we know of at least one boat part-registered by a Carrickfergus trader which was wrecked off Beaumaris in 1308 with a cargo of wine from Gascony. And although the pottery kiln located during the excavation of a site in High Street is likely to have predated 1250 the pottery was probably still being produced there in the later middle ages along with iron objects. There is also documentary evidence of the existence of two mills there as late as 1406.[47]

All this evidence for Ulster, although limited in extent, does indicate that the larger urban settlements of the earldom were weathering the problems of the fourteenth century. During this century and the first half of the succeeding one the Irish recovered control over four out of five counties of the earldom and this eventually led to the gradual disintegration of the Anglo-Norman lordship over the region. This chronology put forward by McNeill goes counter to the traditional explanation of the end of the earldom, usually attributed to the Bruce invasion and the murder of the Earl in 1333. He suggested that what probably happened was that, as the Anglo-Norman lords in Ulster, unlike in south-eastern parts of Ireland, were essentially a resident rentier class, the Irish eventually replaced them on the land. Thus the original Irish-based agriculture still continued, with the same renders still being exacted from their landholdings which were then sold through the ports as before.[48]

There is also some historical evidence to show that the major ports along the eastern coastline successfully responded to the changes in the rural economy of Ireland in the later middle ages – the shift from a mainly arable bias towards one of pastoral husbandry. Thus the exports of cereals gave way increasingly to shipments of Irish herds, hides and wool. In this way ports such as Waterford and New Ross which responded quickly to these changes in the pattern of overseas trade survived throughout the later middle ages, whilst other towns, such as Wexford, went into a steep decline. Archaeologically, it is impossible to prove either a decline or survival because of the lack of excavations. This lack of traceable archaeological occupation in the fifteenth and sixteenth centuries was identified by Sweetman in his excavation of a small site at Shop Street, Drogheda, Co. Louth, and he suggested that the 'hiatus in the activity on the quayside might be the result of depopulation and contraction of the occupied area due to the Black Death'.[49]

On the other hand, the documentary evidence of the economic well-being of Waterford in the later middle ages, as evinced by the surviving customs returns, would suggest that the city was prospering in spite of the general economic recession. However, the archaeological evidence is, at best, conflicting, because at the Lady Lane site excavated by Moore in 1982–3 there was no identifiable fifteenth-century occupation debris although there was evidence for every other century from the twelfth to the nineteenth. But at other archaeological sites in the city there is some archaeological evidence surviving from this problematic century. According to B. Murtagh it is possible that the southern part of the extension of the city begun in the reign of King John was not completely walled until the fifteenth century.[50] And in the heart of the original pre-Norman city centre

C. O'Rahilly and M. O'Sullivan have revealed that the thirteenth-century crypt in the Deanery Garden was extensively enlarged in the fifteenth and sixteenth centuries.[51] The 'hiatus' or gap in the archaeological record for the occupation of medieval sites in Ireland in the later middle ages is both a common and puzzling feature to the medieval archaeologist. Fanning remarked on this in his Clontuskert report as the small finds from the fifteenth century, apart from some iron keys, were very limited. And this is at direct variance with both the documentary evidence and with the amount of extant sculptural carving in the priory itself. The pattern of coin loss also reveals a gap at this period.[52] At many of the Anglo-Norman stone castles, such as Trim and Ferns, there is also a lack of occupation evidence for the fourteenth century. Of course this gap could be explained simply by highlighting the degree of population decrease in this period as a direct result of the political and economic disorders. However, in such a disturbed period of history people would surely be drawn to sheltering in solidly built stone structures such as castles and religious houses and so, theoretically, there should be much more evidence for late medieval settlement than there is at the present time. Perhaps the excavations in such sites as castles and religious houses as well as in urban areas have not been on a large enough scale to produce this evidence, or perhaps a re-examination is required of the chronology of medieval small finds and especially of medieval pottery. This would either lead to the gap being effectively closed or, alternatively, re-emphasize and reinforce its existence with all the attendant ramifications for the medieval settlement pattern generally in the later middle ages.

It would also seem that not all the major east coast ports were flourishing. Apart from the particular problems of Wexford,[53] the available evidence would suggest that Cork was also going through a very depressed time at the end of the medieval period. Excavations in the medieval city such as the one directed by C. Papazian in 1984 at Tobin Street on the backyards of thirteenth- and fourteenth-century houses which fronted onto the street indicated that the period of medieval occupation was quite short, dating from the mid-thirteenth to the second or third decade of the fourteenth century.[54] This would confirm the historical record that also showed that Cork was badly hit by plague, political unrest and the economic recession which affected so many aspects of the late medieval urban life. Earlier excavations by Twohig of UCC in 1975 behind the medieval street frontage on South Main Street revealed occupation there between 1200 and 1400, similar to that found at Tobin Street.[55] Of course, this is not to say that there was no development at all in Cork city in the later middle ages as Twohig also revealed the remains of Skiddy's Castle, a tower-house erected in 1445, and the fragmentary foundations of the College of the Holy Trinity, built in 1482, in other excavations.[56] Perhaps the very fact that tower-houses were now being erected in urban areas such as Cork indicates the growing problem of law and order in the late medieval period.

Indeed the construction of these tower-houses all over Ireland in the later middle ages in both rural and urban environments is one indicator that there were the necessary resources available on a large scale to construct such substantial stone edifices. It must also be remembered that the fifteenth century saw the construction of over forty new friaries mainly in the west of the country. These two developments alone should be sufficient to make scholars wary of classing the fourteenth and fifteenth centuries in Ireland as a period of complete economic decline and consequent social chaos and disorder. What these tower-houses and friaries do indicate, rather, is the shift away from centralized authority, whether in Dublin or Westminster, towards the growth in regional power bases, such as that exercised by the great Anglo-Irish families, including the Ormonds or the Kildares, or powerful Gaelic families such as the O'Neills. This character-ized the period from the beginning of the fourteenth century until the Elizabethan reconquest. This retreat in the area under the sway of the English Crown or its Irish representatives is nowhere better illustrated than in the constant shrinking of the area around Dublin to be fortified by a static line of defence comprising a bank and an interior fosse, known as the 'Pale'. Although there are several documentary references from the mid-fifteenth century to a Pale ditch being dug to defend the Anglo-Irish heartland against the worst ravages of the Gaelic Irish, it is unlikely that a continuous line of defence was erected all along its probable length from around Ardee, Co. Louth, in the north to the port of Dalkey just south of Dublin (fig. 36).[57] Although taxes were levied in order to assist in the expenses of building this barrier it was obviously not to be the equivalent of the modern-day Berlin Wall. Money and labour were often diverted into other projects such as the erection of tower-houses or frittered away due to corruption and inefficiency. Thus only a few actual lengths of ditch were probably dug, such as the still surviving portion at Clongowes, Co. Kildare.[58]

There appear to have been several tower-houses built along the supposed line of the Pale which were probably erected by the landlord of the area as a strongpoint to which he could retreat if necessary. For instance at Kilteel in Co. Kildare near to a medieval church there are the remains of a preceptory of the Knights Hospitallers which was probably founded by the Fitzgeralds in the thirteenth century. Its most impressive remaining structure is a fifteenth-century five-storied tower-house and gateway. It is an impressive defensive feature and from its roof what would seem to be another part of the Pale ditch runs in an easterly direction towards its eventual end on the coast south of Dalkey where, incidentally, there are three surviving urban tower-houses. This ditch and other associated earthworks can be seen in the aerial photograph which Manning used to help illustrate his church excavation report (pl. 21 and fig. 37). It is probable, therefore, that this preceptory functioned as an important border stronghold on the Pale in the later middle ages at this vulnerable point where it bends eastward from its southwards progress.[59]

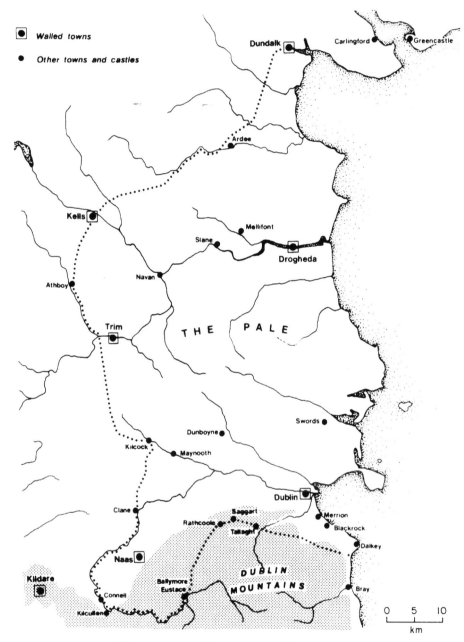

Figure 36 Map of the Pale in the fifteenth century

Plate 21 Aerial photograph of Kilteel Church, Co. Kildare, showing remains of the Pale ditch to the west and south

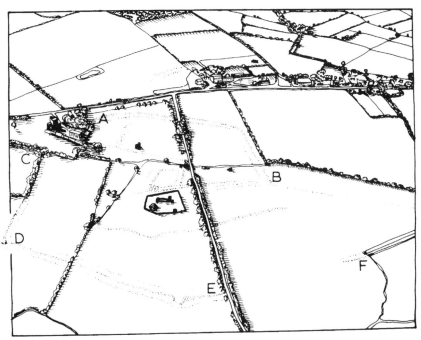

Figure 37 Interpretative tracing of Kilteel aerial photograph (plate 21)

Plate 23 Tower house at Castlegrove, Co. Galway

In the interpretive tracing of Kilteel (fig 37) letters A and B indicate the remains of a large enclosure, probably of medieval date, while letters C, D, E and F mark the linear earthwork which is almost certainly part of the Pale. Its ditch is up to 3.5 m wide and 60 cm deep, and its interior bank is up to 6.5 m wide and 60 cm high.

These tower-houses were a compromise between the large stone castles of the Anglo-Norman period and the undefended Elizabethan mansions, as exemplified by the one surviving example erected about 1568 by Thomas, Earl of Ormond, beside the River Suir at Carrick-on-Suir, Co. Tipperary (pl. 22). Altogether it has been calculated that the overwhelming majority of the 3,000 castles in Ireland would have been tower-houses. This would have made Ireland the most heavily castellated part of the British Isles by the seventeenth century.[60] The main element of such a dwelling was a single tower (pl. 23) which was the most cost-effective form of defence for an individual of fairly limited means who needed such a fortified structure to protect himself and his family against raiding or the minor outbreaks of warfare which seem to have been such a common occurrence in late medieval Irish society. In many cases there would also have been a bawn or a fortified enclosure either surrounding the tower or joined on to the tower itself. The examples that survive, such as at Knockkelly, Co. Tipperary, are of stone but there are documentary references to them being constructed of wooden palisades, wattled walls or even out of earthen sods or hedges.[61] Within these bawns would have been located the ancillary domestic or agricultural buildings normally associated with the manor house of an influential family. It must be remembered, too, that there were also some very fine massive tower-houses in Counties Clare, Cork and Galway, such as Bunratty, Co. Clare and Blarney, Co. Cork. Until recently it was believed that tower-houses mainly date to the period immediately after the 1429 grant of a £10 subsidy to the King's 'liege men' in Dublin, Meath, Kildare and Louth who built towers to at least the minimum size of 20 by 16 ft in plan and 40 ft or more in height. The success of this subsidy can be gauged by the fact that twenty years later, in 1449, a limit was imposed upon their erection. However, in a recent PhD thesis, C. T. Cairns has shown for Co. Tipperary that there is some limited historical evidence for the construction of some of these towers in the fourteenth century, although the peak of their popularity was between 1400 and 1650.[62] He also almost doubled Leask's original figure to 410 definite and 63 possible examples in the county, although only about 20 per cent could be safely dated.[63] Nevertheless, Cairns suggests that tower-houses began to be built around 1300 in Ireland. Documentary evidence for 1300 and 1305 for Counties Offaly and Wexford show that there was already an established procedure for the subsidizing of 'fortalices', which were essentially tower-houses, either by the Dublin or local government. There are also references to fortalices guarding the marches in 1343–4 and 1358–9. Further references to the construction of castles in Ulster in 1352, only two years after the end of the Black Death in

Ireland, shows that there was not a significant hiatus in their construction at any time in the fourteenth century.[64]

If Cairns's figures for Co. Tipperary could be tentatively extrapolated for the country as a whole it would give even greater emphasis to counties such as Galway, Clare and Limerick which, although largely outside Anglo-Irish control, have the densest distribution patterns of tower-houses (fig. 38). It is

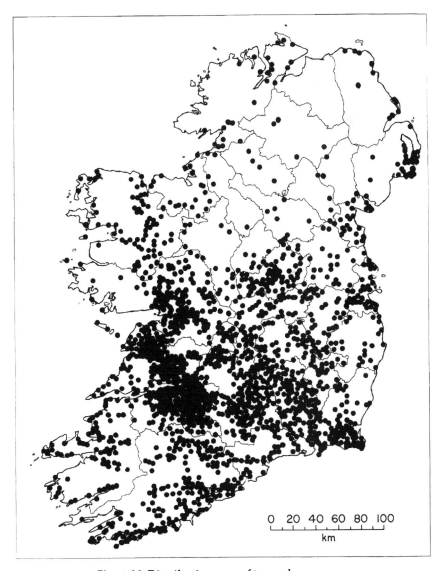

Figure 38 Distribution map of tower-houses

interesting to note that although Cairns suggests an Anglo-Norman origin for the earliest tower-houses they became even more popular in Gaelic areas in the later middle ages, probably because they were the ideal combination of a comfortable dwelling and a fortified residence.

There has been much debate about the probable origins of tower-houses, with O'Danachair proposing that their inspiration was 'undoubtedly' from parts of continental Europe. He also argued that Irish examples had no direct link with Scottish towers and this conclusion is borne out by their distribution as there are relatively few examples in Ulster, the closest part of Ireland to Scotland and because the architectural design of the towers in both countries was also very different.[65] Scotland and Ireland do, however, share a common architectural tradition which is different from that of contemporary England. This has led writers such as C. T. Cairns and J. J. Smith to suggest that these towers were being constructed in Northumberland, Scotland and Ireland as a response by those who could afford the outlay to build houses with some defensive capabilities in the insecure society in which they found themselves. Thus their general consensus is that these towers evolved multilaterally in many parts of the world to meet specific defensive needs in an economically viable fashion.[66]

O'Danachair believes, however, that Irish towers evolved in generally peaceful times and that their major function was not defensive. This theory does not really hold up when the distribution maps of tower-houses are examined for the whole of Britain and Ireland, as Ireland, Scotland and northern England all have concentrations of towers, while Wales and the rest of England had the more residential hall-houses in the more secure society that flourished there in the later middle ages. Obviously the defensive element in their construction was of primary importance and in some cases, such as the 1429 subsidy and the erection of some towers along the Pale, there were even military factors which were of importance. A. Davin's research on the towers of the Pale has revealed that in Counties Kildare, Meath and Louth they were concentrated along the borders of the Pale. However, in Co. Dublin, although the towers to the south of the River Liffey were mainly to be found at the base of the Wicklow mountains where the Anglo-Irish settlements were most open to attack, the towers to the north of the river were generally larger and more elaborate.[67]

There is at least one other area where it would appear that the siting of tower-houses was governed by strategic considerations. This was the line erected along the northern borders of the two southernmost baronies of Forth and Bargy in Co. Wexford, probably as a defence against the encroachment of the MacMurrough Kavanaghs in the fifteenth century.[68] But in the other regions where their distribution pattern has been examined more closely it has generally been found that they were primarily located in areas with good agricultural land which also had easy communications. For instance, research by Cunningham has shown that the O'Carrolls did not seem to have sited their eleven known towers in places where they could have protected the lands they owned in Ely O'Carroll in Co. Offaly and northern Tipperary. For Tipperary as a whole Cairns has found that these same locational factors also operated for he wrote that 'there seems to have been little effort at co-ordinated territorial defence by groups of towers'.[69] Thus he found that they were concentrated in the most fertile areas of Tipperary, around towns such as Nenagh, Thurles, Clonmel, Cashel and Fethard.

There has also been research by Murtagh on the urban tower-houses of Ireland which has elucidated several aspects of their chronology and function.[70] But what is needed now is a work of synthesis encompassing the roles played by rural, urban and ecclesiastical towers in the late middle ages in Ireland. For instance there has yet to be an examination as to how these urban and ecclesiastical towers differed in architectural and functional terms from their more common rural counterparts. Many more regional studies also need to be undertaken, similar to those for the Pale counties of Dublin, Kildare, Meath and Louth as well as for Co. Tipperary, to see whether the distribution and chronology of the towers in these regions are directly comparable with the situation in the rest of the country.

There has only been one fully published excavation of a tower-house in recent years, that of Dunboy Castle, Co. Cork. However, there have been short interim reports on at least two others: one situated beneath the later seventeenth-century Parke's Castle in Co. Leitrim, and another of a tower-house bawn on Aughinish Island, Co. Limerick. The excavation by Foley of the OPW at Parke's Castle, Co. Leitrim, from 1972–4 discovered the foundations of a fifteenth- to sixteenth-century tower-house under the cobbled courtyard of a later Plantation castle which had been the source of stone for the later building. Its dimensions were 12.05 m long and 9.05 m wide and it was divided into two rooms. Interestingly enough, she also located an 8 m-wide and 2 m-deep moat associated with the tower-house, a feature that does not often survive into the modern landscape. A gully was also discovered close to the south wall of the tower which was probably where the garderobe deposits collected. The small finds associated with this period of occupation included horseshoes, knives, buckles and bronze harp pins and showed that the windows had glass in them. The finding of an Edward IV coin also helped with the dating of this first phase of occupation into the fifteenth century.[71]

In another small excavation in 1974 Lynch, then of the Department of Archaeology, UCC, excavated the bawn of a late-sixteenth- to early-seventeenth-century tower-house sited in a roughly circular enclosure on Aughinish Island, Co. Limerick. A section cut across the north bawn wall revealed that it was well built, 2.2 m thick, and constructed directly on the limestone bedrock. Other trial trenches traced the full line of the bawn wall which was roughly circular in plan with no evidence for flankers. The entrance was on the south side and was 3.5 m wide. No evidence for a ditch was located to the exterior of the bawn although the remains of what was interpreted as a domed oven were excavated in its northern section. A curious feature was the discovery of thirty-one skeletons, mostly concentrated in the northern half of the bawn, which were mainly of young children and babies. As well as sherds of late medieval and post medieval pottery, iron objects, clay pipe fragments, a blue glass bead, a bronze disc-headed pin, and a 1683 Irish halfpenny were also located.[72]

Excavations during the summer months of 1967–73 at Dunboy Castle, Co. Cork, by the late E. M. Fahy of the Department of Geography, UCC, uncovered a complex sequence of occupation dating from the fifteenth to the eighteenth century. The first phase was represented by the stump of a tower-house which was dated by the late-fifteenth-century pottery fragments uncovered by the excavation. Its walls were of green–grey sandstone on solid rock foundations and had a slight external batter. The approximate external dimensions were 16.8 by 12.8 m, and its arrangement of mural staircase, windows, and guard cells were all comparable to those found in surviving examples in the county. It was probably c.20 m in height with three upper floors if it was broadly similar to the majority of tower-houses known in Co. Cork. The bawn wall which was probably contemporary with the tower was traced along the southern and eastern sides of the site and was found to have a width of c.1.3 m with two external towers. Then in the spring of 1602 when it became clear to O'Sullivan Beare, its owner at the time, that it would be besieged, a secondary bawn wall was constructed. Part of this wall along the east side of the tower lay across a large rock-cut pond of the first phase of occupation, and water could be drawn from it through a slab covered opening at its base, probably for use in a siege. The later history of this site falls outside the chronological compass of this book but it is of some interest to note that the castle was besieged in 1602 and was eventually replaced by a star-plan fort in the middle of the seventeenth century.[73]

These excavations have not really added much to our general knowledge of the subsidiary buildings likely to be found in the tower-house bawns. As these subsidiary buildings are often less soundly constructed than the tower itself they do not usually survive into the present landscape. Often it is only by a study of the later documents, and especially from the seventeenth-century Civil Survey, when it survives, that some idea can be reached about the buildings that once surrounded many tower-houses. We know, for instance, that some towers in Co. Tipperary had up to twenty 'cabins' associated with them. Other features mentioned in the Civil Survey were grist or corn mills as well as gardens and orchards. Sometimes towers have houses beside them which are of the same scale or indeed larger than the original tower. Such examples as Carrick, Kilcash, Ballynakill and Loughmoe are all signs of expansion in the last century or so of the tower-building period.[74]

Apart from the tower-house the other major type of new construction in the later middle ages was the friaries. Leask has calculated that over forty new friaries of the Franciscan, Dominican and Augustinian orders were established in Ireland between 1400 and the beginning of the sixteenth century.[75] The Franciscan Third Order or Tertiaries also set up around forty houses for both sexes in the first half of the fifteenth century.[76] This success is in marked contrast to the situation in England where there were no known houses of Tertiaries, and Scotland where only two were set up in the middle ages. It would seem that the ethos of the order appealed to the Irish, so much so that it was most popular in Connacht where the Gaelic Irish were in the ascendancy. However, their houses have often not survived to the present day, mainly because they were often small in size and did not possess many domestic buildings. Leask was, nevertheless, so impressed by the numbers of these late houses surviving that he wrote: 'It is evident, indeed, that the economic condition of the country had improved after the passing of the calamitous years of the fourteenth century.'[77]

One of the very few of these late friaries to have been excavated is St Mary's Priory on Devenish Island in Co. Fermanagh, an Augustinian house which may have been founded as early as the twelfth century; the surviving remains of the church and cloister, though, are of fifteenth- to early-sixteenth-century date (fig. 39). It is possible that the original twelfth-century monastery may have been sited on lower ground below the fifteenth-century buildings but this is only conjectural at present as it is based on a number of carved Romanesque stones found in the general area. The excavations proper concentrated upon the east range and only uncovered three stratified finds which could have been earlier than the fifteenth century: two sherds of English glazed pottery and a twelfth-century bronze ringed pin. In the church there survives an inscription which records building work here in 1449 but the excavations showed that this was disrupted later in the century by a serious fire. In the east range the fire can be dated to c.1500 or soon after from the imported pottery found there, and this was given added weight by a radiocarbon date ranging from 1470 to 1520 for the destruction level. It was difficult for Waterman to be sure how long the east range remained in use although they might still have been in an inhabitable condition as late as the beginning of the seventeenth century.[78]

Another example of a late friary to have been excavated, again in Ulster, was Massereene in Co. Antrim, a house of the Franciscan Third Order, but which has no visible remains today. It was reputedly founded in Antrim town in about 1500 by one of the O'Neills and it was eventually located by Lynn of the Historic Monuments Branch, Ministry of Finance (NI) in advance of a new bypass road which was to be constructed around the western side of the town. During the two seasons of excavation in 1973–4 the entire outline of the church foundations was revealed. It was a simple rectangle, with external dimensions of 29.25 by 8.5 m, and with its walls ranging in width from 80 cm to 1.15 m. As the interior of the church was full of burials none of the original floor survived, and no architectural details,

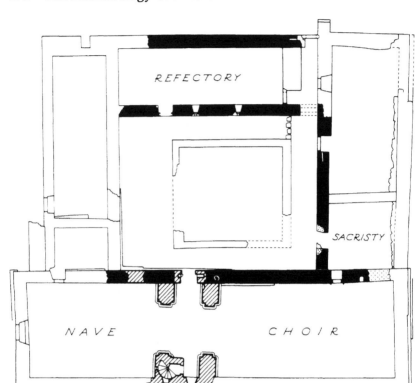

Figure 39 Plan of St Mary's Priory, Devenish, Co. Fermanagh

internal structures or even the position of a door were located. However, evidence was found at its south-east end for the construction of a tower-house-type structure.[79]

At the western end of the church Lynn located a V-shaped ditch, 2–3 m wide and 2 m deep, which was dated by the finding of eleven coins in its silt which were probably in circulation from 1501 to 1505. It did not fully enclose the church but swung off to the north to join the Six-Mile-Water, and therefore its purpose seems to have been primarily for drainage rather than defence. Evidence for the position of an entrance causeway over this ditch was found some 10 m south of the west end of the church and it would also have appeared that the ditch was roughly paved over while the church was still in use.[80]

The archaeological evidence for this friary is of interest as everything found there seemed to have been very reliably restricted in date to the sixteenth century. In the church itself an almost complete everted-rim cooking pot was found along with some iron knives and a buckle, as well as eleven coins of AD 1601 which were situated in the base of the topsoil. In the ditch more everted-rim pottery was located along with an iron coulter pushed into a plough-sock. Cartographic and documentary evidence would suggest that the friary was remodelled later in the sixteenth century to become a fort of the Elizabethan wars but there was no direct archaeological evidence for this.

Apart from these two excavations there were also excavations of the important Cistercian Abbey of the Holy Cross in Co. Tipperary in the 1960s, and although they have yet to be published we know from the surviving remains that the abbey was virtually rebuilt by the Earls of Ormond in the fifteenth century. The extensive reconstruction included a new chancel and transept with a graceful east window and ribbed vaulting. Inside the chancel there is a structure which probably housed the relic of the True Cross that the monastery held in the middle ages. The north transept also has a fifteenth-century mural of a hunting scene. The church has recently been extensively reconstructed for modern worship and work is also proceeding on the sizeable remains of the claustral buildings of the monastery.

Another Cistercian foundation, Kilcooly Abbey in north Co. Tipperary, was almost completely levelled by an armed force of men in 1444. Here again the Ormond Butlers instigated a programme of reconstruction which removed the nave aisles and added a new north transept and tower. Other religious houses that underwent extensive rebuilding in this century include the Augustinian priory at Clontuskert, Co. Galway (see chapter 6), and cathedrals such as St Mary's in Limerick.

However, it was the new wave of the construction of Franciscan friaries in the south and west throughout the fifteenth century that probably had the greatest single impact on late medieval religious settlement patterns. With these later foundations it would appear that construction proceeded often in a piecemeal fashion as funds became available from the nearby lay communities. This was in almost complete contrast to the monasteries of the early middle ages which were often founded by rich and powerful patrons. Thus the buildings of these later friaries were often simple and more easily adaptable to the rapidly changing conditions of the later period. There are also other differences between these and thirteenth-century foundations, such as the fact that the domestic buildings of the new foundations usually lie to the north of the church. Also, whereas the older houses were set up in towns, fifteenth- and sixteenth-century houses were founded in rural areas, either close to small towns or to the chief settlement of their Irish founders. But in their general layout the friaries generally followed the Cistercian plan: a quadrangular cloister garth bounded on one side by the church and on the other sides by three ranges of domestic buildings. In many cases there were additional attached structures and also a few extra courtyards surrounded by more buildings. The functions of these additional buildings is often not very clear and this is one area in which archaeological investigations might help to provide some useful answers.

One such friary that symbolized the break from the past is Quin, Co. Clare, which was constructed after 1433 by the Macnamaras on top of the remains of a thirteenth-century de Clare castle which had been captured by the family in the early fourteenth century (fig. 40). Thus its siting illustrates the dominance of the Gaelic tradition over the Anglo-Irish with the earlier castle providing the building-stone necessary for the friary. The southern

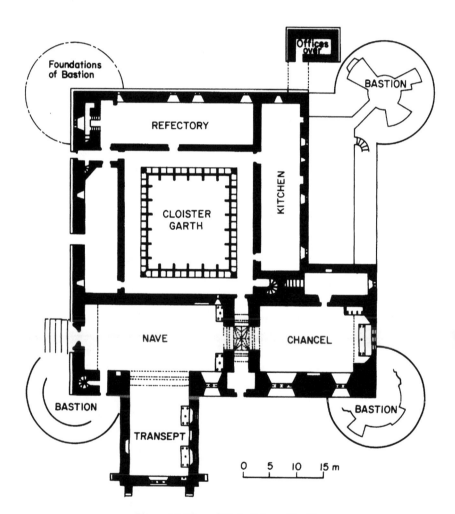

Figure 40 Plan of Quin Friary, Co. Clare

curtain wall of the castle was reutilized as the south wall of the nave and chancel church, and the east and west ends of the church were also built on to the corresponding walls of the castle. At the east end the thick castle wall had to be considerably altered to accommodate the triple-light window. A very tall tower separated the nave and the chancel and there was also the usual nave extension. Finally, the claustral buildings here have extensive remains: cloisters with slightly pointed arches in pairs with buttresses separating them.[81] Other major Franciscan friaries in the west include Ross Errilly, Co. Galway, probably not begun before 1498, which was the largest and best preserved of these fifteenth-century foundations. As de Breffny correctly emphasized, 'Its size in a fairly isolated and sparsely populated region bears witness to the popularity of the Franciscans and the upsurge of monastic vocations at this time.'[82] Other impressive remains include the friary at Askeaton, Co. Limerick, probably built between 1420 and 1440, and Muckross near Killarney, Co. Kerry, founded in 1448 and completed within fifty years. All these houses as well as those that are either less completely preserved or especially those of which no trace is now visible would repay archaeological excavation to elucidate their chronological development.

The later middle ages also saw the construction of new parish churches and substantial additions to existing ones. In Ulster this patronage by Gaelic chiefs was an especial feature of the western parts of the Province. In Co. Fermanagh, for instance, Carrick Church was founded by Gilbert O'Flanagan and Margaret Maguire in the late fifteenth century, while the church at Aghalurcher was an important burial ground for the Maguires, although only the basal foundations of its east end now survive. But it was within the Pale that some of the largest new churches were erected, often with much English influence on their window designs. They were usually simple nave and chancel churches although with fortified towers at their west end. There is a famous group of three such churches at Killeen, Dunsany, and Rathmore, all in Co. Meath which were built by the powerful Plunket family. In Howth, Co. Dublin, the eastern part of the south aisle of the late medieval collegiate parish church of the Blessed Virgin Mary (pl. 24) was remodelled by the St Lawrences in the fifteenth century to serve as a family chantry. In it still stands the tomb of Sir Christopher St Lawrence, thirteenth Baron of Howth, who died in 1462, and his wife Anna Plunket of Ratoath, Co. Meath. Outside the Pale it is hardly surprising that a strong residential tower was *de rigueur* by the fifteenth century. Examples of these are to be found at the churches of Kiltinan, Co. Tipperary, and Taghmon, Co. Westmeath.

Finally in this chapter some consideration must be given to the question of where the Gaelic Irish population was living in the later middle ages, or at least that sizeable part of it that was not either dwelling in tower-houses or living in Anglo-Irish towns and villages. Of course, if the theoretical possibility of the existence of 'proto-clachans' in the medieval period is

Plate 24 St Mary's Church, Howth, Co. Dublin

accepted, then these undefended house clusters would have accounted for much of the indigenous rural population, and especially the lower stratum of that population. K. W. Nicholls has put forward the suggestion that transient settlement features may have been an important component in the Irish landscape in the later middle ages.[83] These 'impermanent agglomerations' would have comprised flimsy house structures that could be taken up quickly when the inhabitants moved from summer to winter pasturage or vice versa. It would be valuable to assess what proportion of the rural settlement pattern of the later medieval period was made up of these transient settlements, especially in the area beyond the Pale. Several sixteenth-century writers make some mention of this type of settlement. For instance, in 1596 Bishop Lyons of Cork wrote that 'the people of Munster do commonly dwell dispersed'.[84] Any attempts to trace the evidence for these transient settlements archaeologically would be almost impossible without the remote sensing techniques now available. Perhaps a refinement of the scientific methods for tracing phosphate deposits as employed by F. W. Hamond at the medieval nucleated settlement of Newcastle, Co. Dublin, might be very helpful in tracing such settlements as long as their approximate location is known.[85]

In this chapter I have tried to deal with the problem of what happened to the medieval settlement pattern, whether Anglo-Irish or Gaelic or indeed an admixture of both cultures, in the fourteenth and fifteenth centuries. These two centuries saw the dramatic reduction in the area of Ireland directly controlled by the English Crown through its officer in Dublin and the re-emergence of Gaelic influence and culture. This latter phenomenon is well reflected in the large numbers of tower-houses to be found in the west of the country and by the many friaries founded under the protection of the greater Gaelic families. But this Gaelic resurgence is a much more complex process than has hitherto been realized. Gone are the days when historians saw it in terms of the Anglo-Irish lordship slowly being pushed eastwards by the victorious Gael. Long before the middle of the fourteenth century there were large pockets of Irish within the bounds of the lordship, whether in the 'Irishtowns' of Kilkenny or Waterford or in their betagh settlements within the rural manors of the Anglo-Normans. By the later middle ages the processes of acculturation had resulted in there being at least three 'nations': the Irish, the Anglo-Irish and the English.[86] Thus to see the ebb and flow of settlements purely in terms of one side or the other gaining the upper hand is too simplistic an analysis in an island which was made up of a patchwork of many divided loyalties.

It is true, nevertheless, that the net result of the Bruce invasion, the Great Famine and the Black Death (all of which occurred in the first half of the fourteenth century) was to weaken or to destroy elements of the Anglo-Norman settlement pattern. Pressure by the Irish on the boundaries of the lordship also added to these forces, leading to the desertion of some small villages and boroughs in these localities. However, at the present stage of research, with only Counties Meath and Westmeath systematically examined for deserted medieval villages, it is not yet possible to quantify the scale and scope of these desertions. We do know, however, that by the 1350s the royal castles of Rinndown and Roscommon in Connacht were finally abandoned, and that the borough at Rinndown was probably deserted at the same period. Within about ten years the junior branches of the De Burgos also abandoned their last attempts to collect rents from their lands in west Connacht.[87] Further east in the Butler lordship of Tipperary and Kilkenny, although we know that the major towns were surviving behind their solid walls, in the countryside there appears to have been widespread depopulation and the abandonment of sizeable freeholdings.[88] But Nicholls sees the revival as only making sense in the long run in terms of economic utilization and land use by the switch from a predominantly tillage to a pastoral economy. I would further agree with him that any conclusions about the settlement pattern of late medieval Ireland can only be of an interim nature as the 'geographical manifestations [of the Gaelic resurgence] in the retreat alike of royal authority and colonial settlement patterns and the emergence of the autonomous lordships based on a largely pastoral economy . . .'[89] have been largely under-researched.

8 Future horizons

This book has been an attempt to show that medieval archaeology as a discipline has come of age in Ireland over the last thirty years or so. However, it must also be apparent that for a country so rich in medieval sites and monuments, research in Ireland has really only scratched the surface of the available evidence. How this might be improved in the future is difficult to say without a massive increase in both the funding and manpower of the principal state archaeological service, both in the Office of Public Works and in the National Museum of Ireland in the Republic of Ireland, and in the Historic Buildings and Monuments Section of the Department of the Environment and the Ulster Museum in Northern Ireland. The legislation protecting monuments was also in urgent need of updating as the original National Monument Act of 1930, as amended in 1954, was woefully inadequate to protect them against the encroachment of developers, whether rural or urban. An amendment act was passed in 1987 primarily to control metal detectors and underwater archaeology, and to increase the penalties for all infringements of the acts. A further amendment act is currently under discussion in the Dáil.

Another major problem is that we do not, as yet, possess either a complete listing or, indeed, a description of all archaeological sites throughout the country. In Northern Ireland the legislation is also currently being up-dated, but is generally only effective in protecting a number of the more important archaeological sites. Progress has recently been made in this area in both Northern Ireland where one county, Down, had had its sites published[1] and where the Archaeological Survey of Northern Ireland hopes to publish Armagh in the near future. Lists of all sites, known as sites and monuments records, for the other four counties have also been produced,[2] and the Republic sites and monuments inventories have recently been produced by the Archaeological Survey of Ireland for the counties of Louth, Meath and Monaghan. These will also be produced for every other county in the country, although County Louth has had a full survey published recently.[3] The archaeology departments of UCC and UCG are co-operating in surveys for Counties Cork and Galway, and an Urban Archaeological Survey is currently being carried out by Bradley. In 1985, in order to speed up the progress of the Survey a 'paper survey', employing only maps and published sources, was set up for a further sixteen counties.[4] As well as this there have been archaeological surveys carried out in various parts of the country.[5] As a result of all of this activity surveys of smaller more manageable areas such as baronies will be a feature of future publications outside the Archaeological Survey of Ireland. Thus by the early 1990s we should be in a much better position to know the number and quality of archaeological monuments throughout the country.

But if we are to narrow our focus to medieval sites in Ireland one of the major problems about archaeological research on them is the lack of any co-ordinated policy for future excavations. The great majority of excavations mentioned in this book have been 'rescue' projects, designed to test the archaeological horizons before a particular site is destroyed. Thus there are no 'research' excavations of important medieval sites in Ireland to parallel, for example, the long-term excavations of the important prehistoric passage graves of Newgrange and Knowth on the River Boyne in County Meath. There is also the school of thought that would argue that as the pace of destruction is so great, especially in urban areas, medieval archaeologists could profitably spend their whole time just doing rescue excavations. However, this book should have shown how many problems still remain to be answered by the archaeologist before we can hope to understand the socio-economic framework of the medieval past. Thus excavations and field-work in the future need to be problem-orientated so that key sites can be investigated in order to try and answer particular questions. Of course, one of the fascinations and indeed problems of archaeological exploration is the fact that until the excavation has been started it is impossible to know whether material remains at a site will be sufficient to answer any particular hypothesis. There also still remains the dichotomy between those archaeo-logists who believe a particular and entire site should be excavated to try and answer these questions and those who maintain that a whole range of sites should just be sampled to test several hypotheses.[6]

Future research in medieval archaeology in Ireland needs to be concen-trated into projects such as a co-ordinated programme of excavations on the large scale reuse of indigenous settlement sites by the Anglo-Normans for their military strongholds. Much more research also needs to be carried out into the ringwork castles and the linear earthworks in this first phase of the Anglo-Norman invasion. But perhaps even more than that, our almost complete lack of knowledge of the Gaelic Irish settlement pattern of the medieval period needs to be investigated, both within and beyond the borders of the Anglo-Irish lordship. Our current state of knowledge of even the types and forms of the Anglo-Norman villages and rural boroughs is also lamentably small. Despite the existence of the Group for the Study of Irish Historic Settlement set up by R. E. Glasscock in 1969 very little progress has been made in excavating other possible deserted medieval villages since the investigations at Caherguillamore in the early 1940s.[7] And our knowledge of the industrial processes of medieval Ireland, both rural and urban, is negligible in comparison with the situation in England. It is in the area of medieval urban archaeology that our knowledge of the socio-economic conditions of the major medieval ports, such as Dublin, Cork, Limerick and Waterford, has grown enormously over the past decade because of the large-scale excavations within them. And despite the overwhelming importance of the Church on medieval society our archaeological knowledge is dependent upon some limited excavations of Cistercian and Augustinian houses in the country with very little research upon the contribution of the other monastic orders or indeed upon the considerable impact of the friars, especially in the west. Also, there has been far too little attention paid to the development of the secular churches in both rural and urban environments.

Archaeology has, as yet, only made a very limited contribution to the debate on what was happening to settlement patterns in the later middle ages. It is still not possible to analyse fully the effects of such events as the Bruce invasion and the Black Death either on the towns or indeed on rural sites. It was at some juncture in the later middle ages that tower-houses became popular, probably with the Anglo-Normans first and then with the Gaelic nobility, but we are not sure exactly when and how this switch occurred. At this time also, several Anglo-Irish towns were being fortified against the 'Irish enemy' and a Pale ditch was constructed around the environs of Dublin to protect the area of English influence and to prevent cattle being raided from within that area, although we are still unsure of its actual extent.[8]

As to how future research into medieval archaeology in Ireland would best be co-ordinated, this is problematic at the present time because the state archaeological services in the Republic of Ireland may be restructured in the near future. However, whether this will entail some internal reorganization of the various bodies, or whether archaeology will come under the umbrella of a semi-state body such as a Heritage Council much on the lines of English Heritage has yet to be established. It is a moot point whether medieval – especially urban – sites will be given any higher priority than at present, because of the very high costs of such excavations. Perhaps an added impetus might be given to this if a department of medieval archaeology were set up in one of the universities in Ireland or in one of the other institutions of higher education. This would help somewhat to redress the imbalance that presently applies, as the prehistoric and the Early Christian periods currently have the most attention paid to them by the academic archaeological community. It would, however, be beyond the resources of one department to establish a strategy for future research and to carry it out. But it could at least help to bring the necessary pressure to bear in the right quarters for such a programme to become a feasible possibility.

Some idea of the progress such a development could make to the study of medieval archaeology can be gained by an examination of the work of several voluntary bodies over the last few years. Perhaps the one with the highest public profile is the 'Friends of Medieval Dublin', who became closely associated with the fight to have the important Viking and early medieval site at Wood Quay and Fishamble Street in Dublin adequately excavated and preserved. They may not have fully succeeded in their twin aims but they did mobilize thousands of people in two protest marches through Dublin to try and save the site. They were also very successful as a pressure group in changing people's opinion about the positive aspects of the Viking presence in Ireland.

The nearest equivalent in Ireland to the Medieval Settlement Research Group is the Group for the Study of Irish Historic Settlement, which holds an annual conference in different regions of Ireland on various aspects of historic settlement. Central to the group's interests is medieval settlement, and 1985 has seen the publication of the first monograph in a series, *Irish Settlement Studies*, on 'Anglo-Norman settlement in Ireland' by B. J. Graham, the current president. The earlier *Bulletin* of the Group also tended to concentrate upon the medieval period while not forgetting post-medieval developments. It is a pity that because of the many other commitments of its committee the group could not increase both the number and the diversity of its activities, especially in regard to increasing an awareness among the community as a whole about the importance of medieval and post-medieval settlement forms.

Since the 1970s the Dublin Historic Settlement Group has met regularly during term time in UCD to hear papers read on different aspects of settlement history. This has meant that historians, archaeologists, historical geographers and other interested academics have had the opportunity to discuss these papers within a mutually beneficial interdisciplinary environment. At its inception the Group planned to study the settlement evolution of a particular area, that of Co. Meath, and also to publish the papers in a single volume. However, it has since developed away from this original plan and its seminar papers now cover all aspects of settlement in Ireland.

All these three organizations have acted as pressure groups in the preservation of medieval monuments and in calling for new legislation to protect them in the future. However, there is no Irish equivalent to the Society for Medieval Archaeology, although this London-based society does publish articles on Ireland and has recently begun to include the island in the summaries of excavation reports published in each volume of their journal, *Medieval Archaeology*.[9] Indeed over the past four years (during which Ireland has been included in these summaries) there has been a remarkable amount of work reported. This large number of medieval excavations, the majority of which were 'rescue digs', has meant that the data base for medieval archaeology in Ireland is rapidly growing all the time. However, with the rising costs of printing and publishing generally it is difficult to see how many of these excavations will be adequately reported in the archaeological journals. Nevertheless, there have recently been some encouraging developments such as the publication of the first volume in the Archaeological Monograph Series of the Royal Irish Academy on Knowth[10] which will be followed by some medieval titles. There is also the imminent publication of a series of monographs on the excavations in Dublin by the National Museum of Ireland, also in association with the RIA.[11] Additionally, there is the increasing trend for published excavation reports to contain the minimum amount of data for the reader to understand the interpretation of a particular site by the archaeologist, and to include all the detailed information in microfiche cards in a pocket at the back of the publication. Alternatively the publication will state where the field notes, plans, drawings, photographs and artefacts can be consulted by interested scholars.

Despite the problems facing archaeology in Ireland in the foreseeable future there have also been many areas of spectacular growth and achievement. Of these, the most useful to the medieval archaeologist are the increasing interdisciplinary research on medieval settlement by historians and historical geographers alongside the archaeologists; advances in scientific dating methods and especially dendrochronology; the impact of environmental archaeology; the increasing use of computers both on site and later for the analysis and retrieval of data; and, finally, an increasing public awareness of our heritage in a rapidly changing world. For all these reasons, despite the many problems of site destruction and the export of antiquities, the future looks bright for medieval archaeology in Ireland and we can agree with the sentiments of A. Simms that 'with a sigh of relief we can now say that medieval archaeology in Ireland has come of age'.[12]

Notes

1 Introduction

1 MacNiocaill 1975.
2 'Survey of the memoranda rolls . . .',
   51–134.
3 *Ormond Deeds, 1172–1603.*
4 *CDI.*
5 *Hist. and mun. doc. Ire.*
6 *Cal. Alen's Reg.*
7 *Knights' fees.*
8 *CDI*, I, no 1176.
9 Sweetman 1978a, 130.
10 ibid., 187.
11 ibid.
12 *Chartul. St Mary's, Dublin.*
13 *Acc. Roll Holy Trinity, Dublin.*
14 *Reg. St Thomas, Dublin.*
15 *Ir. chartul. Llanthony.*
16 *Reg. Tristernagh.*
17 'Chart. Duiske, Kilkenny'.
18 *Acc. Roll Holy Trinity, Dublin*, 36–40.
19 ibid., 60–1.
20 ibid.
21 ibid., 55, and see p. 99.
22 ibid., 61.
23 PRO, S.C. 6, 1237–9.
24 Mills 1892.
25 Hore 1900–11.
26 Lyons 1984.
27 Lydon 1973, and see p. 87.
28 Hand 1957, 274.
29 Barry 1977, 128.
30 'Cal. Liber Ruber'.

31 Barry 1977; McNeill 1973; Walton 1980.
32 Barry 1977, 131.
33 Armagh, Reeve MSS (safe).
34 See p. 122.
35 See pp. 47–8.
36 *Ann. of Ire.*
37 ibid., 38.
38 MacNiocaill 1975, 37–9, 41.
39 *Ann. Con.*
40 *Ann. Inisf.*
41 *ALC.*
42 *AU.*
43 K. W. Nicholls, conference paper,
   25 February 1985, TCD.
44 Ó Ríordáin and Hunt 1942.
45 Especially Mr Leo Swan and Ms
   Daphne Pochin-Mould.
46 Herity 1983.
47 BKS, and Irish Air Surveys, Balgriffin,
   Co. Dublin.
48 Dolley 1972; Nicholls 1972; Lydon 1973.
49 Frame 1981; Cosgrove 1981.
50 Barker 1977, 203.
51 Mook and Waterbolk 1985.
52 Baillie 1982.
53 Baillie 1985, 22.
54 Tebbutt, Rudd and Moorhouse 1971.
55 Wilson 1982.
56 Alcock 1972.
57 Woodman 1981–2.

2 Pre-Norman settlement *c*.1000–1169

1 Ó Ríordáin 1979, 29.
2 Evans 1964, 235.
3 O'Kelly 1962b.
4 Co. Donegal: Lacy 1983; Co. Down:
  ASCD 1966; Co. Louth: Buckley 1986;
  Co. Meath: Moore 1987; Co.
  Monaghan: Brindley 1986; Ikerrin: Stout 1984; *Corca Dhuibhne*: Cuppage 1986.
5 Barrett 1972; 1980.
6 O'Kelly 1970.
7 Barrett and Graham 1975.
8 Jones-Hughes 1970, 247.
9 Nicholls 1972.
10 O'Corráin 1972.
11 Proudfoot 1977, 90.
12 Pers. comm., Mr J. Bradley, Urban
  Archaeology Survey.
13 Jope 1952.
14 Baillie 1979, 72.
15 Barry 1981a, 314.
16 Buckley 1986, 69–70 and pers. comm.,
  Mr P. D. Sweetman.
17 Proudfoot 1977, 93.
18 Barrett 1972.
19 McErlean 1983, 333.
20 ibid., 332.
21 Barrett 1982, 252.
22 Price 1963.
23 Jones-Hughes 1970, 253.
24 Flanagan 1978.
25 Graham 1979.
26 Proudfoot 1959, 110.
27 Norman and St Joseph 1969.
28 Pers. comm., Mr P. D. Sweetman.
29 Barrett 1980, 35.
30 ibid.
31 ibid., 36.
32 Herity and Eogan 1977, 226.
33 O'Corráin 1972, 52–61.
34 Ó Ríordáin 1979, 66.
35 Mr P. Gosling, conference paper,
  30 April 1983, Dundalk.
36 Williams 1985, 75.
37 Baillie 1975, 26.
38 Baillie 1979, 82.
39 ibid.
40 Manning 1983–4.
41 Fanning 1981b, 158.
42 ibid.
43 O'Kelly 1958.
44 Fanning 1981b, 160.
45 Swan 1983, 273–7.
46 Hurley 1979. 74.
47 *AU* I, 425; II, 87, 151–3.
48 Brown and Harper 1984.
49 *Frag. Ann.* 167.
50 Clarke and Simms 1985, 685.
51 *Cogadh Gaedhel re Gallaibh*, 12–13.
52 Wallace 1978, 24.
53 Wallace 1982, 140–1.
54 Graham-Campbell 1976, 40.
55 Hall 1984.
56 Wallace 1985b.
57 Wallace 1978, 24.
58 Unpublished prelim. report, OPW,
  9–11.
59 ibid., 11–13.
60 ibid., 12–13.
61 ibid., 13–15.

3 Anglo-Norman military fortifications

1 McNeill 1980, 102–3.
2 Ó Ríordáin 1979, 56.
3 Barry 1983.
4 ibid., 299, 308.
5 Orpen 1911–20, II.
6 Glasscock 1975.
7 Graham 1980b.
8 Pers. comm., Mr P. D. Sweetman, 1986.
9 Caulfield forthcoming.
10 *Chart. St. Mary's, Dublin*, II, 279, 312.
11 Barker and Barton 1977.
12 Talbot 1972.
13 McNeill 1980, 84–5.
14 Lynn 1981–2, 99.
15 Culleton and Colfer 1974–5.
16 Barry, Culleton and Empey 1984.
17 Waterman 1959a.
18 Hope-Taylor 1950.
19 *Oibre* 1965, 22.
20 Clough: Waterman 1954a, 119;
  Lismahon: Waterman 1959a, 147.
21 Dromore: Waterman 1954b; Clough:
  Waterman 1954a.
22 *ASCD*.

206 The Archaeology of Medieval Ireland

23 Waterman 1959a, 164–9.
24 Glasscock and McNeill 1972, 29.
25 McNeill 1980, 86–9.
26 *Excavations 1975–6*, 27.
27 Pers. comm., Mr M.Moore, 1986.
28 *ASCD*.
29 ibid.
30 Barrett and Graham 1975, 36.
31 Pers. comm., Ms Anna Brindley, 1985.
32 *CDI* I, no. 2760.
33 Lismahon: Waterman 1959a; Clough: Waterman 1954a.
34 Twohig 1978.
35 King and Alcock 1969, 104.
36 *Exp. Hib.*, 298 note 58.
37 ibid., 84.
38 ibid., 85.
39 Alcock 1966.
40 *Exp. Hib.*, 53.
41 Orpen 1907, 244.
42 Bennett 1984–5.
43 Sweetman 1978a.
44 *Song of Dermot*, lines 3222–5.
45 Fanning 1973–4.
46 Alcock 1966.
47 *Excavations 1974*, 18.
48 O'Kelly 1962a.
49 Talbot 1972.
50 Twohig 1978.
51 Sweetman 1978b.
52 Sweetman 1979, 224.
53 Rynne 1961.
54 Fanning and O'Brien 1973–4.
55 Waterman 1959b.
56 ibid., 85.
57 Twohig 1978, 8.
58 Buckley 1986, 69–70.
59 Glasscock 1975.
60 King and Alcock 1969, 104.
61 Rynne 1963.
62 Barrett and Graham 1975.
63 Pers. comm., Mr M. Moore, 1985.
64 McNeill 1975.
65 Lynn 1975a, 45–6.
66 Lynn 1975c.
67 de Paor 1976.
68 Barrett and Graham 1975, 37.
69 Leask 1973, 6; O'Corráin 1974.
70 O'Corráin 1974, 73.
71 Leask 1973, 6.
72 Murtagh 1986, 5.

73 ibid.
74 Saunders 1977, 2.
75 O'Corráin 1974, 70.
76 McNeill 1980, 9.
77 ibid.
78 ibid.
79 McNeill 1981, 22–7.
80 ibid., 39–40.
81 Sweetman 1978a, 186.
82 ibid.
83 ibid., 187.
84 ibid., 148–52.
85 ibid., 156–61.
86 ibid. 177–84.
87 ibid. 188.
88 Sweetman 1980a.
89 *Excavations 1972*, 12.
90 Lynn 1976.
91 McNeill 1980, 24–7.
92 Lynn 1976.
93 ibid.
94 'Irish pipe roll'.
95 Waterman 1951.
96 McNeill 1980, 22.
97 Renn 1973, 303.
98 Leask 1973, 42.
99 ibid., 41–2.
100 ibid., 43.
101 Waterman 1955.
102 ibid., 93.
103 *Med. Archaeol.* 1983 and 1984.
104 Waterman 1951.
105 Sweetman 1979.
106 ibid., 218.
107 ibid., 240.
108 ibid.
109 ibid., 241.
110 ibid., 225–6.
111 ibid., 241.
112 Stalley 1971, 49.
113 Pers. comm., OPW, 1984.
114 Pers. comm., Dr Ann Lynch and Mr Con Manning, 1986.
115 Sweetman 1980.
116 ibid., 210.
117 See p. 45.
118 Leask 1973, 57.
119 Stout, 1983–4.
120 Walton 1980, 361.
121 Sweetman forthcoming.
122 Stalley 1971, 52–7.

123 ibid., 53–4.
124 Claffey 1969–75.
125 ibid., 72.
126 de Paor 1962.
127 ibid., 9.

128 ibid., 5–7.
129 Cairns 1984.
130 Lynn 1981–2, 155.
131 ibid., 159–60.

4 Anglo-Norman rural settlement

1 Glasscock 1970, 171.
2 Graham 1980a, 15.
3 Otway-Ruthven 1968, 117.
4 Glasscock 1970; 1971.
5 Graham 1977b; 1978; 1979; 1985a.
6 Bradley 1985b; 1985c.
7 Ó Ríordáin and Hunt 1942.
8 ibid., 62.
9 ibid., 51–2, 54.
10 ibid., 60.
11 Glasscock 1970.
12 Excavations 1973, 14–15.
13 Pilsworth 1958, 33.
14 Glasscock 1970, 170.
15 PRO, S.C. 11. 794.
16 Rot. pat. Hib. 91, no. 52.
17 Graves 1868, 11–14.
18 ibid., 13.
19 Cal. pat. rolls, no. 52.
20 PRO, S.C. 11. 794.
21 See pp. 7⁵–6.
22 Otway-Ruthven 1965, 80.
23 Extents Ir. mon. possessions, 183.
24 PRO, S.C. 11. 794.
25 Ormond Deeds, 1584–1603, 89.
26 NLI, M 2506, f. 55.
27 Corish, 1976, 346.
28 Cleary 1982; 1983; 1984.
29 Cleary 1983, 64.
30 ibid., 65; Westropp 1906–7, 180.
31 Brannon 1984, 169.
32 ibid., 168.
33 ibid., 165.
34 Simms 1979, 139.
35 ibid., 172.
36 Edwards, Hamond and Simms 1983.
37 Curtis 1936; O'Loan 1961.
38 Meenan 1985.
39 Barry 1977, 159.
40 ibid., 36.
41 Westropp 1897.
42 Barry 1977, 176.

43 Pers. comm., Dr E. Plunkett-Dillon.
44 Yates 1983a, 12.
45 Barry 1977; Co. Waterford: Barry 1979;
   Co. Wicklow: Barry 1980; Counties
   Cork and Limerick: Barry 1981b.
46 Barry 1981b, 71.
47 PRO, S.C. 6 1247–9; Hore 1900–11, I,
   26–31.
48 Ó Ríordáin 1936.
49 Med. Archaeol. 1968, 196–7.
50 Sweetman 1981.
51 ibid., 200, 203.
52 But see p. 98.
53 Barry 1981b, 78.
54 Med. Archaeol. 1983, 220.
55 Med. Archaeol. 1983, 218.
56 Pers. comm., Ms M. Cahill, NMI.
57 ibid.
58 Barry 1977.
59 ibid., 112.
60 Empey 1982, 335.
61 Red Bk. Ormond, no. 73.
62 Barry, Culleton and Empey 1984, 163.
63 Empey 1982, 332.
64 Red Bk. Ormond, no. 13.
65 Med. Archaeol. 1983, 218.
66 Ryan 1973.
67 McNeill 1980, 53.
68 For instance, see Wallace 1981a, 253.
69 Waterman 1958.
70 McNeill 1981, 199.
71 Wallace 1981a, 253–8.
72 McNeill 1980, 56.
73 Wallace 1981a.
74 Pers. comm., Mr M. Moore, Office of
   Public Works.
75 Sweetman 1984, 182–3.
76 Excavations 1975–6, 27.
77 Pers. comm., Mr P. D. Sweetman, OPW.
78 See p. 91.
79 Ferns: Sweetman 1979; Trim:
   Sweetman 1978a; Cork: Excavations

1975–6, 27, Hurley and Power 1981, Hurley 1985; Drogheda: Sweetman 1984; Dublin: Wallace 1981a.
80 Allen 1983, 200–1. Cork: Hurley and Power 1981, 9–11; Drogheda: Sweetman 1984; Dublin: Wallace 1981a.
81 Limerick: Lynch 1984; Adare: Sweetman 1980a; Ferns: Sweetman 1979; Limerick: Sweetman 1980b; Trim: Sweetman 1978a.
82 Wallace 1981a, 257.
83 Trim: Sweetman 1978a; Drogheda: Sweetman 1984.
84 Wallace 1981b, 118. For other examples see Hurst forthcoming.
85 Exp. Hib., 67.
86 Lynn 1981–2, 114.
87 ibid.
88 Downpatrick: Pollock and Waterman 1963; Carrickfergus: Simpson et al. 1979.
89 Sweetman 1980a, 4.
90 Pers. comm., Mr A. MacDonald, University College, Cork.
91 Clough: Waterman 1954a; Ballynarry: Davison 1961–2; Lismahon: Waterman 1959a.
92 Pollock and Waterman 1963.
93 Lynn 1981–2, 114.
94 Simpson et al. 1979, 41–52.
95 McNeill 1980, 113.
96 Wallace 1981a, 254–6.
97 Sweetman 1978a, 171–5.
98 Sweetman 1979, 230–2.
99 Sweetman 1984, 183–6.
100 Manning 1981–2; O'Floinn 1976.
101 Fanning 1981a.
102 ibid., 14.
103 ibid., 16.
104 ibid., 16.
105 Pers. comm., Mr K. Campbell.
106 Fanning 1981a, 16.
107 Sweetman 1979, 232–3.
108 Duiske: Bradley and Manning 1981; Kells: Excavations 1973, 16; Mellifont: de Paor 1969; Swords: Fanning 1975; Kilteel: Manning 1981–2.
109 Swords: Fanning 1975; Kilteel: Manning 1981–2.
110 Med. Archaeol. 1984, 253.
111 Drogheda: Med. Archaeol. 1985, 256; Kilferagh: Med. Archaeol. 1983, 218; Lough Gur: Cleary 1983, 67–8.
112 Caherguillamore: Ó Ríordáin and Hunt 1942; Trim: Sweetman 1978a, 180; NMI 1973, 14.
113 High Street: Ó Ríordáin 1976, 140; Rigsdale: Sweetman 1981, 201.
114 Ó Ríordáin 1971, 73.
115 Dublin: NMI 1973, 14; Cork: pers. comm., Mr D. Twohig.
116 Wallace 1978, 4.
117 NMI 1973, 48.
118 Ó Ríordáin 1971, 76.
119 Sweetman 1979, 239.
120 Bradley 1985a.
121 McComish 1968, 25.
122 Ó Ríordáin 1971, 73.
123 Wallace 1981a, 258.
124 Pers. comm., Dr A. Lynch, OPW.
125 Sweetman 1984, 195–7.
126 Clarke 1984, 139.
127 Grand Parade: Hurley and Power 1981 87; Holy Trinity: Excavations 1975–76, 9.
128 Simpson and Dickson 1981, 87.
129 Ó Ríordáin 1971; Wallace 1981a, 1985a
130 Cal. pat. rolls 1281–92, 322.
131 Gleeson 1937, 103.
132 Pers. comm., Mr W. Colfer.
133 RIA Halliday coll., II, 178–9.
134 Quoted in O'Sullivan 1935.
135 McComish 1968, 65.
136 PROI Ferguson coll., II, 178–9.
137 Cal. Close Rolls, 1364–8, 8.
138 O'Kelly 1962b.
139 Ó Ríordáin 1971; Ó Ríordáin 1976, 140
140 Stalley 1977.
141 McNeill 1980, 113.
142 Waterman 1959a, 152.
143 Cleary 1982, 90–2; Cleary 1983, 64–5.
144 Med. Archaeol. 1985, 214.
145 Med. Archaeol. 1984, 253.
146 Simpson and Dickson 1981, 80.
147 Excavations 1975–6, 26.
148 Seaby 1970.
149 Reynolds 1978.
150 Ó Ríordáin 1976, 137.
151 NMI 1973, 16.
152 Wallace 1981a, 259.
153 O'Meadhra, 1979.

154 *Excavations 1972*, 10.
155 Baillie 1982, 147.
156 Murray 1983; Wallace 1981a, 251; *Med. Archaeol.* 1973, 152; 1974, 206.
157 Wallace 1981b.
158 Wallace 1981a, 262.
159 Baillie 1977, 260.
160 NMI 1973, 14.
161 Trim: Sweetman, 1978a, 179; Rigsdale: Sweetman 1981, 202.
162 Dublin: Wallace 1981a, 262; Adare: Sweetman 1980a, 6; Trim: Sweetman 1978a, 184–5; Kilmagoura: *Med. Archaeol.* 1968, 196.
163 Wallace 1985b, 406.
164 Dublin: Wallace 1981a, 258; Ferns: Sweetman 1979, 239.
165 McComish 1968, 57.
166 Orpen 1911–20, IV, 275–6.
167 McComish 1968, 55.
168 *Cal. Close Rolls, 1402–1405*, 456.
169 de Paor and de Paor 1958.
170 McNeill 1980, 43.
171 ibid.

172 Stalley 1980, 335.
173 Stalley 1971, 24.
174 ibid.
175 Leask 1973, 32.
176 Fanning 1976, 154.
177 Wallace 1981b, 113.
178 Hurley and Power 1981, 5.
179 Pers. comm., Mr M. Moore, OPW.
180 Lynch 1984, 287.
181 Stalley 1971; Stalley 1978.
182 Stalley 1971, 75–80.
183 ibid., 18–19.
184 ibid., 108.
185 *Tresors d'Irlande* 1983, 219.
186 Mellifont: de Paor 1969, 157; Kells: *Excavations 1972*, 18; Clontusket: Fanning, 1976; Duiske: Bradley and Manning 1981, 419.
187 Bradley and Manning 1981, 419.
188 Dublin: pers. comm., Dr. A. Lynch; Trim: Sweetman 1978a, 185.
189 Ó Ríordáin 1971, 76.
190 Clarke 1984, 129.
191 ibid.

5 The growth of medieval towns

1 Barry 1978, 13.
2 See Graham 1977b, 29.
3 McNeill 1980, 89–90.
4 Stephenson 1933, 134.
5 Wallace 1978, 24.
6 Wallace 1978.
7 ibid.
8 ibid.
9 *Chronica Magistri Rogeri de Houedene*, II, 32.
10 Pers. comm., Mr K. Campbell.
11 See pp. 101–15.
12 Wallace 1981a, 260–1.
13 Ó Ríordáin 1971, 77.
14 Mitchell 1987.
15 *Chartul. St Mary's, Dublin*, II, 332.
16 *Ann. of Ire.*, 35.
17 Lydon 1973, 78.
18 *Acc. Roll Holy Trinity, Dublin*, 23.
19 *Excavations 1972*, 4.
20 Simpson and Dickson 1981, 82–3.
21 *Excavations 1974*, 12.
22 *Excavations 1975–6*, 26–7.
23 Hurley and Power 1981.

24 *Exp. Hib.*, 67.
25 Graham 1977b, 41.
26 Moore 1983, 54.
27 Pers. comm., Dr P. Wallace.
28 Unpublished prelim. report, OPW, 15.
29 ibid., 15–19.
30 Moore 1983, 54.
31 See p. 35.
32 *Exp. Hib.*, 57.
33 Drogheda: Sweetman 1984, 185.
34 Carus-Wilson 1954, 14. [And see Hurley 1988.]
35 *CDI* IV, no. 726; Orpen 1911–20, IV, 275–6.
36 *38th Rep. Dep. Keeper*, 42.
37 *Cal. Inq. Post Mortem*, IV, 340.
38 ibid., VI, 326.
39 Pers. comm., Mr A. B. Ó Ríordáin.
40 *Excavations 1973*, 28.
41 *Excavations 1974*, 28.
42 Cahill and Ryan 1980–1.
43 *Exp. Hib.*, 33, 35.
44 Graham 1977b, 41.
45 Pers. comm., Mr N. Ross.

46 *Excavations 1975–6*, 33.
47 Sweetman 1984.
48 *Med. Archaeol.* 1983, 218–19.
49 Bradley 1978.
50 Graham 1977b.
51 Bradley 1978.
52 ibid.
53 *Excavations 1975–6*, 14–15.

54 Lynch 1984.
55 Pers. comm., Dr A. Lynch, OPW.
56 *Excavations 1975–6, 7*, 24–5.
57 ibid., 25–6.
58 Lynn 1975b; and see p. 159–60.
59 *Med. Archaeol.* 1985, 212.
60 Pollock and Waterman 1963; Mr N. F. Brannon, public lecture, 5 May 1984.

6 The archaeology of the medieval church

1 Nicholls 1971, 62.
2 Buckley 1986, 71–81 and information from the Archaeological Survey of Ireland.
3 Leask 1966, 85.
4 ibid., 153–4.
5 McNeill 1980, 50.
6 Waterman and Hamlin 1976, 35–7.
7 *Med. Archaeol.* 1983, 217.
8 DART 1981.
9 McNeill 1980, 61.
10 Stalley 1971, 58–68.
11 ibid., 68.
12 Barry 1985.
13 Stalley 1971, 84–7.
14 Rahtz and Hirst 1976.
15 Stalley 1987.
16 de Paor 1969.
17 Stalley 1980.
18 *Med. Archaeol.* 1984, 259.
19 Stalley 1980, 353.
20 Bradley and Manning 1981.
21 ibid., 425.
22 *Med. Archaeol.* 1983, 221; *Med. Archaeol.* 1984, 258–9.
23 *Med. Archaeol.* 1984, 218.
24 *Med. Archaeol.* 1985, 215.
25 Stalley 1971, 100.
26 ibid., 104.
27 ibid., 125.
28 ibid., 126.
29 Fanning 1976.
30 Empey 1984.
31 Fanning 1976, 161.
32 ibid.
33 ibid., 162.
34 Empey 1984, 150.
35 *Excavations 1972*, 18.
36 *Excavations 1973*, 15.
37 *Excavations 1974*, 19.

38 ibid., 20.
39 Stalley 1971, 110–16.
40 Hamlin 1983, 53.
41 *Bull. GSIHS* 1970, 34.
42 *Excavations 1975*, 10.
43 *Excavations 1973*, 5.
44 Yates 1983b, 54.
45 ibid.
46 Ivens 1984, 106.
47 ibid., 107.
48 See p. 191.
49 *Excavations 1973*, 28.
50 Empey 1984.
51 ibid., 138. The Fourth Lateran Council (1215) banned enclosed religious orders from taking on parochial duties.
52 Otway-Ruthven 1968, 127.
53 *Excavations 1975*, 14.
54 Stalley 1971, 136.
55 Lynn 1975b, 65.
56 ibid., 71–80.
57 ibid., 71.
58 Simpson and Dickson 1981, 82.
59 *Med. Archaeol.* 1985, 216.
60 Harbison 1970, 97, 137.
61 Manning 1981–2.
62 *Med. Archaeol.* 1985, 215.
63 *Med. Archaeol.* 1983, 218–19; *Med. Archaeol.* 1984, 256.
64 'Chart. Duiske, Kilkenny', 124–5.
65 Bradley and Manning 1981, 398.
66 J. Bradley, unpublished report for RIA, 1983.
67 O'Conbhui 1962.
68 Conway 1958, 122.
69 Bradley 1980–1.
70 Fanning 1976, 121–3.
71 ibid., 121.
72 See p. 142.
73 See pp. 149, 151.

74 Pers. comm., Mrs Mary McMahon.
75 Stalley 1987.
76 Kells: *Excavations 1972*, 18; Mellifont:

de Paor 1969, 125.
77 See p. 156.
78 Pers. comm., Dr Ann Lynch.

7   The later middle ages: growth or decline?

1 Postan 1972.
2 Bridbury 1962.
3 Empey 1970.
4 Frame 1981; Otway-Ruthven 1968.
5 See p. 72.
6 Lecture to Dublin Historic Settlement Group, Dr D. Denecke.
7 Graham 1977a, 17.
8 See pp. 127–8.
9 Gosling 1982, 18–22.
10 See p. 130.
11 *CDI*, 1302–7, 666.
12 *38th Rep. Dep. Keeper*, 42.
13 See p. 91.
14 Glasscock 1987, 239.
15 Glasscock 1971, 293.
16 Empey 1970, 148.
17 ibid., 144.
18 ibid., 231.
19 ibid., 231–2.
20 ibid., 232.
21 ibid., 238.
22 ibid., 328–9.
23 ibid., 239.
24 ibid., 151.
25 ibid., 507–8.
26 Walton 1980.
27 Stalley 1978, 43.
28 Meenan 1985, 95–6.
29 Orpen 1911–20, IV, 179.
30 Otway-Ruthven forthcoming.
31 *Ann. of Ire.*, 37.
32 Otway-Ruthven forthcoming.
33 Westropp 1917, 14–15.
34 Otway-Ruthven forthcoming
35 See pp. 7–8.
36 *Ann. of Ire.*, 35.
37 Lyons 1984, 37–8.
38 ibid., 37.
39 Glasscock 1970, 1971; Graham 1980a; Meenan 1985.
40 *CDI*, 1252–84, no. 2028.
41 Otway-Ruthven 1968, 252.
42 Feehan 1983, 370–1.

43 ibid., 370.
44 McNeill 1980, 91.
45 ibid., 91–4.
46 ibid.
47 ibid., 93.
48 McNeill 1980.
49 Sweetman 1984, 198.
50 *Med. Archaeol.* 1985, 216.
51 *Med. Archaeol.* 1985, 218.
52 Fanning 1976, 161, 168.
53 See p. 130.
54 *Med. Archaeol.* 1985, 213.
55 *Excavations 1975*, 9.
56 *Excavations 1975*, 8.
57 Cosgrove 1981.
58 Devitt 1899–1902.
59 Manning 1981–2.
60 Cairns 1984, 152.
61 ibid., 250–1.
62 ibid., 178–89.
63 ibid., 155.
64 ibid., 186–7.
65 O'Danachair 1977–9.
66 Cairns 1984; Smith 1969.
67 Davin 1982.
68 Hadden 1964.
69 Cairns 1984, 47.
70 Murtagh 1982.
71 *Excavations 1972*, 19–20; *1973*, 16–17; *1974*, 20.
72 *Excavations 1974*, 22.
73 Gowen 1978.
74 Cairns 1984, 357, 362, 275, 380.
75 Leask 1971, 1.
76 De Breffny and Mott 1976, 99.
77 Leask, 1971, 1.
78 Waterman 1979.
79 *Excavations 1973*, 4; *1974*, 9.
80 ibid.
81 De Breffny and Mott 1976, 97–8.
82 ibid., 99.
83 Nicholls 1982.
84 K. W. Nicholls, conference paper, 25 February 1985, TCD.

85 Edwards, Hamond and Simms 1983.
86 Lydon 1984, 1–26.
87 Walton 1980.

88 Nicholls 1982, 401.
89 ibid., 392–3.

8 Future horizons

1 *ASCD* 1966.
2 Pers. comm., Ms C. Foley.
3 Louth: Buckley 1986, Buckley and Sweetman 1991; Meath: Moore 1987; Monaghan: Brindley 1986.
4 Duffy 1985.
5 See p. 16.

6 Binford 1964.
7 See pp. 72–4.
8 See pp. 181–2.
9 *Med. Archaeol.* 1983 onwards.
10 Eogan 1985.
11 Pers. comm., Dr P. Wallace.
12 Simms 1978, 207.

Bibliography

Manuscript sources

Armagh Public Library
  Reeve MSS (safe).

National Library of Ireland
  Down Survey (1654–6) parish and barony maps.
  M2506, f. 55.

Public Records Office, Ireland
  Books of Survey and Distribution (1641–1701).
  Ferguson collection.

Public Record Office, London
  C 47 Chancery Miscellaneous.
  SC 6 Special Collection.
  SC 11 Special Collection.

Royal Irish Academy
  Halliday Collection.
  OS Letters.

Printed sources

Account Roll of the Priory of the Holy Trinity, Dublin, 1337–46, ed. J. Mills, Dublin, 1891.
The Annals of Connacht, ed. A.M. Freeman, Dublin, 1944.
The Annals of Inisfallen, ed. S. MacAirt, Dublin, 1951.
The Annals of Ireland by Friar John Clyn and Thady Dowling, ed. R. Butler, Dublin, 1849.
Annals of the Kingdom of Ireland by the Four Masters, ed. J. O'Donovan, 7 vols, Dublin, 1848–51.
The Annals of Loch Cé, ed. W.M. Hennessy, 2 vols, Dublin, 1871.

Annals of Ulster, ed. W.M. Hennessy and B. MacCarthy, 4 vols, Dublin, 1887–1901.

Annals of Ulster (to AD 1131), eds S. MacAirt and G. MacNiocaill, Dublin, 1984.

Calendar of the Ancient Records of Dublin, ed. J.T. Gilbert, 19 vols, Dublin, 1889–1944.

Calendar of Archbishop Alen's Register, ed. C. McNeill, Dublin, 1950.

Calendar of Close Rolls, 1272–1500, 45 vols, London, 1892–1963.

Calendar of Documents Relating to Ireland, 1171–1307, ed. H.S. Sweetman, 5 vols, London, 1875–86.

Calendar of the Gormanston Register, ed. J. Mills and M.J. McEnery, Dublin, 1916.

Calendar of Inquisitions Post Mortem, London, 1904–74.

Calendar of the Justiciary Rolls of Ireland 1295–1314, ed. J. Mills and M.C. Griffith, 3 vols, Dublin, 1905–14.

'A Calendar of the Liber Niger and Liber Albus of Christ Church Dublin', ed. H.J. Lawlor, *RIA Proc.*, 27C (1908), 1–93.

'Calendar of the Liber Ruber of the diocese of Ossory', *RIA Proc.*, 27C, 1908, 159–208.

Calendar of Ormond Deeds, 1172–1603, 6 vols, Dublin, 1932–43.

Calendar of Patent Rolls, London, 1891–1971.

A Census of Ireland c.1659, ed. S. Pender, Dublin, 1939.

'Charters of the Cistercian Abbey of Duiske in the County of Kilkenny', ed. C.M. Butler and J.H. Bernard, *RIA Proc.*, 35C (1918–20), 1–188.

Chartularies of St Mary's Abbey, Dublin . . . and Annals of Ireland, 1162–1370, ed. J.T. Gilbert, 2 vols, London, 1884–6.

Chronica Magistri Rogeri de Houedene, ed. W. Stubbs, II, 1869, Dublin.

The Civil Survey, ed. R.C. Simmington, 10 vols, Dublin, 1931–61.

Cogadh Gaedhel re Gallaibh: the War of the Gaedhil with the Gaill, or the Invasion of Ireland by the Danes and other Norse men, ed. J.H. Todd, London, 1867.

Dowdall Deeds, ed. C. McNeill and A.J. Otway-Ruthven, Dublin, 1960.

Expugnatio Hibernica: The Conquest of Ireland by Giraldus Cambrensis, ed. A.B. Scott and F.X. Martin, Dublin, 1978.

Extents of Irish Monastic Possessions, 1540–1, ed. N.B. White, Dublin 1943.

Fragmentary Annals of Ireland, ed. J.N. Radner, Dublin, 1978.

Historic and Municipal Documents of Ireland, 1172–1320, ed. J.T. Gilbert, London 1870.

The Irish Cartularies of Llanthony Prima and Secunda, ed. E. St. John Brooks, Dublin, 1953.

'The Irish pipe roll of 14 John', ed. O. Davies and D.B. Quinn, *UJA* 4, 1941, Supplement.

Knights' Fees in Counties Wexford, Carlow and Kilkenny (13th–15th century), ed. E. St John Brooks, Dublin, 1950.

Liber Primus Kilkenniensis, ed. C. McNeill, Dublin, 1931; translated by A.J. Otway-Ruthven, Kilkenny, 1961.

The Red Book of the Earls of Kildare, ed. G. MacNiocaill, Dublin, 1964.

The Red Book of Ormond, ed. N.B. White, Dublin, 1932.

Register of the Abbey of St Thomas the Martyr, Dublin, ed. J.T. Gilbert, London, 1889.

The Register of the Hospital of St John the Baptist, ed. E. St. John Brooks, Dublin, 1936.

Register of the Priory of the Blessed Virgin Mary at Tristernagh, ed. M.V. Clarke, Dublin 1941.

Reports of the Deputy Keeper of the Public Records, Ireland, 35–54, Dublin, 1903–21.

Rotulorum patentium et clausorum cancellariae Hiberniae calendarium, Dublin, 1828.

The Song of Dermot and the Earl, trans. and ed. G.H. Orpen, Oxford, 1892.

The Stafford Inquisition of County Mayo (RIA Ms 24 E 15), ed. W. O'Sullivan, Dublin, 1958

'Survey of the memoranda rolls of the Irish exchequer, 1294–1509', ed. J.F.M. Lydon Analecta Hibernica, 23 (1966), 51–134.

Topographia Hibernica: The History and Topography of Ireland by Gerald of Wales, ed. J.J O'Meara, Harmondsworth, 1982.

Secondary works

AALEN, F.H.A., and WHELAN, K. (eds) 1992. *Dublin City and County: from Prehistory to Present*, Dublin.

ABERG, F.A. and BROWN, A.E. (eds) 1981. *Medieval Moated Sites in North-West Europe*, Oxford.

ALCOCK, L. 1966. 'Castle Tower, Penmaen: Anglo-Norman ring-work in Glamorgan', *Antiq. Jnl*, 46, 178–210.

ALCOCK, L. 1972. *By South Cadbury is that Camelot*, London.

ALLEN, J. 1983. 'The importance of pottery to southern England *c.*1200–1500', in P. Davey and R. Hodges (eds) *Ceramics and Trade: the Production and Distribution of Later Medieval Pottery in North-West Europe*, Sheffield, 193–258.

ALMQUIST, B., and GREENE, D. (eds) 1976. *Proceedings of the Seventh Viking Congress*, Dublin.

An Archaeological Survey of County Down, ed. E.M. Jope, Belfast, 1966.

ANDREWS, J.H. and SIMMS, A. (eds) 1986. *Irish Historic Towns Atlas*, Dublin. No. 1 'Kildare' by J. H. Andrews; No. 2 'Carrickfergus' by P. Robinson.

BAILLIE, M.G.L. 1975. 'A horizontal mill of the eighth century AD at Drumard, County Derry', *UJA*, 38, 25–32.

BAILLIE, M.G.L. 1977. 'The dating of ships' timbers from Wood Quay, Dublin', in Fletcher, J.M. (ed.) *Dendrochronology in Europe*, Oxford, 259–62.

BAILLIE, M.G.L. 1979. 'An interim statement on dendrochronology at Belfast', *UJA*, 42, 72–84.

BAILLIE, M.G.L. 1982. *Tree Ring Dating and Archaeology*, London.

BAILLIE, M.G.L. 1985. 'Irish dendrochronology and radiocarbon calibration', *UJA*, 48, 11–23.

BARKER, P.A. 1977. *Techniques of Archaeological Excavations*, London.

BARKER, P.A., and BARTON, K.J. 1977. 'Excavations at Hastings Castle, 1968', *Archaeol. Jnl*, 134, 80–100.

BARRETT, G.F. 1972. 'The ring-fort: a study in settlement geography with special reference to southern County Donegal and the Dingle area, County Kerry', unpublished PhD thesis, QUB.

BARRETT, G.F. 1980. 'A field survey and morphological study of ring-forts in southern County Donegal', *UJA*, 43, 39–51.

BARRETT, G.F. 1982. 'Aerial photography and the study of early settlement structures in Ireland', *Aerial Archaeology*, 6, 27–38.

BARRETT, G.F., and GRAHAM, B.J. 1975. 'Some considerations concerning the dating and distribution of ring-forts in Ireland', *UJA*, 38, 33–45.

BARRY, S. 1985. 'The architecture of the cathedral', in Empey, C.A. (ed.) *A Worthy Foundation: The Cathedral Church of St Canice, Kilkenny, 1285–1985*, Dublin, 25–48.

BARRY, T.B. 1977. *Medieval Moated Sites of South-East Ireland*, Oxford.

BARRY, T.B. 1978. 'Urban archaeology in the Republic of Ireland', *Bull. GSIHS*, 5, 12–18.

BARRY, T.B. 1979. 'The moated sites of County Waterford', *Decies*, 10, 32–6.

BARRY, T.B. 1980. 'County Wicklow', *MSRG Report*, 7, 31–2.

BARRY, T.B. 1981a. 'Archaeological excavations at Dunbeg Promontory Fort, County Kerry', *RIA Proc.*, 81C, 295–329.

BARRY, T.B. 1981b. 'The shifting frontier: medieval moated sites in Counties Cork and Limerick', in Aberg, F.A., and Brown, A.E. (eds) *Medieval Moated Sites in North-West Europe*, Oxford, 71–85.

BARRY, T.B. 1983. 'Anglo-Norman ringwork castles: some evidence', in Reeves-Smyth, T., and Hamond, F. (eds) *Landscape Archaeology in Ireland*, Oxford, 295–314.

BARRY, T.B. 1988a. 'Medieval moated sites in Ireland: some new conclusions on their chronology and function', in MacNiocaill, G., and Wallace, P.F. (eds) *Keimelia*, Galway, 524–35.

BARRY, T.B. 1988b. '"The people of the country . . . dwell scattered": the pattern of rural settlement in Ireland in the later middle ages', in Bradley, J. (ed.) *Settlement and Society in Medieval Ireland*, Kilkenny, 345–60.

BARRY, T.B. 1993a. 'Late medieval Ireland: the debate on social and economic transformation, 1350–1550', in Graham, B.J., and Proudfoot, L.J. (eds) *An Historical Geography of Ireland*, London, 99–122.

BARRY, T.B. 1993b. 'The archaeology of the tower house in late medieval Ireland', in Andersson, H., and Weinberg, J. (eds) *The Study of Medieval Archaeology: European Teachers of Medieval Archaeology*, Lund Studies in Medieval Archaeology 13, 211–18.

BARRY, T.B., CULLETON, E., and EMPEY, C.A. 1984. 'The motte at Kells, Co. Kilkenny', *RIA Proc.*, 84C, 157–70.

BENNETT, I. 1984–5. 'Preliminary archaeological excavations at Ferrycarrig Ringwork, Newtown Townland, Co. Wexford', *Jnl Wexford Hist. Soc.*, 10, 25–43.

BERESFORD, M.W., and HURST, J.G. (eds) 1971. *Deserted Medieval Villages: Studies*, London.

BINFORD, L.R. 1964. 'A consideration of archaeological research design', *American Antiquity*, 29, 425–41.

BRADLEY, J. 1978. 'The topography and layout of medieval Drogheda', *Jnl Louth Arch. Soc.*, 21, 98–127.

BRADLEY, J. 1980–1. 'St Patrick's Church, Duleek', *Ríocht na Midhe*, 7, 40–51.

BRADLEY, J. 1985a. 'The medieval tombs of St Canice's', in Empey, C.A. (ed.) *A Worthy Foundation: The Cathedral Church of St Canice, Kilkenny, 1285–1985*, Dublin, 49–103.

BRADLEY, J. 1985b. 'The medieval towns of Tipperary', in Nolan, W. (ed.) *Tipperary: History and Society*, Dublin, 34–59.

BRADLEY, J. 1985c. 'Planned Anglo-Norman towns in Ireland', in Clarke, H.B., and Simms, A. (eds) *The Comparative History of Urban Origins in Non-Roman Europe*, Oxford, 411–67.

BRADLEY, J. 1985d. 'The medieval borough of Louth: an archaeological study', *Jnl Louth Arch. Soc.*, 21, 8–22.

BRADLEY, J. 1985e. 'The medieval towns of Tipperary', in Nolan, W., and McGrath, T.G. (eds) *Tipperary: History and Society*, Dublin, 34–59.

BRADLEY, J. 1985–6. 'Excavations at Moynagh Lough, 1984', *Ríocht na Midhe*, 7, no. 4, 79–82.

BRADLEY, J. 1988. *Settlement and Society in Medieval Ireland: Studies Presented to F.X. Martin O.S.A.*, Kilkenny.

BRADLEY, J. 1990. 'The early development of the medieval town of Kilkenny', in Nolan, W., and Whelan, K. (eds) *Kilkenny: History and Society*, Dublin, 63–73.

BRADLEY, J. 1992. 'The topographical development of Scandinavian Dublin', in Aalen, F.H.A., and Whelan, K. (eds) *Dublin City and County: from Prehistory to Present*, Dublin, 43–56.

BRADLEY, J., and HALPIN, A. 1993. 'The topographical development of Scandinavian and Anglo-Norman Cork', in O'Flanagan, P., and Buttimer, C. (eds) *Cork: History and Society*, Dublin, 15–44.

BRADLEY, J., and MANNING, C. 1981. 'Excavations at Duiske Abbey, Graiguenamanagh, Co. Kilkenny', *RIA Proc.*, 81C, 397–426.

BRANNON, N.F. 1984. 'A small excavation in Tildarg townland, near Ballyclare, County Antrim', *UJA*, 47, 163–70.

BRIDBURY, A.R. 1962. *Economic Growth: England in the Later Middle Ages*, London.

BRINDLEY, A.L. 1986. *Archaeological Inventory of Co. Monaghan*, Dublin.

BROWN, C.G., and HARPER, A.E.T. 1984. 'Excavations on Cathedral Hill, Armagh, 1968, *UJA*, 47, 109–61.

BUCKLEY, V.M. (ed.) 1986. *Archaeological Inventory of Co. Louth*, Dublin.

BUCKLEY, V.M., and SWEETMAN, P.D. (eds) 1991. *Archaeological Survey of County Louth*, Dublin.

BUTLIN, R.A. (ed.) 1977. *The Development of the Irish Town*, London.

CAHILL, M., and RYAN, M.F. 1980–1. 'An investigation of the town wall at Abbey Street, Wexford', *Jnl Old Wexford Soc.*, 8, 56–64.

CAIRNS, C.T. 1984. 'The tower houses of County Tipperary', unpublished PhD thesis, TCD.

CAMPBELL, K. 1985. 'A medieval tile kiln site at Magdalene Street, Drogheda', *Jnl Louth Arch. Soc.*, 21, 48–54.

CARRIGAN, W. 1905. *The History and Antiquities of the Diocese of Ossory*, 4 vols, Dublin.

CARUS-WILSON, E.M. 1954. *Medieval Merchant Ventures*, London.

CLAFFEY, J.A. 1969–75. 'Ballintubber Castle, Co. Roscommon', *Old Athlone Society Jnl*, 1, 143–6; 218–21.

CLARKE, H. 1984. *The Archaeology of Medieval England*, London.

CLARKE, H.B. (ed.) 1978. 'Focus on medieval Dublin', in *Dublin Arts Festival 21–30 April 1978*, Dublin.

CLARKE, H.B. and SIMMS, A. (eds) 1985. *The Comparative History of Urban Origins in Non-Roman Europe*, Oxford.

CLEARY, R.M. 1982. 'Excavations at Lough Gur, Co. Limerick: part II', *JCHAS*, 87, 77–106.

CLEARY, R.M. 1983. 'Excavations at Lough Gur, Co. Limerick: part III', *JCHAS*, 88, 51–80.

CLEARY, R.M. 1984. 'Excavations at Lough Gur, Co. Limerick: part IV', *JCHAS*, 89, 33–54.

CLEARY, R.M., HURLEY, M.F., and TWOHIG, E.A. (eds) 1987. *Archaeological Excavations on the Cork–Dublin Gas Pipeline (1981–82)*, Cork.

COLFER, W. 1986. 'Anglo-Norman settlement in medieval Shelburne, 1169–1307', unpublished M. Litt. thesis, TCD.

COLFER, W. 1987. 'Anglo-Norman settlement in County Wexford', in Whelan, K. (ed.) *Wexford: History and Society*, Dublin, 65–101.

CONWAY, Rev. Fr Colmcille 1958. *The Story of Mellifont*, Dublin.

CORISH, P.J. 1976. 'The Cromwellian Conquest, 1649–53', in Moody, T.W., Martin, F.X., and Byrne, F.J. *A New History of Ireland*, vol. 3, Oxford, 336–52.

COSGROVE, A. 1981. *Late Medieval Ireland, 1370–1541*, Dublin.

COSGROVE, A. (ed.) 1987. *A New History of Ireland*, vol. 2, 'Medieval Ireland (1169–1534)', Oxford.

CULLETON, E., and COLFER, W. 1974–5. 'The Norman motte at Old Ross, method of construction', *Jnl Old Wexford Soc.*, 5, 22–5.

CUNNINGHAM, G. 1987. *The Anglo-Norman Advance into the South-West Midlands of Ireland 1185–1221*, Roscrea.

CUPPAGE, J. (ed.) 1986. *Corca Dhuibhne. Dingle Peninsula Archaeological Survey*, Ballyferriter.

CURTIS, E. 1936. 'Rental of the Manor of Lisronagh, 1333, and notes on "Betagh" tenure in medieval Ireland', *RIA Proc.*, 43C, 41–76.

CURTIS, E. 1938. *A History of Medieval Ireland From 1086 to 1513*, London.

DART 1981. *Preliminary Report and Recommendations on the Site of St Michael le Pole and Surrounding Areas*, Dublin.

DAVIN, A.K. 1982. 'Tower houses of the Pale', unpublished M.Litt. thesis, TCD.

DAVISON, B.K. 1961–2. 'Excavations at Ballynarry, Co. Down', *UJA* 23, 39–87.

DE BREFFNY, B., and MOTT, G. 1976. *The Churches and Abbeys of Ireland*, London.

DE PAOR, L. 1962. 'Excavations at Ballyloughan Castle, Co. Carlow', *RSAI Jnl*, 42, 1–14.

DE PAOR, L. 1969. 'Excavations at Mellifont Abbey, Co. Louth', *RIA Proc.*, 68C, 109–64.

DE PAOR, L. 1976. 'The Viking towns in Ireland', in Almquist, B., and Greene, D. (eds) *Proceedings of the Seventh Viking Congress*, Dublin.

DE PAOR, M. and L. 1958. *Early Christian Ireland*, London.

218 The Archaeology of Medieval Ireland

DEVITT, M. 1899–1902. 'The ramparts of the Pale at Clongowes Wood', *Jnl Kildare Arch. Soc.*, 3, 284–8.

DOHERTY, C. 1985. 'Monastic towns in Ireland', in Clarke, H.B., and Simms, A. (eds) *The Comparative History of Urban Origins in Non-Roman Europe*, Oxford, 45–76.

DOLLEY, M. 1972. *Anglo-Norman Ireland*, Dublin.

DUFFY, B.K. 1985. 'The Archaeological Survey of Ireland', *Newsletter of the Group for the Study of Irish Historic Settlement*, 5–8.

EAMES, E.S., and FANNING, T. (eds) 1987. *Decorated Medieval Paving Tiles in Ireland*, 'Monographs in Archaeology', RIA, Dublin.

ECKSTEIN, D. 1984. *Dendrochronological Dating*, Strasbourg.

EDWARDS, K.J., HAMOND, F.W., and SIMMS, A. 1983. 'The medieval settlement of Newcastle Lyons, Co. Dublin: an interdisciplinary approach', *RIA Proc.*, 83C, 351–76.

EDWARDS, N. 1990. *The Archaeology of Early Medieval Ireland*, London.

EMPEY, C.A., 1970. 'The Butler lordship in Ireland, 1185–1515', unpublished PhD thesis, TCD.

EMPEY, C.A. 1982. 'Medieval Knocktopher: a study in manorial settlement – part I', *Old Kilkenny Review*, 2, no. 4, 329–42.

EMPEY, C.A. 1984. 'The sacred and the secular: the Augustinian priory of Kells in Ossory, 1193–1541', *IHS*, 24, 131–51.

EMPEY, C.A. (ed.) 1985. *A Worthy Foundation: The Cathedral Church of St Canice, Kilkenny, 1285–1985*, Dublin.

EOGAN, G. 1985. *Excavations at Knowth – I*, Dublin.

EVANS, E.E. 1964. 'Ireland and Atlantic Europe', *Geographische Zeitschrift*, 52, 224–41.

Excavations. Summary accounts of archaeological work in Ireland, Association of Young Irish Archaeologists, Belfast 1970–6.

FANNING, T. 1973–4. 'Excavations of a ringfort at Pollardstown, Co. Kildare', *Jnl Kildare Arch. Soc.* 15, 251–61.

FANNING, T. 1975. 'An Irish medieval tile pavement: recent excavations at Swords Castle, County Dublin', *RSAI Jnl*, 105, 47–82.

FANNING, T. 1976. 'Excavations at Clontuskert Priory, Co. Galway', *RIA Proc.*, 76C, 97–169.

FANNING, T. 1981a. 'The British Museum catalogue of medieval tiles – a review incorporating Irish evidence', *N. Munster Antiq. Jnl*, 23, 9–16.

FANNING, T. 1981b. 'Excavation of an Early Christian cemetery and settlement at Reask, County Kerry', *RIA Proc.*, 81C, 67–172.

FANNING, T., and O'BRIEN, K. 1973–4. 'Earthworks at Raheen Castle, Co. Limerick', *N. Munster Antiq. Jnl*, 16, 29–32.

FEEHAN, J. 1983. *Laois – An Environmental History*, Ballykilcavan.

FLANAGAN, D. 1978. 'Common elements in Irish place names: Baile', *Bulletin of the Ulster Place-Names Society*, 1, 8–13.

FLATRES, P. (ed.) 1979. *Paysage Ruraux Européens*, Rennes.

FLETCHER, J.M. (ed.) 1977. *Dendrochronology in Europe*, Oxford.

FOLEY, C. 1989. 'Excavations at a medieval settlement site in Jerpointchurch townland, County Kilkenny', *RIA Proc.*, 89C, 71–126.

FRAME, R. 1981. *Colonial Ireland, 1169–1369*, Dublin.

GLASSCOCK, R.E. 1970. 'Moated sites and deserted boroughs and villages: two neglected aspects of Anglo-Norman settlement in Ireland', in Stephens, N., and Glasscock, R.E. (eds) *Irish Geographical Studies*, Belfast, 162–77.

GLASSCOCK, R.E. 1971. 'The study of deserted medieval settlements in Ireland (to 1969)', in Beresford, M.W., and Hurst, J.G. (eds) *Deserted Medieval Villages: Studies*, London, 279–301.

GLASSCOCK, R.E. 1975. 'Mottes in Ireland', *Château-Gaillard*, 7, 95–110.

GLASSCOCK, R.E. 1986. 'Land and people, c.1300', in Cosgrove, A. (ed.) *A New History of Ireland*, vol. 2, 'Medieval Ireland (1169–1534)', Oxford, 205–39.

GLASSCOCK, R.E. and MCNEILL, T. 1972. 'Mottes in Ireland: a draft list', *Bull. GSIHS*, 3, 27–51.

GLEESON, D.F. 1937. 'The silver mines of Ormond', *RSAI Jnl*, 67, 101–16.

GOSLING, P. 1982. *Dundalk: A Survey and Report on the Archaeology of the Town and District*, Dundalk.

GOWEN, M. 1978. 'Dunboy Castle, Co. Cork', *JCHAS*, 83, 1–49.

GRAHAM, B.J. 1977a. 'The documentation of medieval Irish boroughs', *Bull. GSIHS*, 4, 9–20.

GRAHAM, B.J. 1977b. 'The towns of medieval Ireland', in Butlin, R.A. (ed.) *The Development of the Irish Town*, London, 28–60.

GRAHAM, B.J. 1978. 'The documentation of medieval Irish boroughs', *Bull. GSIHS*, 5, 41–5.

GRAHAM, B.J. 1979. 'The evolution of urbanisation in medieval Ireland', *Journal of Historical Geography*, 5, 111–25.

GRAHAM, B.J. 1980a. *Medieval Irish settlement, A Review*, Norwich.

GRAHAM, B.J. 1980b. 'The mottes of the Norman liberty of Meath', in Murtagh, H. (ed.) *Irish Midland Studies*, Athlone, 39–56.

GRAHAM, B.J. 1985a. 'Anglo-Norman manorial settlement in Ireland: an assessment', *Ir. Geog.*, 18, 4–15.

GRAHAM, B.J. 1985b. *Anglo-Norman Settlement in Ireland*, Athlone.

GRAHAM, B.J. 1987–90. 'Twelfth- and thirteenth-century earthwork fortifications in Ireland', *Irish Sword*, 17, 225–43.

GRAHAM, B.J. 1988a. 'Medieval timber and earthwork fortifications in western Ireland', *Med. Archaeol.*, 32, 110–29.

GRAHAM, B.J. 1988b. 'Medieval settlement in County Roscommon', *RIA Proc.*, 88C, 19–38.

GRAHAM, B.J. 1993. 'The high middle ages: c.1100 to c.1350', in Graham, B.J., and Proudfoot, L.J. (eds) *An Historical Geography of Ireland*, London, 58–98.

GRAHAM, B.J., and PROUDFOOT, L.J. 1993. *An Historical Geography of Ireland*, London.

GRAHAM-CAMPBELL, J. 1976. 'The Viking-age silver hoards of Ireland', in Almquist, B., and Greene, D. (eds) *Proceedings of the Seventh Viking Congress*, Dublin, 39–74.

GRAVES, J. 1868. 'Proceedings', *RSAI Jnl*, 7, 11–14.

GREENE, J.P. 1992. *Medieval Monasteries*, Leicester.

HADDEN, G. 1964. 'Some earthworks in Co. Wexford', *JCHAS*, 69, 118–22.

HALL, R.A. 1984. *Viking Dig: The Excavations at York*, London.

HALPIN, A. 1986. 'Irish medieval swords, c.1170–1600', *RIA Proc.*, 86C, 183–230.

HAMLIN, A. 1983. *Historic Monuments of Northern Ireland*, Belfast.

HAND, G.J. 1957. 'Dating of the early fourteenth century ecclesiastical valuation of Ireland', *Irish Theological Quarterly*, 24, 271–4.

HARBISON, P. 1970. *Guide to the National Monuments of the Republic of Ireland*, Dublin.

HERITY, M. 1983. 'A survey of the royal site of Cruachain in Connacht', *RSAI Jnl*, 113, 121–42.

HERITY, M. and EOGAN, G. 1977. *Ireland in Prehistory*, London.

HOPE-TAYLOR, B. 1950. 'The excavation of a motte at Abinger, Surrey', *Archaeol. Jnl*, 107, 15–43.

HORE, H.F. 1900–11. *A History of the Town and County of Wexford*, 6 vols, London.

HUGHES, K. 1966. *The Church in Early Irish Society*, London.

HURLEY, M.F. 1985. 'Excavations of part of the medieval city walls at Grand Parade, Cork', *JCHAS*, 90, 65–90.

HURLEY, M.F. 1986. 'Excavations in medieval Cork: St Peter's Market', *JCHAS*, 41, 1–25.

HURLEY, M.F. 1988. 'Recent archaeological excavations in Waterford city', *Archaeology Ireland*, II (1), 17–21.

HURLEY, M.F. 1989. 'Excavations at Grand Parade, Cork, II', *JCHAS*, 44, 278–45.

HURLEY, M.F. 1990. 'Excavations at Grand Parade, Cork, II', *JCHAS*, 45, 64–87.

HURLEY, M.F. 1992. 'Late Viking settlement in Waterford City', in Nolan, W., and Power, T. (eds) *Waterford: History and Society*, Dublin, 49–72.

HURLEY, M.F. and POWER, D. 1981. 'The medieval town wall of Cork', *JCHAS*, 86, 1–20.

HURLEY, V. 1979. 'The distribution, origins and development of Temple as a church name in the south-west of Ireland', *JCHAS*, 84, 74–94.

HURST, J.G. 1988. 'Medieval pottery imported into Ireland', in MacNiocaill, G., and Wallace, P.F. (eds) *Kemelia, Studies in Archaeology and History in Memory of Tom Delaney*, Galway, 229–53.

HYDE, D. 1993. *Building on the Past – Urban Change and Archaeology*, Dublin.

IVENS, R. 1984. 'Movilla Abbey, Newtownards, County Down: excavations 1981', *UJA*, 47 71–108.

JENKINS, J.G. (ed.) 1969. *Studies in Folk-Life: Essays in Honour of Iorwerth C. Peate*, London.

JONES-HUGHES, T. 1970. 'Town and Baile in Irish place-names', in Stephens, N., and Glasscock, R.E. (eds) *Irish Geographical Studies*, Belfast, 244–58.

JOPE, E.M. 1952. 'Review of "Excavations at Island MacHugh" by Oliver Davies . . .', *UJA*, 15, 134–7.

KING, D.J.C., and ALCOCK, L. 1969. 'Ringworks of England and Wales', *Château-Gaillard*, 3, 90–127.

LACY, B. 1983. *Archaeological Survey of County Donegal*, Donegal.

LAING, L. (ed.) 1977. *Studies in Celtic Survival*, Oxford.

LANG, J.T. 1988. *Viking-Age Decorated Wood*, Dublin.

LEASK, H.G. 1966. *Irish Churches and Monastic Buildings*, II, 'Gothic architecture to AD 1400', Dundalk.

LEASK, H.G. 1971. *Irish Churches and Monastic Buildings*, III, 'Medieval Gothic: the last phase', Dundalk.

LEASK, H.G. 1973. *Irish Castles and Castellated Houses*, Dundalk.

LEWIS, S. 1837. *A Topographical Dictionary of Ireland*, 2 vols, London.

LUCAS, A.T. 1967. 'The plundering and burning of churches in Ireland, 7th to 16th century', in Rynne, E. (ed.) *North Munster Studies*, Limerick, 172–229.

LYDON, J.F.M. 1972. *The Lordship of Ireland in the Middle Ages*, Dublin.

LYDON, J.F.M. 1973. *Ireland in the Later Middle Ages*, Dublin.

LYDON, J.F.M. 1984. 'The middle nation', in *The English in Medieval Ireland*, ed. J.F.M. Lydon, Dublin, 1–26.

LYNCH, A. 1984. 'Excavations of the Medieval Town Defences at Charlotte's Quay, Limerick', *RIA Proc.*, 84C, 281–331.

LYNN, C.J. 1975a. 'The dating of raths: an orthodox view', *UJA*, 38, 45–7.

LYNN, C.J. 1975b. 'Excavations in the Franciscan Friary Church, Armagh', *UJA*, 38, 61–80.

LYNN, C.J. 1975c. 'The medieval ring-fort – an archaeological chimera!' *Ir. Arch. Res. Forum*, 2, 29–36.

LYNN, C.J. 1976. 'Appendix: the iron objects from Greencastle, County Down', *UJA*, 39, 52.

LYNN, C.J. 1981–2. 'The excavation of Rathmullan, a raised rath and motte in County Down', *UJA*, 44 and 45, 65–171.

LYONS, M.C. 1984. 'Manorial administration and the manorial economy in Ireland, c.1200–c.1377', unpublished PhD thesis, TCD.

LYONS, M.C. 1989. 'Weather, famine, pestilence and plague in Ireland, 900–1500', in Crawford, E.M. (ed.) *Famine: the Irish Experience, 900–1900: Subsistence Crises and Famines in Ireland*, Edinburgh, 31–74.

MC COMISH, W.A. 1968. 'Irish overseas trade in the later middle ages', unpublished BA (Mod.) thesis, TCD.

MCERLEAN, T. 1983. 'The Irish townland system of landscape organisation', in Reeves-Smyth, T., and Hamond, F. (eds) *Landscape Archaeology in Ireland*, Oxford, 315–40.

MCGRAIL, S. 1993. *Medieval Boat and Ship Timbers from Dublin*, Dublin.

MCMAHON, M. 1988. 'Archaeological excavations at the site of the Four Courts extension, Inns Quay, Dublin', *RIA Proc.*, 88C, 271–319.

MCMAHON, M. 1991. 'Archaeological excavations at Bridge Street Lower, Dublin', *RIA Proc.*, 91, 41–71.

MCNEILL, T.E. 1973. 'History and archaeology of the Anglo-Norman earldom of Ulster', unpublished PhD thesis, QUB.

MCNEILL, T.E. 1975. 'Medieval raths? An Anglo-Norman comment', *Ir. Arch. Res. Forum*, 2, 37–9.

MCNEILL, T.E. 1980. *Anglo-Norman Ulster*, Edinburgh.

MCNEILL, T.E. 1981. *Carrickfergus Castle*, Belfast.

MCNEILL, T.E. 1981–2. 'Anglo-Norman Ireland and the dating of English medieval pottery', *UJA*, 44 and 45, 198–200.

MCNEILL, T.E. 1990. 'Trim Castle County Meath; the first three generations', *Archaeol. Jnl*, 147, 308–36.

MCNEILL, T.E. 1992. *Castles*, London.

MACNIOCAILL, G. 1964. *Na Buirgéisí XII–XV Anois*, 2 vols, Dublin.

MACNIOCAILL, G. 1975. *The Medieval Irish Annals*, Dublin.

MACNIOCAILL, G. (ed.) forthcoming. *Collected Papers of A.J. Otway-Ruthven*, Galway.

MACNIOCAILL, G. and WALLACE, P.F. (eds) 1988. *Kemelia, Studies in Archaeology and History in Memory of Tom Delaney*, Galway.

MALLORY, J.P., and MCNEILL, T.E. 1991. *The Archaeology of Ulster*, Belfast.

MANNING, C. 1981–2. 'Excavations at Kilteel Church, Co. Kildare', *Jnl Kildare Arch. Soc.*, 16, 173–229.

MANNING, C. 1983–4. 'Excavations at Glendalough', *Jnl Kildare Arch. Soc.*, 16, 342–7.

MANNING, C. 1985. *Irish Field Monuments*, Dublin.

MANNING, C. 1989–90. 'Clogh Oughter castle', *Breifne*, 8, no. 1, 20–61.

MEENAN, R. 1985. 'The deserted medieval villages of County Westmeath', unpublished M.Litt. thesis, TCD.

MILLS, J. 1892. 'Accounts of the earl of Norfolk's estates in Ireland, 1279–94', *RSAI Jnl*, 22, 50–62.

MILNE, G., and HOBLEY, B. (eds) 1981. *Waterfront Archaeology in Britain and Northern Europe*, London.

MITCHELL, G.F. 1987. *Archaeology and Environment in Early Dublin*, Dublin.

MOODY, T.W., MARTIN, F.X., and BYRNE, F.J. 1976. *A New History of Ireland*, vol. 3, 'Early Modern Ireland, 1534–1691', Oxford.

MOOK, W.G., and WATERBOLK, H.T. 1985. *Radiocarbon Dating*, Strasbourg.

MOORE, D. (ed.) 1970. *The Irish Sea Province in Archaeology and History*, Cardiff.

MOORE, M. 1983. 'City walls and gateway at the site of St Martin's Castle', *Decies*, 23, 50–61.

MOORE, M. 1987. *Archaeological Inventory of Co. Meath*, Dublin.

MURRAY, H. 1983. *Viking and Early Medieval Buildings in Dublin*, Oxford.

MURTAGH, B. 1982. 'The fortified town houses of the English Pale in the later Middle Ages', unpublished MA thesis, UCD.

MURTAGH, H. (ed.) 1980. *Irish Midland Studies*, Athlone.

MURTAGH, H. 1986. 'Tudor, Stuart and Georgian Athlone', unpublished PhD thesis, UCG.

National Museum of Ireland 1973. *Viking and Medieval Dublin*, Dublin.

NICHOLLS, K.W. 1971. 'Rectory, vicarage and parish in the western Irish dioceses', *RSAI Jnl*, 101, 53–84.

NICHOLLS, K.W. 1972. *Gaelic and Gaelicised Ireland in the Middle Ages*, Dublin.

NICHOLLS, K.W. 1982. 'Anglo-French Ireland and after', *Peritia*, 1, 370–403.

NOLAN, W. (ed.) 1985. *Tipperary: History and Society*, Dublin.

NOLAN, W., and POWER, T. (eds) 1992. *Waterford: History and Society*, Dublin.

NOLAN, W., and WHELAN, K. (eds) 1990. *Kilkenny: History and Society*, Dublin.

NORMAN, E.R., and ST JOSEPH, J.K. 1969. *The Early Development of Irish Society*, Cambridge.

O'CONBHUÍ, C. 1962. 'The lands of St Mary's Abbey, Dublin', *RIA Proc.*, 62C, 21–84.

O'CORRÁIN, D. 1972. *Ireland before the Normans*, Dublin.

O'CORRÁIN, D. 1974. 'Aspects of early Irish history', in Scott, B.G. (ed.) *Perspectives in Irish Archaeology*, Dublin, 64–75.

O'CORRÁIN, D. (ed.) 1981. *Irish Antiquity*, Cork.

O'DANACHAIR, C. 1977–9. 'Irish tower houses', *Béaloideas*, 45–7, 158–63.

O'FLANAGAN, P. 1981. 'Surveys, maps and the study of rural settlement development', in O'Corráin, D. (ed.) *Irish Antiquity*, Cork.

O'FLOINN, R. 1976. 'Medieval cooking pottery in Leinster, thirteenth to fourteenth century', unpublished MA thesis, UCD.

O'FLOINN, R. 1988. 'Handmade medieval pottery in S.E. Ireland – "Leinster cooking ware"', in MacNiocaill, G., and Wallace, P.F. (eds) *Keimelia*, Galway, 325–48.

Oibre 1965. Official journal of the Office of Public Works, Dublin, No. 2.

O'KEEFE, T. 1987. 'Rathnageeragh and Ballyloo: a study of stone castles of probable fourteenth to early fifteenth century date in County Carlow', *RSAI Jnl*, 117, 28–49.

O'KELLY, M.J. 1958. 'Church Island, near Valencia, Co. Kerry', *RIA Proc.*, 59C, 57–136.

O'KELLY, M.J. 1962a. 'Beal Boru, Co. Clare', *JCHAS*, 67, 1–27.

O'KELLY, M.J. 1962b. 'Two ring-forts at Garryduff, County Cork', *RIA Proc.*, 63C, 17–124.

O'KELLY, M.J. 1970. 'Problems of Irish ring-forts', in Moore, D. (ed.) *The Irish Sea Province in Archaeology and History*, Cardiff, 50–4.

O'LOAN, J. 1961. 'The manor of Cloncurry, County Kildare and the feudal system of land tenure in Ireland', *Department of Agriculture Journal*, 58, 14–36.

O'MEADHRA, U. 1979. *Early Christian, Viking and Romanesque Art: Motif Pieces from Ireland*, Stockholm.

O'NEILL, T. 1987. *Merchants and Mariners in Medieval Ireland*, Dublin.

OPW 1984. *Sites and Monuments Record, Co. Louth*, Dublin.

OPW 1985. *Sites and Monuments Record, Co. Meath*, Dublin.

OPW 1985. *Sites and Monuments Record, Co. Monaghan*, Dublin.

OPW 1985. *Sites and Monuments Record, Co. Westmeath*, Dublin.

OPW 1986. *Sites and Monuments Record, Co. Carlow*, Dublin.

OPW 1986. *Sites and Monuments Record, Co. Wicklow*, Dublin.

Ó RÍORDÁIN, B. 1971. 'Excavations at High Street and Winetavern Street, Dublin', *Med. Archaeol.*, 15, 73–8.

Ó RÍORDÁIN, B. 1976. 'The High Street excavation', in Almquist, B., and Greene, D. (eds) *Proceedings of the Seventh Viking Congress*, Dublin.

Ó RÍORDÁIN, S.P. 1936. 'Excavations at Lissard, County Limerick, and other sites in the vicinity', *RSAI Jnl*, 66, 173–85.

Ó RÍORDÁIN, S.P. 1979. *Antiquities of the Irish Countryside*, London.

Ó RÍORDÁIN, S.P. and HUNT, J. 1942. 'Medieval dwellings at Caherguillamore, County Limerick', *RSAI Jnl*, 72, 37–63.

ORPEN, G.H. 1907. 'Mottes and Norman castles in Ireland', *English Historical Review*, 22, 228–54.

ORPEN, G.H. 1911–20. *Ireland under the Normans, 1169–1333*, 4 vols, Oxford.

O'SULLIVAN, M.D. 1935. 'The exploitation of the mines of Ireland in the sixteenth century', *Studies*, 24, 442–62.

OTWAY-RUTHVEN, A.J. 1965. 'The character of Norman settlement in Ireland', *Historical Studies*, 5, 75–84.

OTWAY-RUTHVEN, A.J. 1968. *A History of Medieval Ireland*, London.

OTWAY-RUTHVEN, A.J. forthcoming. 'The medieval Irish town', in MacNiocaill, G. (ed.) *Collected Papers of A.J. Otway-Ruthven*, Galway.

PILSWORTH, W.J. 1958. 'Newtown Jerpoint', *Old Kilkenny Rev.*, 10, 31–5.

POLLOCK, A.J., and WATERMAN, D.M. 1963. 'A medieval pottery kiln at Downpatrick', *UJA*, 26, 79–104.

POSTAN, M.M. 1972. *The Medieval Economy and Society: An Economic History of Britain in the Middle Ages*, London.

POWER, D. *et al.* 1992. *Archaeological Inventory of County Cork*, vol. 1, 'West Cork', Dublin.

PRICE, L. 1963. 'A note on the use of the word *baile* in place-names', *Celtica*, 6, 119–26.

PROUDFOOT, V.B. 1959. 'Clachans in Ireland', *Gwerin*, 2, 110–22.

PROUDFOOT, V.B. 1977. 'Economy and settlement in rural Ireland', in Laing, L. (ed.) *Studies in Celtic Survival*, Oxford, 83–106.

RAHTZ, P.A., and HIRST, S.M. 1976. *Bordesley Abbey*, Oxford.

REEVES-SMYTH, T., and HAMOND, F. (eds) 1983. *Landscape Archaeology in Ireland*, Oxford.

RENN, D.F. 1973. *Norman Castles in Britain*, London.

REYNOLDS, M. 1978. 'Irish combs from the ninth to the thirteenth century', in Clarke, H.B. (ed.) 'Focus on medieval Dublin', in *Dublin Arts Festival 21–30 April 1978*, Dublin, 15–20.

ROESDAHL, E. 1991. *The Vikings*, London.

RYAN, M.F. 1973. 'Native pottery in early historic Ireland', *RIA Proc.*, 73C, 619–45.

RYAN, M.F. (ed.) 1983. *Treasures of Ireland*, Dublin.

RYNNE, C. 1993. *The Archaeology of Cork City and Harbour from the Earliest Times to Industrialisation*, Cork.

RYNNE, E. 1961. 'Was Desmond Castle, Adare, erected on a ringfort?', *N. Munster Antiq. Jnl*, 8, 193–202.

RYNNE, E. 1963. 'Some destroyed sites at Shannon airport, County Clare', *RIA Proc.*, 63C, 245–77.

SAUNDERS, A.D. 1977. 'Five castle excavations – Introduction', *Arch. Jnl*, 134, 1–10.

SCOTT, B.G. (ed.) 1974. *Perspectives in Irish Archaeology*, Dublin.

SCOTT, B.G. (ed.) 1982. *Studies on Early Ireland*, Belfast.

SEABY, P. 1970. *Coins and Tokens of Ireland*, London.

SIMMS, A. 1978. Review article in *Ir. Geog.*, 11, 206–7.

SIMMS, A. 1979a. 'Settlement patterns of medieval colonisation in Ireland: the example of Duleek in County Meath', in Flatres, P. (ed.) *Paysage Ruraux Europeéns*, Rennes, 159–77.

SIMMS, A. 1979b. 'Medieval Dublin; a topographical analysis', *Ir. Geog.*, 12, 25–41.

SIMMS, A., and SIMMS, K. 1990. *Kells*, Irish Historic Towns Atlas No. 4, Dublin.

SIMPSON, M.L., BRYAN, P.S., DELANEY, T.G., and DICKSON, A. 1979. 'An early thirteenth century double-flued pottery kiln at Carrickfergus, County Antrim: an interim report', *Medieval Ceramics*, 3, 41–51.

SIMPSON, M.L. and DICKSON, A. 1981. 'Excavations in Carrickfergus, County Antrim, 1972–9', *Med. Archaeol.*, 25, 78–89.

SMITH, J.T. 1969. 'The concept of diffusion in its application to vernacular buildings', in Jenkins, J.G. (ed.) *Studies in folk-life: Essays in Honour of Iorweth C. Peate*, London, 59–78.

STALLEY, R.A. 1971. *Architecture and Sculpture in Ireland, 1150–1350*, Dublin.

STALLEY, R.A. 1977. 'Irish art in the Romanesque and Gothic periods', in *Treasures of Early Irish Art 1500 BC to AD 1100*, New York, 187–220.

STALLEY, R.A. 1978. 'William of Prene and the royal works in Ireland', *Jnl Brit. Archaeol. Assoc.*, 131, 30–49.

STALLEY, R.A. 1980. 'Mellifont Abbey: a study of its architectural history', *RIA Proc.*, 80C, 14–354.

STALLEY, R.A. 1987. *The Cistercian Monasteries of Ireland*, New Haven, Conn.

STEPHENS, N., and GLASSCOCK, R.E. (eds) 1970. *Irish Geographical Studies*, Belfast.

STEPHENSON, C. 1933. *Borough and Town: A Study of Urban Origins in England*, Cambridge, Mass.

224 Bibliography

STOUT, G. 1983–4. 'Trial excavations at Roscrea Castle, County Tipperary', *Eile*, 2, 29–42.

STOUT, G. 1984. *Archaeological Survey of the Barony of Ikerrin*, Roscrea.

SWAN, D.L. 1983. 'Enclosed ecclesiastical sites and their relevance to settlement patterns of the first millennium AD', in Reeves-Smyth, T., and Hamond, F. (eds) *Landscape Archaeology in Ireland*, Oxford, 269–94.

SWEETMAN, P.D. 1978a. 'Archaeological excavations at Trim Castle, County Meath, 1971–4', *RIA Proc.*, 78C, 127–98.

SWEETMAN, P.D. 1978b. 'Excavation of medieval "field boundaries" at Clonard, County Meath', *RSAI Jnl*, 108, 10–22.

SWEETMAN, P.D. 1979. 'Archaeological excavations at Ferns Castle, County Wexford', *RIA Proc.*, 79C, 217–45.

SWEETMAN, P.D. 1980a. 'Archaeological excavations at Adare Castle, County Limerick', *JCHAS*, 85, 1–6.

SWEETMAN, P.D. 1980b. 'Archaeological excavations at King John's Castle, Limerick', *RIA Proc.*, 80C, 207–29.

SWEETMAN, P.D. 1981. 'Excavations of a medieval moated site at Rigsdale, County Cork, 1977–8', *RIA Proc.*, 81C, 103–205.

SWEETMAN, P.D. 1984. 'Excavations at Shop Street, Drogheda, County Louth', *RIA Proc.*, 84C, 171–224.

SWEETMAN, P.D. 1985–6. 'Archaeological excavations at Ballymote Castle, County Sligo', *Galway Archaeological Journal*, 40, 114–24.

SWEETMAN, P.D. 1986. 'Archaeological excavations at Kilcash church, Co. Tipperary', *N. Munster Antiq. Jnl*, 26, 36–43.

SWEETMAN, P.D. 1987. 'Archaeological excavations at Abbeyknockmoy, Co. Galway', *RIA Proc.*, 87C, 1–12.

SWEETMAN, P.D. 1992. 'Aspects of early thirteenth century castles in Leinster', *Château-Gaillard*, 15, Caen, 325–33.

TALBOT, E.J. 1972. 'Lorrha motte, County Tipperary', *N. Munster Antiq. Jnl*, 15, 8–12.

TEBBUTT, C.F., RUDD, G.T., and MOORHOUSE, S. 1971. 'Excavations of a moated site at Ellington, Hunts', *Proc. Camb. Antiq. Soc.*, 63, 31–74.

THOMAS, A. 1992. *The Walled Towns of Ireland*, 2 vols, Dublin.

Treasures of Early Irish Art 1500 BC to AD 1100, 1977. New York.

Trésors d'Irlande 1983. Paris.

TWOHIG, D.C. 1978. 'Norman ringwork castles', *Bull. GSIHS*, 5, 7–9.

WALLACE, P.F. 1978. 'Recent discoveries at Wood Quay', *Bull. GSIHS*, 5, 23–6.

WALLACE, P.F. 1981a. 'Anglo-Norman Dublin: continuity and change', in O'Corráin, D. (ed.) *Irish Antiquity*, Cork, 247–67.

WALLACE, P.F. 1981b. 'Dublin's waterfront at Wood Quay: 900–1317', in Milne, G., and Hobley, B. (eds) *Waterfront Archaeology in Britain and Northern Europe*, London, 109–54.

WALLACE, P.F. 1982. 'The origins of Dublin', in Scott, B.G. (ed.) *Studies on Early Ireland*, Belfast, 129–42.

WALLACE, P.F. 1985a. 'The archaeology of Anglo-Norman Dublin', in Clarke, H.B., and Simms, A. (eds) *The Comparative History of Urban Origins in Non-Roman Europe*, Oxford, 379–410.

WALLACE, P.F. 1985b. 'The archaeology of Viking Dublin', in Clarke, H.B., and Simms, A. (eds) *The Comparative History of Urban Origins in Non-Roman Europe*, Oxford, 103–45.

WALLACE, P.F. 1986. 'The English presence in Viking Dublin', in Blackburn, M.A.S. (ed.) *Anglo-Saxon Monetary History*, Leicester, 201–21.

WALLACE, P.F. 1992. *The Viking Age Buildings of Dublin*, 2 vols, Dublin.

WALTON, H. 1980. 'The English in Connacht, 1171–1333', unpublished PhD thesis, TCD.

WATERMAN, D.M. 1951. 'Excavations at Dundrum Castle, 1950', *UJA*, 14, 15–29.

WATERMAN, D.M. 1954a. 'Excavations at Clough Castle, County Down', *UJA*, 17, 103–63.

WATERMAN, D.M. 1954b. 'Excavations at Dromore Motte, County Down', *UJA*, 17, 164–8.

WATERMAN, D.M. 1955. 'Excavations at Seafin Castle and Ballymoney Motte and Bailey', *UJA*, 18, 83–104.

WATERMAN, D.M. 1958. 'Excavations at Ballyfounder rath, County Down', *UJA*, 21, 39–61.

WATERMAN, D.M. 1959a. 'Excavations at Lismahon, County Down', *Med. Archaeol.*, 3, 139–76.

WATERMAN, D.M. 1959b. 'Piper's Fort, Farranfad, County Down', *UJA*, 22, 83–7.

WATERMAN, D.M. 1979. 'St Mary's Priory, Devenish excavation of the east range, 1972–4', *UJA*, 42, 34–50.

WATERMAN, D.M., and HAMLIN, A. 1976. 'Banagher church, County Derry', *UJA*, 39, 25–41.

WESTROPP, T.J. 1917. 'Notes on the primitive remains (forts and dolmens) in central County Clare', *RSAI Jnl*, 47, 1–20.

WESTROPP, T.J. 1906–7. 'The ancient castles of the County of Limerick', *RIA Proc.*, 26C, 143–200.

WESTROPP, T. J. 1917. 'Notes on the primitive remains (forts and dolmens) in central County Clare', *RSAI Jnl*, 47, 1–20.

WILLIAMS, B.B. 1985. 'Excavation of a rath at Coolcran, County Fermanagh', *UJA*, 48, 69–80.

WILSON, D.R. 1982. *Air Photo Interpretation for Archaeologists*, London.

WOODMAN, P.C. 1981–2. 'Sampling strategies and problems of archaeological visibility', *UJA*, 44 and 45, 179–84.

YATES, M.J. 1983a. 'Excavations at Carnaghliss', *MSRG Report*, 10, 12.

YATES, M.J. 1983b. 'Preliminary excavations at Movilla Abbey, County Down, 1980', *UJA*, 146, 53–66.

Place index

All places in Ireland with some archaeological remains still surviving have been given six figure National Grid references in brackets. Those sites in the Republic of Ireland also have the relevant sheet number of the ½ inch Ordnance Survey map preceding the letter. References to illustrations are in *italics*.

Subject and name index

Printed in the USA/Agawam, MA
February 5, 2010